Radical Politics

 Heretical Thought

HERETICAL THOUGHT

Series editor: Ruth O'Brien,
The Graduate Center,
City University of New York

Radical Politics

On the Causes of Contemporary Emancipation

PETER D. THOMAS

OXFORD
UNIVERSITY PRESS

OXFORD
UNIVERSITY PRESS

Oxford University Press is a department of the University of Oxford. It furthers
the University's objective of excellence in research, scholarship, and education
by publishing worldwide. Oxford is a registered trade mark of Oxford University
Press in the UK and certain other countries.

Published in the United States of America by Oxford University Press
198 Madison Avenue, New York, NY 10016, United States of America.

© Oxford University Press 2023

Library of Congress Cataloging-in-Publication Data
Names: Thomas, Peter D., author.
Title: Radical politics : on the causes of contemporary emancipation / Peter D. Thomas.
Description: New York, NY : Oxford University Press, [2023] |
Series: Heretical thought |
Includes bibliographical references and index.
Identifiers: LCCN 2023007082 (print) | LCCN 2023007083 (ebook) |
ISBN 9780197528075 (hardback) | ISBN 9780197528099 (epub)
Subjects: LCSH: Political participation. | Social movements. |
Radicalism. | State, The. | Political science—Philosophy. |
Gramsci, Antonio, 1891–1937.
Classification: LCC JF799 .T55 2023 (print) | LCC JF799 (ebook) |
DDC 303.48/4—dc23/eng/20230321
LC record available at https://lccn.loc.gov/2023007082
LC ebook record available at https://lccn.loc.gov/2023007083

DOI: 10.1093/oso/9780197528075.001.0001

Printed by Sheridan Books, Inc., United States of America

O wonder!
How many goodly creatures are there here!
How beauteous mankind is! O brave new world,
That has such people in't

The Tempest, Act V, Scene I, ll. 203–220

"The master's tools will never dismantle the master's house"
Audre Lorde

Contents

Acknowledgments

The themes explored in this book were developed over many years in a variety of conference papers, seminar presentations, publications and conversations. I am grateful for the stimulating criticisms and suggestions that I received on all of those occasions, by comrades, interlocutors and critics too numerous to mention. A year spent in the School of Social Science at the Institute for Advanced Study, Princeton, provided the space and distance needed to think seriously about the overall conceptual architecture of my argument. I am grateful to Didier Fassin for the opportunity to participate in that distinctive scholarly environment. I owe a special debt to Joan Scott for her unwavering moral and intellectual support, and to the members of the reading group that she convened throughout a memorable year: Johanna Bockman, Peter Covielo, John Modern, Julie Orlemanski, and Angela Zimmerman. As always, my most unpayable debts, and deepest thanks, are to Sara R. Farris, Mira, and Nadia.

This book is dedicated to the teacher and friend whose concrete example first inspired me to try to understand the deep structures of feeling and response that are embodied in self-emancipatory politics: Daniel Francis Patrick O'Neill, il miglior fabbro e maestro di color che sanno.

Introduction

Radical Politics against the New World Order

> Besides, it is not difficult to see that ours is a birth-time and a pe-
> riod of transition to a new era. Spirit has broken with the world it has
> hitherto inhabited and imagined, and is of a mind to submerge it in
> the past, and in the labour of its own transformation. Spirit is indeed
> never at rest but always engaged in moving forward.[1]

Hegel's reflections in the midst of the great events that inaugurated
global political modernity—a revolution against slavery, the dissolution of the feudal order, the vindication of the rights of women, among
so many others—might seem to speak also to the immense political
transformations of our own times. The early years of the twenty-first
century have witnessed wave after wave of protests and rebellions
against the "New World Order" that was proclaimed with the fall of the
Soviet Bloc and the consolidation of what has become known as "neoliberalism" on a global scale. From the clarion call of the Zapatista's
uprising in the early 1990s; the alternative globalization movement
straddling the turn of the new century; anti-war protests throughout
its first decade; the "pink tide" of progressive governments in Latin
America; revolutionary upsurges in the "Arab Spring"; anti-austerity
campaigns; and the "Intersectional Sociopolitical Movements" that
have defined popular responses to the latest round of capitalist crisis
internationally, the depoliticization and neutralization frequently
foretold or feared by the auguries of both right and left over the last
30 years have failed to appear.[2]

Recent decades have instead witnessed a proliferation of radical
emancipatory social and political movements. They have been "radical" not in the sense of merely extreme (such as when, e.g., the term

Radical Politics. Peter D. Thomas, Oxford University Press. © Oxford University Press 2023.
DOI: 10.1093/oso/9780197528075.003.0001

is used to characterize supposedly "radical" right-wing politics) but in its more profound sense as a fundamental questioning of the nature and causes of the manifold experiences of injustice within the current order. "To be radical," as Marx wrote, "is to grasp the root of the matter"; in a world such as ours that continues to be structured by generalized relations of exploitation, subjugation, and subalternization, to be radical means in the first instance to work for emancipation from all such conditions wherever they are encountered.[3] It is precisely this task that the most dynamic of contemporary movements have set themselves.

Sometimes these radical emancipatory movements have been punctual and sometimes delayed, sometimes ephemeral in appearance and sometimes subterranean in effect; but their stubbornly persistent emergence and re-emergence signifies the development of new forms of conflict and struggle of the popular or subaltern social groups and classes.[4] The new century seems to be characterized by a progressive accumulation of accelerated political cycles on a variety of terrains and in different geopolitical regions, as if it were only through the exhaustion of spirit in one of its incarnations that it might gather the strength to spring forth afresh elsewhere, clothed in different garbs yet cut from the same cloth.

These movements of resistance and revolt may not have issued in many unambiguous victories. Their failures may not even have been of an important type. And the significance of whatever modest successes these movements may have enjoyed in their own moments has been continually found wanting when measured against standards derived from previous and wholly different political conjunctures.

At the beginning of each upsurge of struggles, it has not been difficult to hear voices hopefully declaring the end of a long season of defeats and the opening of a new chapter in the universal history of the forward march of popular movements. Retrospect, even at a short remove, seems quickly to deflate such enthusiasms, seeing in what was yesterday's novelty merely an eventual exception that does not disprove the continuing rule of the party of order. Indeed, in some cases, it even appears to have been strengthened, particularly when xenophobic, racist, and nationalist mobilizations or revivals of the far right have been able to fill the vacuum left by the defeat or demobilization of emancipatory projects.

The spectacular irruption and subsequent fierce repression of revolutionary initiatives in the Arab Spring constitutes the most tragic and significant example of this negative dialectic. The brief flowering of the Occupy movement in the heart of the imperialist powers in the early years of the second decade of the century and its equally rapid "dispersion"—in both figurative and literal senses—followed something of the same pattern, albeit on a lesser scale. In a longer-term perspective, the sequential election of progressive governments in Venezuela, Brazil, and Bolivia raised hopes for the inauguration of a "socialism for the twenty-first century." In each case, initial enthusiasms more or less gradually subsided, when they were not abandoned, as those movements and their domestic and international supporters confronted the sober realities and contradictions of governing what remained societies fundamentally structured by capitalist social relations, of socialization just as much of production.[5]

In a similar fashion, the hopes of the European Left have migrated over the last decades, with specific, nationally based political formations appearing to represent—at least for a season—a paradigm for a more general continental recomposition of progressive forces. These exemplary instances have included *Rifondazione comunista* in Italy, at the height of "the movement of movements" in the early years of the century; *Die Linke* in Germany in the wake of the movements against the invasions of Afghanistan and Iraq at the midpoint of the first decade; the foundation of the *Nouveau Parti anticapitaliste* in France in 2009 embodying hopes for leftist recomposition that were soon dashed; *SYRIZA*'s revolt against the creditors in Greece before its capitulation to the Troika's dictates in 2015; Podemos's ongoing traversal of the contradictions of the austerity-riven and disintegrating Spanish nation state; or the enthusiasm for Jeremy Corbyn's leadership of the Labour Party in the UK, echoing and echoed by the mobilizations around Bernie Sander's bids for the Presidency in the United States. Most recently, this accumulative cycle has been shadowed by a revival of the extreme right across the continent and around the globe not entirely incomparable to the dynamics of the 1930s.

We seem to live in something of an interregnum, as elements of the old tenaciously hold back the emergence of the new, as hopes are raised and just as soon dashed, hanged on the expectation of plenty. As

Antonio Gramsci noted in a very different period, with a formulation that seemed to become ubiquitous since the global financial crisis in 2007–2008, "the crisis consists precisely in the fact that the old is dying and the new cannot be born; in this interregnum a great variety of morbid symptoms appear."[6] Yet whatever strange beasts slouch toward Bethlehem today, and however much reactionary currents seem to have grown in strength in recent years in particular national contexts, at least one thing seems to be clear when considering the global situation over the longer, extended generational period that runs from the 1990s until today: something fundamental has shifted in the exhausted structures of feeling and response that were dominated by the experience of defeats for emancipatory politics in the final phases of the twentieth century.

The type of "left melancholia" that corralled critical political energies for more than a generation no longer exerts the same mesmerizing fascination that dominated so many leftist responses from the 1980s onward.[7] For those who have been active in the movements and mobilizations of the nascent oppositional political cultures of the last decades, such an orientation can only seem strangely dated, if not even narcissistic. From these younger standpoints, the horizons of the present no longer appear as pale reflections of the past or menacing shadows of its traumatic repetition, but are populated by figures of the new, and of the unexpected.

This novelty derives in the first instance from changed conditions of contemporary politics, characterized by a unique conjugation of crises on multiple fronts: expansive capitalist globalization in a unipolar world accompanied by increasing imperialist interventionism around the globe, accelerating environmental catastrophes on an apocalyptic scale coinciding with the pulverization of autonomous institutions of popular industrial and political organization, the redefinition of the sites of injustice and its contestation occurring alongside technological reconfigurations of social space and time. But the distinctiveness of this period also owes something to the way in which contemporary movements have confronted its challenges as discrete instances of protest, nevertheless in some way linked together in their revolt against everything that is "the contemporary" itself. Albeit unevenly, failing and recommencing in turn, frustratingly patient in their broken rhythms, our times are marked by a revival of popular struggles and new political practices on a scale not witnessed since the "long 1960s." Piece by piece, the new world order seems to be dissolving before our eyes. A new product of spirit, Hegel might have said, is being prepared.[8]

Contemporary Emancipatory Politics

It is not surprising that the punctual tempo of recent political movements and their cycles has given rise to more provisional and strategic forms of thought than the type of melancholic brooding over epochal transformations that so entranced an earlier generation. How is this particular movement to be built, in the here and now? What are the social groups and actors most likely to become involved in this initiative? How can they be encouraged to move from passive support to active participation in the movement's development? These are questions that, in the simplicity of their formulation and their orientation to the resolution of particular problems, are both more particular than any periodizing narrative but also more general than any temporal distinction. It is almost as if these movements, in their commonalities and in their differences, have been searching for responses to the questions posed by the conjunctures themselves, questions simultaneously generic in their import yet specific in each of their modes of formulation.

It has been the repetition of these questions, different in their sameness, which has been the most striking continuity across the specificities of each discrete political cycle. It is almost as if, unsatisfied, these questions demand to be revisited, reformulated and reposed in each new moment. The emergence of every wave of protest and resistance over the last 25 years has posed the problem of attempting to "translate" experiences and insights from immediately preceding cycles, not simply or even primarily in terms of their responses but perhaps even more in terms of their modes of posing these questions. It is a dialectic of simplification and clarification that descends down—or ascends up—toward the "basic problems" of political action, grasped in the specific formulations of the contemporary conjuncture.

At least four such questions have been repeatedly posed in distinct but related forms by the movements of the last 25 years. These four questions focus on the goal, nature, method, and organizational forms of political action. I propose to consider the articulation of these questions as a potential "aitiology of contemporary emancipation."

Aitiology is today perhaps most commonly associated with a medical vocabulary, a sounding of the depths that correspond to the surface symptoms identified by its twin science of pathology. Other readers may recall its usage in Freud's early attempt to delineate a foundational method for what would only later become psychoanalysis.[9] In this book, it is instead intended as one of its original Greek and above all Aristotelian meanings: that is, an account of the final, material, efficient, and formal "causes" [aitíai] of radical political engagement.[10]

It is true that a notion of causation derived from a thinker who infamously justified slavery as both natural and necessary may not seem, at first sight, to be the most promising way to focus on the challenges of contemporary emancipation. The great strength of the Aristotelian tradition, however, is that it enables us to avoid the reductions of those modern notions of cause (frequently inspired by David Hume's approach) that consider it in a restrictive sense as an "origin" of a (potential) effect, with the various intentionalist or even subjectivist deviations that follow from this premise. The more expansive notion of an aitiology—a study of a thing's "causes," or the modes of explaining its constitution—offers us a more differentiated sense of all those features that can help us to explain why and how something has come to be that which it is: or even more importantly, why and how it might have the potential to become something else.

The four questions of such an aitiology of contemporary emancipation can be formulated in a condensed fashion in the following ways:

- First, in terms of emancipatory politics' "final" cause, or the end that it seeks to achieve, what is the terrain on which emancipatory political activity today should concentrate its efforts? Should the seizure of state power still constitute the immediate or even ultimate goal of political action, or has the centrality of "traditional" state power been superseded or displaced by the emergence of other rationalities or regions of (political, social, ethical . . .) power and its contestation?

- Second, regarding the "material" cause of emancipatory politics, or the stuff of which it is made, what constitutes the distinctive nature of emancipatory politics? Can it be conceived as the sublation, completion, or inheritor of political modernity, or is it properly understood as oppositional and antagonistic to all forms of political order hitherto?

- Third, in terms of emancipatory politics' "efficient" cause, or the way in which it is done, what methods of "political work" might help emancipatory political movements to be built? Are these methods to be derived from known models of political action, or do the goals of these movements necessitate a different way of conceiving how politics itself might be done?

- And fourth and finally, as the "formal" cause of emancipatory politics, or that which gives it its distinctive shape, what are the forms of organization most likely to deepen and extend the dynamics that led to the emergence of these movements of resistance and rebellion in the first place? Can a form of the political party still be enabling, or would contemporary political activity be better comprehended, theoretically and practically, in terms of other forms of organization, association, and relationality?

Translating Gramsci

This book explores the ways in which the implicit and explicit responses of the political movements of the twenty-first century to these four questions might be brought into productive dialogue with the thought of Antonio Gramsci and the various conflicting interpretative traditions that have grown up around it. It is admittedly not immediately obvious why a reference to a figure from the past, however interesting on their own terms, may be the most useful way to pose these questions. If we wish to clarify the conditions and potentials of contemporary emancipatory movements, would it not make more sense to begin instead directly from the debates that are actually happening today? Doesn't such a "return" to a known thinker risk becoming yet another flight from the contradictions of the present rather than an attempt to resolve them in the active construction of a different future?

Yet a historically significant figure such as Gramsci has a claim on our attention today for a variety of reasons, each of them compelling in its own way and none of them exhaustive on its own of his multifaceted contemporaneity. Gramsci appeals to readers today, for instance, due to his undoubted historical importance as one of the most sophisticated theoretical expressions to have emerged from the plurality of experiences, struggles, and discourses often too rapidly condensed into the myth of a unitary or purportedly "classical" Marxism and its supposedly Western aftermath. Similarly, while not as clearly "canonical" as his near contemporaries Max Weber or Carl Schmitt (at least for some influential currents of academic discussion), Gramsci is undoubtedly today ranked among the major political thinkers of the twentieth century. The fact that the most recent philological and historical studies have substantially increased our knowledge of his thought, revealing previously unnoted sources, structures, and implications, suggests that revisiting the *Prison Notebooks* today could prove to be generative of new insights and perspectives not only for the history of political thought but also for contemporary emancipatory politics.[11]

Gramsci's continuing significance is due not only to his formative influence on the political culture of the New Left, particularly in the 1960s and 1970s, and many of its later derivations and afterlives, including cultural studies, postcolonial theory, and subaltern studies. Equally, the ongoing diffusion of some of the key themes and concepts of the *Prison Notebooks*—above all, that of hegemony—across almost all humanistic and social-scientific academic disciplines, and a global prominence in all the major linguistic-cultural zones of theoretical debate, is not the only reason that he might be regarded as an unavoidable point of reference. Finally, it is not only because Gramsci's thought has constituted an important reference for some of the most dynamic political movements and formations of our time, from Venezuela to Bolivia, from Greece to Spain, that he might be thought a fitting interlocutor for an attempt to reflect on the theoretical and practical challenges that those movements have posed.

The argument of this book is both more general and more specific. In terms of the former, I wish to demonstrate that a reading of some of the central themes associated with Gramsci's thought and the debates that have shaped its reception can provide us with clarifying critical perspectives on these four central questions regarding the distinctive goals, nature, method, and organizational forms of emancipatory politics. There are immediate historical reasons why a thinker such as Gramsci is particularly well placed to help us to respond to questions of this nature. For whatever his various afterlives and the truncated political, national, and disciplinary receptions to which his writings have been subjected, Gramsci was above all else a political practitioner and professional revolutionary directly engaged in seeking answers to similar questions in the movements of his own time. All of his writings both before and after his imprisonment remained inextricably tied to this context.

The extensive reflections on seemingly "other" forms of social life that define the encyclopedic nature of the *Prison Notebooks*— literature, culture, history, philosophy, sociology, anthropology, and folklore, among many others—were not subordinated to this primacy of politics but enabled by it. As historical documents, the distinctive answers that Gramsci provided to the questions posed by the world-historical events in his own period undoubtedly continue to have a cardinal importance in the record of revolutionary movements in the twentieth century. It is only in this optic that any true measure can be taken of the nature of Gramsci's achievements in his own historical context.

Yet in the *Prison Notebooks*, Gramsci aimed to produce a political theory that could not only explain the determining features of his particular historical moment, one marked by the involution of a revolutionary upsurge and the rise of extreme forms of fascist reaction. He also sought to comprehend the deeper historical processes that had produced and were condensed in that distinctive moment. By so doing he formulated not a *philosophia politica perennis*, at the heights of universalist abstraction, nor simply a description of the conditions that obtained in Italy and Europe in the interwar years, in a modestly nominalist fashion. Rather, he produced what can be regarded— using his own terms—as a "translatable" theory of the possibilities of emancipatory political action in societies dominated by the capitalist mode of production and structured as processes of subalternization.[12]

The translatability of the political theory of the *Prison Notebooks* derives not from its presentation of an ensemble of generic concepts, immediately good for all seasons. Their translation must be actively attempted, based in the first instance on their potential for meaningful reformulation in the vocabularies of the present. The intensity of Gramsci's immersion in the particular concrete conditions of his own time enabled him to outline a singular critical perspective on political modernity as processes of "subalternization" and their contestation. Part of the reason that so many different political and national conjunctures over the last 70 years have repeatedly thought to find in Gramsci a "guide to action" may be because such subalternization remains the "destiny" against which emancipatory politics constitutively and necessarily struggles. One dimension of this book will therefore explore the extent to which such a critical perspective on subalternization drawn from Gramsci's carceral research might be translated once again today in order to clarify some of the central debates of contemporary emancipatory politics.

The "Strategic Method" of Hegemony

The fundamental argument of this book, however, is that there is also a more specific reason why Gramsci might be productively translated in relation to the questions that have emerged within contemporary movements. As Walter Benjamin argued, translatability never simply inheres in an original text but is always a relation that is produced in the work of translation itself, in its distinctive combination of retrospection and projection.[13] In this sense, it is less a question of translating Gramsci *into* the present in order to enlighten it than of being attentive to what might emerge when Gramsci is translated *by* the present— that is, of how the concerns of the present might illuminate previously obscured radical potentials that were neglected by the now canonical interpretations of his thought elaborated in previous political cultures.

This book therefore not only aims to propose a certain type of "Gramscian" analysis of radical emancipatory politics today. Rather, the central debates of our contemporary intersectional sociopolitical movements also here provide an optic with which we can attempt to read Gramsci in new ways. In their turn, these new readings are then proposed as a potential basis for distinctive responses to the four questions of an aitiology of contemporary emancipation. In this perspective, much more important than any of Gramsci's specific concepts or analyses is thus the general approach with which he confronted the challenges of his own time. It is this "strategic method" that is here proposed as an example of an enabling way to respond to the questions dominating our own conjuncture.

In a defeat much deeper than any our own times have known (because the intensity of defeat is always measured in relation to the frustration of a future that had been anticipated), Gramsci did not passively suffer the terms in which his conjuncture posed its short-sighted questions to him and to his contemporaries: to choose between an adventurist impatience or the sobriety of an Olympian distance, between the opportunism of too immediate tactics or the compromises of disembodied long-term strategy. Whichever alternative was accepted, the result was the same: to subordinate emancipatory politics to the rhythms and priorities of the dominant order and its theoretical comprehension rather than subjecting them to a fundamental theoretical and practical critique.

Gramsci's response was instead to beg those questions and to refuse their false choices. Rather than being dominated by the demands of his conjuncture, he actively confronted it with his own set of interrogatives. These questions were articulated in a strategic perspective, focused on the resolution of concrete organizational challenges and grounded in an understanding of the self-emancipation of the subaltern social classes as the project of constructing the future out of the incoherence and contradictions of the present. Each problem that Gramsci confronted was considered in this open-ended futural perspective and not subordinated to the periodizing and organizing imperatives of an existing order wedded to the repetition of its own past.

The questions that the *Prison Notebooks* posed to their conjuncture aimed to clarify the concrete possibilities for emancipatory political action in the specific conditions of that moment; but the strategic method by which they did so, in its assumption and construction of the self-emancipation of the subaltern social classes as the process of their "autonomization" from the existing sociopolitical order, constitutes a methodological discovery of a potentially more general validity. This strategic method can be characterized as a categorical imperative continually to "translate" the challenges of a given conjuncture into the terms of the organizational forms and practices that represent their real critique and resolution.

This categorical imperative was concretized in a distinctive, strategically focused understanding of "hegemony" as a process of "desubalternization." It is a perspective developed already in Gramsci's political activism prior to imprisonment and further elaborated in the *Prison Notebooks* as a "method of political work." This strategically focused understanding of hegemony should be rigorously distinguished from the ways in which the term is usually understood today in radical political thought (to say nothing of the word's conventional geopolitical usage in mainstream international relations theory and journalistic commentary). More often generically invoked rather than precisely defined, hegemony has frequently been understood in two interrelated senses.

On the one hand, it has been presented as an analytic concept that describes the functioning of modern political systems founded on the formation of "consent," conceived either tacitly, as effective passivity, or actively, as the 'occupation' of the interiority of a "subject" by impulses and dispositions originating outside it. In this case, hegemony is understood as a theory of the intersubjective foundations of domination.

On the other hand, hegemony has also been posited as a sophisticated historical account of the emergence of the modern state and the forms of neutralization, integration, and legitimation on which it depends. In this case, hegemony is effectively presented as a leftist variant of, or alternative to, the modern theory of sovereignty.

Variously weighted articulations of these dimensions are strongly present in the most influential understandings of hegemony in radical political thought today, derived from readings and uses proposed 40 years ago by figures such as Stuart Hall, Ranajit Guha, Giovanni Arrighi, and perhaps above all Ernesto Laclau and Chantal Mouffe with their notion of the hegemonic articulation of chains of equivalence and the formation of a "collective will," conceived as a "political subject."[14] Ultimately, this understanding of hegemony represents a delicate synthesis of the two great modern theorists of political form, Rousseau and Hobbes, integrating the former's emphasis on the immediacy of unity (in the rapid transition from the "will of all" to the "general will" necessary to prevent the emergence of seditious factions) with the latter's decisionistic act of transcendental ordering (in the foundational and exhaustive status of the instituted sovereign). Hegemony, that is, is presumed to be a theory of unity, universalization, and—ultimately—of political order.

One of the arguments proposed in this book is that hegemony, at least in Gramsci's most significant and strategically focused formulations, contains a very different political logic—and a way of thinking much closer to what we need to confront the challenges of our movements today. Hegemony here is understood not as an abstract theory of a consent-based social system or a generic notion of state power. It is not, that is, a general model of politics, to be applied ready-made to particular cases. Rather, a strategic understanding of hegemony views it as simultaneously the goal, nature, method, and form of self-emancipatory politics.

- *Goal*: To engage in hegemonic politics means to construct the novel relations of force and institutional forms capable of representing a viable alternative to the hierarchies and exclusions of the existing state of affairs; it means, that is, unashamedly to engage in the construction of a "new order."
- *Nature*: Such a practice of hegemonic politics implies a conception of historical progress understood as a concrete process, that is, not as the implementation of a normative standard but as the valorization of the critical acts immanent to the contradictions that define existing sociopolitical relations.
- *Method*: Hegemony understood in this sense is a practice of political leadership conceived not as an instance of command but as a process of experimentation with political proposals and programs that aim to increase the subaltern social classes' capacity to act as an autonomous political force, within but against the current order.

- *Form*: The organizational elaboration of this strategic method of
  political work represents something akin to a "pedagogical laboratory" for collectively unlearning the habits of subalternity and
  discovering new forms of conviviality, mutuality, and collective
  self-determination.

In its fullest sense, this strategic understanding of hegemony can be
comprehended as an open-ended constituent process that aims to construct a future, autonomous new order within and by means of the
forms of struggle in the present. Hegemony as a strategic method of
political work, in short, signifies the revolutionary project of the always ongoing self-emancipation of the subaltern social groups and
classes: a constitutive path rather than definitive destination.

It is in this perspective that Gramsci will appear in the pages of this
book, that is, as the practitioner of this distinctive strategic method
of the autonomization of self-emancipatory politics embodied in the
practice of hegemony. Gramsci the historical figure may appear to us
today as a type of Machiavellian "exemplar," providing us with general
lessons derived from his particular case about the nature of the political
forms that secure and consolidate the ongoing dominance of the capitalist mode of production. Considering Gramsci instead as a "strategic
methodologist," on the other hand, might be able to teach us a more
specific lesson: namely, how to break with the self-defeating structures
of feeling and response that remain subaltern to the demands of our
age, and to begin the construction of the unprecedented and the new.
The urgency of this lesson cannot be overemphasized; for it has been
precisely such a failure to refuse the terms of the conjuncture's own self-
comprehension that has for so long deformed emancipatory politics.

A "Weberian Tone"

The dialogue with Gramsci proposed in this book thus functions in
the first instance as a critical rejection of the pessimistic and melancholic strains wafting in from the recent past that sound so discordant
among the cacophonous melodies of contemporary movements. It
would indeed be difficult to imagine an orientation more unsuited to

comprehending the challenges and questions of our conjuncture than what could be characterized as the "Weberian tone" that dominated much political and theoretical discussion in the final decades of the twentieth century. Taking aim against "mystagogues" engaged in "fanaticism" [*Schwärmerei*], Kant famously satirized an "overlordly" or "superior" [*vornehmen*] "tone" that could be heard on the philosophical *Kampfplatz* of the Enlightenment. It was, according to Kant, not simply a discordant tone but a way of speaking that frustrated itself; this "new tone in philosophy," while declaring its inspired and easy access to philosophy's goals, in effect resulted in dispensing with philosophy as such, signaling not its ennoblement but its end.[15]

A tone similar in pitch if not in timbre can be found at work in the way Max Weber attempted to confront the transformations wrought by capitalist modernity in late nineteenth-century Germany as he sought to secure the ideological conditions of the dominance of the bourgeois class to which he continually declared he proudly belonged.[16] Weber's tone fluctuated between über-aristocratic bravura and a despairing sigh. Modernity's inexorable decline into bureaucratic mediocrity could only be held in check, he opined, through some extraordinary moment of charismatic political leadership. Yet the further back Weber frantically searched through history for exemplary instances of such saving power, the more it seemed to him that the historical roots of rationalization struck so deep as to be well-nigh fate. In his famous metaphor, an "iron cage," an encasing as hard as steel [*stahlhartes Gehäuse*], closed in around political modernity as something inevitable and unavoidable, something against which we moderns might struggle, but that which would thereby merely be affirmed in its increasing substantiality as our inexorable destiny.[17]

The "Weberian tone" of our more recent *fin de siècle* began with a similar "dying fall," acting out its own particular "ends." One of the responses to the decline of the social and political struggles that had marked the experience of the New Left, beginning in the 1970s but accelerating throughout the 1980s and 1990s, was the declaration that something was coming to an end, if it had not already passed— but what? Was it merely a mythical "Fordist" phase of the capitalist mode of production that was thought to be over? If it was not merely literary and artistic modernism that had come to an end, perhaps it was modernity as such? Later it would be claimed that not even history itself had been spared from its completion. The multiplication of philosophies of the "post" in the ensuing decades only seemed to take for granted precisely that which might be thought to be in need of explanation: namely, how could that fallen time that we *Nachgeborene* (those following in the wake) had been so lucky to escape really be so radically different from our own present, when we still seemed to need to look to it as if it were our own mirror?

Nevertheless, as if mere repetition on its own had the force of innovation, claims regarding the unprecedented novelty of the present continued to proliferate. So-called new social movements rose up, new political actors stepped onto center stage, and politics itself seemed to have found a new relation to "Life." Each of these claims was premised on a constant reference to what was taken to be the "past," constructed as everything that the present was not or should not be. For this perspective, novelty was thus not ultimately conceived as the "really new" but instead as the mere exhaustion of the past. It was a teleological narrative that sought to comfort the present, that although it thought itself to be unprecedented, its coming had nevertheless been foretold. Among the frantic and ironically derivative attempts to "make it new" of the 1980s and 1990s there thus lurked a profound "anxiety of actuality," as if one could only become truly "of the present" by loudly asserting one's contemporaneity.

The most striking example of this performative contradiction was the moment of so-called post-Marxism, living in the empty time of a break with a past that remained uncertain of a future. As a discursive formation and strategy, what became known, not unproblematically, as post-Marxism was characterized by the curious fact that it could neither entirely dispense with "historically existing" Marxism, but nor could it tolerate it either. It needed repeatedly to "reactivate" the "sedimentation" of the Marxism to which it constitutively referred.[18] In order to affirm its own novelty, post-Marxism continually recalled its illustrious ancestor, eulogizing it, condemning it, relativizing it, absolutizing it—in short, mourning it, but in a perversely melancholic way.

Marxism was here constrained to assume the function of a temporal index against which the contemporaneity of post-Marxism would seemingly become spontaneously apparent. It this sense, post-Marxism shared with all philosophies of" "the post" the fact that it constitutively arrived both too late and too early: too late to resurrect the objects of its obsessions but too early to have found a new attachment that would efface the memories of loves lost. It was a parasitic and narcissistic relationship, in a strict sense: a present that could only relate to itself, or be present to itself, by repeatedly distinguishing itself from the past it anxiously claimed not to be. Rather than an enabling orientation to the new, what these constructions of the post offered was often only this obsessive relation to a past they could no longer change but merely ceaselessly replay. The new became a mere variation of the old, verified in its simulation of novelty by the distance it proposed to take from that which came before.

Freud's understanding of the paradoxically active passivity of endless melancholy, rather than the terminable work of mourning, is the metaphor best suited to capture this structure of feeling.[19] Just as melancholy remains linked to the lost object, as its afterlife, or as the form in which an object is forced to live beyond itself, so some of the most significant discursive formations of the 1980s and 1990s remained linked to a cycle of real and perceived defeats of the previous conjuncture of the New Left. They summoned them up again and again in order to exorcise them, thinking that the full presence of the present would thereby be assured. But by so doing, they merely tended to confirm the continuing presence of the past, leaving the present anxious before those forms with which it supposedly needed to break in order to become itself. In its own way, such an always uncertain present soon became an iron cage just as suffocating as anything imagined by Weber in his darkest moments.

From *Zeitdiagnose* to Militant Nostalgia

The "post" generations of the 1980s and 1990s were dominated by the type of *Zeitdiagnose* (diagnosis of the contemporary) that aspires to provide an almost clinically detached reading of the pathologies of the present. Such maudlin tales of a lamentable decline or resentful reconciliation with the existing order, however, are narratives unlikely to have much to say to many of those active in radical politics today, particularly to younger generations either unencumbered by expectations of defeat or happily oblivious to their postlapsarian state. The energies of movements over the last 20 years have in fact shown themselves to be rather reluctant to engage in such "epic" or even tragic modes of self-comprehension. Our age seems to demand different tones and different orientations in thought.

The melancholic attachments that still flare up today with each ebb in the tide of movements seem increasingly minoritarian, if not instances of generationally determined territorialization and capture; they suffice to produce a self-satisfied commentary at the end of one cycle, but don't offer any propulsive force for the projection of the next. Not even enthusiastic negations of such dystopias, with frantic flights toward utopian futures, seem capable of constituting an enduring pole of attraction for the accelerations and recompositions that have characterized the cycle of political movements in the early twenty-first century. Just as historicist and teleological as the melancholic orientations that they claim to oppose, they also share a fundamentally speculative relation to the present, as if it could only be grasped at a distance, narrativized into a past or a future that are equally far away from the concrete challenges that contemporary movements have been attempting to confront.

Rather than narratives tracing out the conditions of possibility of our current misery, it has instead been a thinking of the specificity of the present that has generated more excitement in recent political movements. This is not to deny that theories of the new, of periodization, or even full-blown philosophies of history continue to constitute an important tendency in wider forms of political, social, and cultural critique. Structures of feeling formative for entire generations rarely disappear overnight but are only worked through and metabolized into new formations and orientations slowly, in relations of generational inheritance and disavowal.[20] Yet it is not this type of theoretical perspective that, on the whole and in general, has been adopted as a mode of self-understanding within the movements themselves.

It has instead been the prospect of some type of viable "grammar" of contemporary political mobilizations that has animated the most creative theoretical projects, even when they have remained invested in the rhetoric of periodization and notions of the new. It is less a case of describing the present in terms of a *Zeitdiagnose*, that is, than it is a matter of attempting to comprehend the present in terms closer to a Machiavellian *occasione*, as an opportunity for an intervention that could open the present to the future.

But how can the tasks of the present be comprehended if not in the optic of the new that defines itself through disavowal of the old? Are we forced to declare a type of decisionistic *tabula rasa* that clears away any meaningful precedents or guiding heritages, forcing us to begin again from the beginning of the austere normative foundations of a political ontology or disembodied philosophical anthropology? The bad conscience of always incomplete disavowal was the path taken by philosophies of the post. Beginning again from the beginning, on the other hand, has effectively been the approach of mainstream—but also some currents in "critical"—political philosophy, implicitly or explicitly, since at least the publication of John Rawls's *A Theory of Justice* and the reconstructive-normative turn of so-called second generation Frankfurtian critical theory.

While such classically systematic approaches have exercised their attractions for some in contemporary radical movements, they have usually been outweighed by perspectives that advance more consciously historical claims, whether in the form of a forensic genealogy, radical historicism, or the construction of critical selective traditions. Here we encounter another of the paradoxical novelties of the recent theoretico-political conjuncture. Rather than a flight from the past, some of the more creative attempts to comprehend the present have increasingly turned instead to the active mobilization and valorization of figures and themes from former days. For this approach, the present is not regarded as the site of the unveiling of a theoretical plenitude denied to an erroneous past. On the contrary, it is precisely the theoretical paucity of the present, or at least its normal forms of "spontaneous" self-comprehension, that has paradoxically seemed an opportunity to search back through the history of critical political thought for types of enabling "futures past."[21]

Such an orientation can be detected in the work of some radical theorists from an older generation who have frequently been referenced in the debates and publications emerging from and around contemporary movements. Antonio Negri's attempt to find in Spinoza's thought the possible "refoundation" of an alternative modernity, for instance, stands as one of the most daring and influential of such projects "to read on the lips of history" (in the pregnant Benjaminian phrase with which Negri concluded *The Savage Anomaly*) the original utopian dream that had been foreclosed by the dominant currents of political modernity.[22]

Something of the same adaptation of a "Benjaminianesque" historical perspective, even if unintentionally, can also be found in Badiou's analysis of the elective affinities with the political challenges of the *Vormärz* of the 1840s, the long arch of peasant revolts in early modernity, or even the paradigmatic uprising led by Spartacus in antiquity, which have opened up for us again after the exhaustion of the "passion for the Real" that marked the twentieth century.[23] Similarly, Agamben or Rancière's very different returns to the past might be regarded as instances of this more general tendency to think the present by means of a detour via the old.[24]

Yet it has perhaps been among younger figures that the most remarkable of these turns to the past has occurred—remarkable because unexpectedly involving a valorization of currents of thought that at least some members of an older generation had come to think were definitively concluded. The rediscovery of various traditions of heretical and forgotten Marxisms has by any measure constituted one of the most significant and vibrant modalities of contemporary radical political thought. The proliferation of new publications, journals, and collective theoretical projects unashamedly claiming affiliation to one or another of the Marxist traditions (expansively conceived) can even be understood as the distinctive feature of the politico-intellectual conjuncture of the last 30 years, sharply demarcating it from the preceding period's distancing from explicitly Marxist themes.[25]

In all these cases, we seem to encounter an attempt to internalize the strengths of the past in order to confront the present, in an almost classically Hegelian-phenomenological fashion: "a slow-moving succession of spirits, a gallery of images," on the way to the "Golgotha" of the present.[26] If some dimensions of this tendency could be characterized as nostalgic, they are nevertheless so in a "militant" rather than melancholic mode. Nostalgia here should thus be understood not in the sense of passive recollection but in terms closer to its original meaning: an Odyssean rather than Proustian quest, not simply the pain of the attempt to return home but the reclaiming of what both is and is not our own, a discovery of unfulfilled but unexhausted promises.

The marker of at least one significant sense of our contemporaneity no longer consists in the anxiety of actuality that defined the 1980s and 1990s, or the feeling that one can never be quite contemporary enough to satisfy the demands of an imperious present. Rather, it is something more like the active cultivation of an "anxiety of influence" that characterizes the energies behind the disparate theoretical and political projects of our times. This orientation involves the deliberate abandonment of a fetishized relation to one's own historical moment and the conscious pursuit of precursors and forerunners.[27] It is as if it were only through imitative familiarity with the past that we could learn how to think the present in excess of itself. The defeated but not destroyed Machiavelli who rejuvenated himself through passionate discourses with the ancients might here provide us with an enabling exemplar of how to relate to the history of our present. "When evening comes," he wrote in a famous letter to Francesco Vettori from his rustication in Sant'Andrea after the fall of the Florentine Republic

> I return home and enter my study; on the threshold I take off my workday clothes, covered with mud and dirt, and put on the garments of court and palace. Fitted out appropriately, I step inside the venerable courts of the ancients, where, solicitously received by them, I nourish myself on that food that alone is mine and for which I was born; where I am unashamed to converse with them and to question them about the motives for their actions, and they, out of their human kindness, answer me. And for four hours at a time . . . I absorb myself into them completely.[28]

As Marx noted in *The Eighteenth Brumaire*, sometimes the present can only learn to speak of itself by imitating the dialects of the past—not in order to parody the old, such as was the case with the farcical second edition of the Eighteenth Brumaire, but rather in order to glorify the new struggles. This was what Marx thought had occurred during the heroic phases of the bourgeois revolutions, with all their acknowledged limitations. The "conjuring up" of the past in these cases aimed to magnify "the given task in the imagination," not to recoil from "its solution in reality"; it sought to find once more the "spirit" [*Geist*] of the revolution, not to make its "ghost" [*Gespenst*] walk again abroad.[29]

Nevertheless, Marx claimed that the social revolution of the nineteenth century could not take its "poetry from the past but only from the future"; it needed to let the "dead bury their dead in order to arrive at its own content."[30] The revival of popular movements and struggles in the early twenty-first century, on the other hand, seems instead to involve an almost specular reversal of perspective. It is precisely a detour via "the apparently accomplished" that today appears to provide the imaginative sustenance to continue "to begin anew" the labor of a genuinely emancipatory politics. As a new day dawns, the light of previous moments of political intensity refracted through contemporary concerns might be one of the ways to illuminate the still shadowy shapes of a present that lies all before us.

Beyond "Classicism"

The attempt to establish a dialogue between the central concerns of contemporary political movements and Gramsci's thought clearly shares something with such attempts to confront the present by drawing on the past. Yet the type of dialogue that I pursue in this book deviates from the main currents of this approach in terms of how it conceives the significance of the "pastness" of the past. Dialogues between past and present have often been conceived as a negotiation of the terms of generational inheritance, as Marx's famous aphorism regarding the "weight of all the dead generations" eloquently illustrates. Such dialogues participate, that is, in a problematic that has come to be known since at least Renaissance humanism as "classicism," for which the distance between past and present is precisely that which is to be overcome.

The type of dialogue that I envisage, however, is less concerned with the distance between past and present than the possibility of an undiscerned proximity; less motivated "to go back" to a foundational primal scene than to discover the concrete forms of its appearance in the present. This approach should thus be distinguished from at least three significant ways in which we might be tempted to relate to Gramsci as a "classic." These are the notions of classicism as permanence and endurance, as recollection and re-proposal, and as "de-foreclusion" and refoundation.

The first sense can be illustrated by Norberto Bobbio's understanding of "classicism."[31] For Bobbio, classic authors are those with whom we never cease to dialogue even when we are unaware of it because their words have become a part of our most spontaneous vocabularies and even of ourselves. They constitute, that is, a permanent presence in our intellectual lifeworld, one that endures beyond any merely seasonal fashions. The status of the classic is here conceived in an almost archaeological sense, as the substrate on which our contemporaneity arises. This type of classic remains present even and especially when it might seem to the untrained eye to be absent. Rather than effaced by time, it is in reality merely concealed in the depths of subterranean layers of the past that sustain the surface of the new.

The notion of classicism as recollection, on the other hand, can be observed in Fredric Jameson's suggestive remarks regarding the contemporary status of the history of Marxism and the "heroic" age of leftist politics in the nineteenth and early twentieth centuries more generally.[32] For Jameson, "classicism" does not inhere in the simple temporal endurance of an author or tradition. It is instead only achieved retrospectively by the attempt to construct a selective tradition at the moment of a thinker's (or tradition's) "absenting" from the present. Recollection here functions as the production of the classic *qua* classic, its transmutation from mere historical debris into signifying artefact. Today, Jameson suggests, the "historically existing" Marxism of which Gramsci might be considered a prime representative has itself become "classical" in this sense, a "golden age of the European left, to be returned to again and again with the most bewildering and fanatical, productive and contradictory results," as a new generation seeks to reinvent an "energizing past for itself."[33]

Finally, an alternative conception of classicism as de-foreclusion can be discerned in approaches like that of Massimiliano Tomba, who

seeks to revisit those possibilities in the past that were not simply neglected or suppressed but constitutively foreclosed as the condition for
the affirmation and consolidation of political modernity.[34] For Tomba,
the negation of this foreclusion rescues these lost potentials from ob-
livion: the insurgent universality of the Declaration of 1793 in the
French Revolutionary process rather than the merely bourgeois claims
of 1789, the expansive 1918 Soviet Constitution in place of that of its
Stalinist shadow of 1936. This rescue also, however, establishes these
potentials as a pantheon of alternative classics by means of which the
present might re-imagine its own emancipatory potentials. Classicism
here signifies almost a turning back to take those roads less traveled by,
in an act of refoundation of the history that flows into—and potentially
beyond—the present.

It is certainly possible to consider Gramsci as a classic in any or all
of these senses, and there already exist a number of significant recent
studies that explore the contemporary relevance of his thought in these
terms.[35] This book, however, has a different aim. Rather than asking
Gramsci to step forward as our illustrious forebear, the dialogue in
which the following chapters engage attempts instead to demonstrate
how Gramsci might be made to appear as our "uncanny contemporary," in our time in a way that is not of our time. It is not the classicism
or "non-actuality" of Gramsci and his problems that is of interest here,
but on the contrary, the possibility that at least some dimensions of his
strategic method of hegemony may already be in excess of our own
moment.

To dialogue with Gramsci understood in this sense is thus not, in
the end, to take a detour via the past in order to return, rejuvenated,
to the challenges of the present. It means instead to search more in-
sistently for those forms and moments today in which the type of
strategic method of self-emancipatory politics developed in his work
might already be operative, rediscovering its preconditions in the
present. In this sense, this book ultimately aims to produce something
like a type of Gadamerian "fusion of horizons" of Gramsci's time and
our own; or more precisely, to situate them both in the shared horizon
of the project of the historical self-emancipation of the subaltern social
classes.

Emancipatory Politics: Goal, Nature, Method, Form

Each of the following chapters on the goal, nature, method, and form of contemporary emancipatory politics proposes a dialogue between the debates that have animated the cycles of radical political movements of the early twenty-first century, on the one hand, and particular dimensions of Gramsci's thought and traditions of interpretation it has inspired, on the other. In each case, I attempt to show how the central concepts, metaphors, and structures of feeling that have shaped contemporary movements might be rethought in relation to significant features of Gramsci's political theory and distinctive strategic method of hegemony. The debates of contemporary radical movements here find themselves reflected and refracted in the "mirror" of the *Prison Notebooks*. Unlike the *specula principum* of early modernity, however, Gramsci's mirror does not merely reveal what the Prince already knows. It instead shows us what we subalterns may become.

Goal (Final Cause)

The relation of emancipatory politics to the state is the focus of this book's first chapter, "Final Cause: Politics Beyond the State." For a brief season around the turn of the century it was claimed by some that the question of what Max Weber thought to be the "destiny" of modern politics—its rationalization, or in other words, its effective "statalization"—could be deferred, if not avoided, through an emphasis on less centralizing metaphors, whether of indeterminate power relations, loose networks, or fluxes and flows of desire. Yet the shared learning experience of recent movements has instead involved increasing engagement with the structures of the contemporary capitalist state, in an experimental mode.

These experiments have ranged from the EZLN's (Zapatista Army of National Liberation) "autonomous zones" in the early 1990s confronting the reality of ongoing and intensifying state interventions and repression over the last two decades, to forms of left governance in Latin America, to the uneven results of the regrouping of leftist forces in coalitions of both electoral and extra-parliamentary types in Europe, to the more or less successful development of recent social protest movements into more or less loosely structured interventions into existing political relations of force (such as proposals to "occupy" the Democratic Party in the United States during Sanders's presidential campaigns, Podemos's interventions in the Spanish electoral process, or the impact of Black Lives Matter movements first in North America and more recently globally on the fundamental terms of our contemporary political languages).

These divergent perspectives have been directly and often influentially echoed in debates in contemporary radical political thought. One tendency has questioned the contemporary viability of perspectives that continue to view the state as the strategic terrain for emancipatory political engagement. It has been continually claimed—and just as continuously contested—that our times are characterized by a fundamental transformation in the nature of state power, which also necessitates the search for a new terrain for emancipatory political action. These transformations, it is suggested, necessitate the adoption of alternative strategies: of refusal, exodus, bypassing, distancing, or subtraction. In effect, they valorize a supposedly non-statal space, whether conceived in traditional terms as the social or the ethical, or as some newly emergent property linked to biopolitical or governmental logics. Figures such as John Holloway, Michael Hardt, Antonio Negri, and Alain Badiou have been only the most prominent among a range of voices, both scholarly and activist, urging this type of reassessment of the left's traditional terrain of operation.

An alternative tendency has taken a diametrically opposed approach. Experiences over the last two decades in Latin America and intermittent revivals of the left's electoral fortunes in Europe (not to mention a longer legacy of practical and contradictory experimentation in south Asia) has revived traditional and contentious debates about the coherence of notions of a "left" or "popular" government as a possible lever to effect radical processes of sociopolitical transformation. In practical politics, the attempt to develop a distinctive mode of engagement with state power has occupied the energies of leftist forces globally in an accelerating fashion over the last 15 years, as wave after wave of protest movements in different geographical locations have found themselves, sometimes unwittingly, washed up on the shores of the state. Brazil, Bolivia, and Greece stand as the most significant examples of this challenge. The "realism" of figures such as Slavoj Žižek and Álvaro García Linera might be taken as representative of a more general theoretical echo of these processes.

Neither of these positions is of course in any sense new. Taken in their necessary dialectical relationship, they constitute the two poles of political engagement that every popular political movement over the last century and more has needed to negotiate. If a unilateral rejection of the state as terrain of political action is today sometimes characterized, echoing Lenin, as an "infantile disorder," engagement with the state, and particularly its representative and supposedly "popular" structures, has with increasing frequency been justified as a mature realpolitik. The distinctive features of the contemporary re-presentation of these traditional positions, I argue, might be more clearly comprehended by means of a reading of a particularly significant moment in the historical elaboration of leftist debates regarding the "realism of the state": namely, the debates about Gramsci's state theory and its potential strategic consequences in the culture of the European New Left of the 1960s and 1970s, particularly in the evolving work of Nicos Poulantzas.

My thesis in this chapter is that a re-reading of Gramsci's often misunderstood notion of the "integral state" can help to clarify the key terms of discussions regarding the specificity of the contemporary state. The state today cannot be understood with the mythological figures of a pure instance of decision or localization of executive power. It should instead be analyzed as the product of long-term processes of "primitive political accumulation" and transformation of social forces into political power. The notion of the integral state was developed in the *Prison Notebooks* precisely in order to comprehend the mechanics of this developmental process throughout the long arch of political modernity. As we will see in the example of Nicos Poulantzas's historically decisive (and representative) missed encounter with the notion of the integral state, the modern state for Gramsci both is and simultaneously is not the "terrain" on which emancipatory politics is constrained to operate.

It is by means of a hegemonic form of politics, Gramsci argues, that the integral state can be dissolved into the "non-place" of a political relation. It is this practical and critical deconstructive relation that opens the way for the emergence of a form of political power "of a completely different type." This perspective enables us to rethink the theoretical foundations of the notion of "dual power," a tradition of critical reflection that is particularly capable of illuminating key dynamics in contemporary extra-parliamentary mobilizations and movements focused on the construction of alternative institutions of emancipatory political engagement.

Nature (Material Cause)

The *differentia specifica* of emancipatory political action has been a continual concern for all recent political movements, whatever their assessment of the viability of engaging with the state. Chapter 2, "Material Cause: The Constitution of the Political," thus begins by exploring a deceptively simple question: What constitutes the distinctive nature of genuinely radical emancipatory politics? If the state no longer represents the privileged terrain of ultimate confrontation with the existing order, what then might be the "ground" of emancipatory political movements? Conversely, if the state remains an unavoidable obstacle that movements ignore only at their peril, in what way can leftist engagements with it be distinguished from the forces they denounce?

For a range of otherwise conflicting political and theoretical positions, the attempt to valorize a form of "politics beyond politics,"—whether conceived normatively, transcendentally, or even anthropologically—has constituted a type of "saving power" that grows there where the danger lies. From Rancière and Badiou's insistence on the rarity of politics, to Daniel Bensaïd's valorization of the political as diagnosis of the incoherence of the merely social, to Chantal Mouffe's invocation of a civil agonism, the notion that a purer political reason may be recovered before, beneath, or beyond "deformed," "official" politics has found widespread assent in contemporary radical thought. A version of "the Political" or its *Doppelgänger* in the notion of "Real Politics" has seemed to offer the guarantees for emancipatory political action that mere mundane politics is unable to provide.

In this chapter 2, I argue that these debates can be thematized in terms of the different philosophical styles by means of which they implicitly engage with one of the fundamental metaphors of the Western philosophical tradition: namely, Plato's allegory of the cave. The notions of the Political and Real Politics both promise, in their different ways, an authentic experience of politics foreclosed by the "cave" of our wretched contemporaneity. One philosophical style has attempted to think this problematic in classically platonic terms, as the search for the essence or foundation of political action. Chantel Mouffe's thought might be taken as representative of this approach, which can also be detected in otherwise very different projects such as those of Jacques Rancière, Raymond Geuss, and Lois McNay.

Another tendency, which I characterize as a "reconstructive-transcendental" approach, ultimately veers toward a paradoxically de-historicizing "historicist-formalism." Badiou's emphasis on exemplary "models" of true and rare politics can be considered as emblematic of this perspective. In both cases, I argue, the search for an "authentic" politics fails to register the extent to which politics itself—that is, politics as such in its historical development, and not merely its supposedly "corrupted" contemporary forms—may represent one of the constitutive forms of the cave in which political modernity has always attempted to confine emancipatory political movements.

A new reading of the *Prison Notebooks*, I argue, can help to clarify some of the implicit presuppositions of these debates. In particular, it provides us with an example of an alternative philosophical style focused not on recovery of an authentic origin of politics but on the problem of its concrete contemporary constitution in the dialectic between "civil" and "political society." What Gramsci characterizes as "political society" does not represent a potential saving power, to be appropriated by the left and wielded against the corrupt institutional forms that have compromised its original and still recoverable purity. On the contrary, the existence of political society, in its distinction from and simultaneous parasitic reliance on civil society, is precisely a symptom and integral part of the central problem of political modernity conceived as a process of subalternization.

The subalternization produced by political society is for Gramsci not equivalent to a functionalist conception of domination or oppression. It refers not to processes of exclusion or prohibition, but on the contrary, to the active mobilization and integration of popular social groups and classes in the expansive political projects of the ruling elites. It is this process of subalternization that founds the constitutive dialectic between civil and political society, as instances of association (from below) and organization (from above). It is subalternizing political society's status as the hidden logic of civil society (i.e., the political institution of "the social") that indicates the constitutive limits of any form of politicism. Rather than searching for the guarantee of an authentic politics, emancipatory political action should instead acknowledge the necessary "impurity" of politics itself, that is, the extent to which it is not located "outside" the cave but always constituted within it. Given this relationship, emancipatory politics within the cave must proceed in the form of deconstructive critique.

Method (Efficient Cause)

If emancipatory politics is not to be conceived as guarantee or purification, as origin or end, is it possible instead to think of it *in media res*, in the rhythm of its development as a process of self-emancipation? Chapter 3, "Efficient Cause: Hegemony as a Method of Political Work," explores the question of the methods of political work that might distinguish anti-systemic, emancipatory politics from the system it seeks to challenge. It is this question, more than any other, that has constituted a type of "ground zero" of the political movements of the twenty-first century and the proliferation of new models and "grammars" of political engagement that have accompanied them.

Debates over prefigurative forms of politics, of formal and informal structures of collaboration and decision-making, or of horizontalist versus verticalist modes of political relationality, have marked the birth of every significant movement from the early 1990s onward. They have continued to accompany those movements in their shorter or longer periods of blossoming, remaining as an unresolved question upon their subterranean dispersion and re-emerging in strikingly similar terms just as soon as new movements arrive to take their place.

For some, the seemingly nascent and inchoate nature of contemporary movements have posed the problem of a coordination of diversity that nevertheless does not negate continuing real differences in principle or practice. This tendency can be noted in Hardt and Negri's notion of "revolutionary intersections" of the often contradictory identity-based affiliations within a singular but not unitary "multitude," or the various forms of coalition building and allyship that have been essayed in what I have characterized as the intersectional sociopolitical movements of today.

For other perspectives, the revival of social and political contestation signals the return of classical questions regarding the formation of unified political actors. Unity is here represented as a Rubicon between ephemeral protest and a more durable political project. Rather than coordination of diversity, this approach argues for a transmutation of multiplicity into and by means of a common form. This understanding of radical politics—an understanding shared by otherwise conflicting theories and tendencies, from invocations of "classical Marxism" to assertions of post-Marxism—receives its most eloquent articulation in Laclau and Mouffe's notion of hegemonic logics as the mechanism for the construction of collective wills, or in short, political subjects.

Hegemony has frequently been understood as a variant of this Hobbesian-Rousseauvian paradigm of political unity, and there are undoubtedly formulations in the *Prison Notebooks* that can be read in this sense. Yet as I argue in chapter 3, when we focus on what Gramsci was "doing" with hegemony as a strategic approach to political action rather than what he was "saying" about it as a theory or concept, we can discern the outlines of a fundamentally different method of political work. The distinctive feature of this understanding of hegemony consists in the priority it gives to the necessarily dynamic and permanently provisional dimensions of political leadership. Hegemony in this sense is not a theory of power. It is rather an experimental practical hypothesis.

Rather than providing a foundation for unity, whether based on notions of consent, legitimation, sovereignty, or universalization, this type of hegemonic politics requires a continual process of differentiation. It introduces a precarious tension between so-called determining and determined instances, between the political and the social, or between the political proposal and the social demand to which a political project seeks to be adequate. Such a strategic understanding of hegemony, as a practice of always provisional leadership without guarantees, continually breaks the bounds of any static systems-theoretical logic. It is based on the proposition that self-emancipatory politics consists in the art of attempting to produce historical progress as an immanent and critical resolution of existing contradictions, beyond the constraints of sovereignty's condensation in the modern state.

Form (Formal Cause)

In chapter 4, "Formal Cause: The Question of Organization," I make the case for the organizational consequences of the "visual angle" of hegemony. In particular, I argue that it can help to clarify the debates regarding the most appropriate organizational forms for the type of movements that have emerged over the last 25 years. The initial waves of mobilization against the post-Cold War consensus were frequently viewed through an optic of lack, particularly when the institutional underdetermination of unmediated protest or resistance was juxtaposed to a mythical party-form that supposedly existed in some Edenic past. The reconstruction of such a party-form would be capable, it was claimed, of resolving the limitations of our contemporary movements, much as the certainty of experience claims to be able to provide good counsel to the intemperance of youth.

Such oppositions have begun to have less purchase on the political imagination in recent years. On the one hand, the diffusion of the "movement of movements" of the early years of the century has given way more recently to novel regroupings of interests and identities in contemporary anti-austerity, anti-racist, and anti-sexist movements. On the other hand, experimentations in leftist and progressivist electoral alliances have produced new organizational proposals that go beyond any merely representative form. The *Organisationsfrage* (the question of organization) is today thus no longer posed in terms of an abstract opposition of parties and movements. Rather, the most recent debates have directly posed the question of the *type* of party that would be capable of deepening and extending the immanent dynamics of the movements currently underway.

In this context, I suggest that a comparison between significant models of organization from the past can help us to comprehend the stakes of the contemporary debate. Derived from the experience of Italian *operaismo* in the 1960s and early 1970s, the notion of a "compositional party" poses the problem of thinking the political organization in a period of the proliferation of demands and movements grounded in diverse experiences of capitalist exploitation and oppression. The conceptualization of the party as a form in which a unitary "political subject" could be forged, on the other hand, was theorized most coherently by Lukács in the early 1920s. This model enables us clearly to see the limitations of the type of political formalism that invokes the political party as a resolution of the contradictions of the social practices that always escape it. In each case, I argue, these responses to the question of organization fail to provide a formulation that can adequately comprehend the dynamism and diversity of contemporary political movements because they remain subaltern to what I characterize as the Janus-faced problematic of political "(in) formalism."

Elaborated in the depths of the anti-fascist struggle in the early 1930s, Gramsci proposed his distinctive conception of the "modern Prince" as both expression and organization of self-emancipatory politics. It was not merely a metaphor for a known type of political party, as has often been thought, but an attempt to rethink the nature of the political party as a harnessing of the inherent conflictuality of political engagement in a process of intensification of associational practice into self-organizational form. This pregnant Machiavellian metaphor extends the notion of hegemony as a method of political work, drawing the organizational conclusions that derive from the dynamic and processual premises of a "constituentism beyond constitutionalization." It was this perspective that constituted the novelty of the figure of the modern Prince in its own historical moment.

Conceived as a mirror of and for the present, however, it also reflects back to us something of the organizational conditions that our struggles today are attempting to rediscover. The modern Prince thereby comes onto the stage of contemporary emancipatory politics not as a destiny but as a new way of doing politics, beyond the iron cage: an organizational practice and form that can extend the expansive horizon of real movements of historical self-emancipation.

1

Final Cause

Politics Beyond the State

After a long season in which the question of state power seemed to have receded back into a vast obscurity somewhere out amongst the dark rolling fields of the republic, the early twenty-first century has been marked by a strong return of what Daniel Bensaïd challengingly called the "politico-strategic question."[1] Declarations of the superannuation of the state as a central terrain of political action, once advanced in theory if never in practice by neoliberal orthodoxy, now seem to be more than a little dated. Whether in positive or negative terms, the central problem for radical politics in the last decades has been the question of how we should relate to the reality of contemporary state power.

Responses within these movements have oscillated between options traditionally described as a leftist "infantile disorder," on the one hand, and a revolutionary realpolitik, on the other. Each has at times claimed—or has been accused of wearing—the other's mantle. Has this been a case, as has sometimes been suggested, of the growth of the often inchoate extra-parliamentary movements in the early years of the century from a state of tutelage to the supposedly more mature project of founding new political formations and parties in order to engage in representative electoral processes?

As tempting as this conveniently teleological narrative may be, the dialectic between "ultra-leftist" and "governmental" perspectives has in reality been a more fraught affair, with each feeding off the other in the growth and decline of different political cycles since the 1990s. One orientation, from the alternative globalization movement at the turn of this century to some of the currents that animated the moment of Occupy in 2011, questioned not only the desirability but also the viability of strategies that posit the centrality of the state. Sometimes this

Radical Politics. Peter D. Thomas, Oxford University Press. © Oxford University Press 2023.
DOI: 10.1093/oso/9780197528075.003.0002

perspective has involved reproposing older (or more recent but now) "classical" positions, deriving from anarchist traditions or radical libertarian currents from the New Left of the 1960s. If John Holloway's call to say "no" to the state's inducements, or Alain Badiou and Jacques Rancière's different but related ways of urging the need to take a "distance" from the state, or even to respond in kind to the state's "indifference," have been among the most prominent theorizations of such a "subtraction" from the state, it has also been a perspective operative in a variety of different recent mobilizations.[2]

At least some of these calls to go beyond the state, however, should be distinguished from more "traditional" reasons for declining to focus on the contestation of a thoroughly corrupted and corrupting state apparatus. The most seductive of such "movementist" perspectives have arguably been those that argue not in terms of theoretical first principles but in eminently realist and arguably even historicist terms. For this position, a continuing focus on the question of the state fails to comprehend that our times are characterized by a fundamentally new terrain for emancipatory political action. Michael Hardt and Antonio Negri's widely influential arguments, for instance, are premised on precisely such a strongly historical narrative. The autonomy of oppositional and alternative movements, beyond the seemingly now eclipsed binary of the state versus civil society, they argue, necessitates other strategies—of exodus, refusal, or even autonomous "entrepreneurship." In effect, they urge the valorization of a supposedly already existing non-statal space in which emancipatory politics should be organized.[3]

Following or preceding this anti-statism, as its shadow and immanent critique, however, is a very different concrete reality. For at the same time that the slogan of "changing the world without taking power" found some resonance among currents in the "movement of movements" in the global North at the turn of this century, a diametrically opposed perspective was motivating significant mobilizations elsewhere. The sequential election in Latin America of the governments of Chavez in Venezuela, Lula in Brazil, and Morales in Bolivia, among others, posed the question of how to relate to state power in particularly urgent terms. Governments elected on the basis of intense social movements attempted to outline programs that could break with the ruling neoliberal consensus. Contentious debates about the coherence of notions of a "left government" as a possible lever to effect radical sociopolitical transformation were revived and put to the test.

Theoretically, legacies of the Latin American reception of Eurocommunism interacted with other traditions of reflection on the specificity of capitalist development in the region, including variants of dependency theory. Theorizations about the roles that state, nation, parliamentary democracy, and popular participation might play in specific contemporary Latin American realities, in their unity and distinction, have been variously greeted in debates outside the region either as harbingers of a new dawn or naïve repetitions of compromises past.[4] In a very real sense, Latin America came to be seen as a "laboratory" for the hopes and fortunes of contemporary emancipatory politics on a global scale.

The division of labor, however, has not been solely between a seemingly "libertarian" North and an increasingly "state-centric" South. Albeit in less immediate forms, the question of the state has also strongly marked European politics over the last decades. The fortunes of the post-Cold War Italian Left are perhaps most emblematic in this regard in its almost classical development and dissolution. Building on a long and intense cycle of social movements, in 2006, *Rifondazione comunista* (Communist Refoundation) put an end to the Italian communists' long banishment from the commanding heights of the central government of the Republic. Yet enthusiasm for participation in a supposed "government of the left" quickly culminated in ostensibly communist parliamentary deputies voting for the continuance of Italian participation in the military occupation of Afghanistan—in open defiance of core sections of its electorate, the most militant antiwar movement in Europe in the early years of the century. Overweening pride was rewarded with its fall. The elections following the fall of the second Prodi government in early 2008 witnessed the exclusion of all *Rifondazione* candidates from a parliament that, for the first time in the history of the Italian republic, included no parties claiming an affiliation with the communist tradition at all.

In Germany, uneven waves of electoral successes of *Die Linke* (The Left) at federal and state levels throughout the 2000s led to increasing tensions within and beyond the party and its social base. In particular, participation in local and state governments implementing neoliberal policies called forth a wide-ranging debate regarding the relations between political and social demands. New parties of the left across Europe, including prominently in France and the Netherlands, experienced similar pressures, as the flow and ebb of protest and resistance movements has cast them up, sometimes unwittingly, upon the shores of the state. The meteoric rise of *SYRIZA* in Greece in the early 2010s and *Podemos* in Spain slightly later also are to be counted among those experiences that have seemed, to some at least, to open up a new path for the tired old European left. In short, the question of the state, for so long rusticated like Machiavelli to San Casciano, is currently witnessing a spectacular return to its own Florence.

It would be easy to regard this emergent season of theoretical and practical debates as a simple updating of the classical debates that have long animated the international workers' movement and emancipatory politics in general, condensed in an all too well-known slogan: reform or revolution? Understood in these cyclical terms, the revival of theorizations of the state in contemporary movements could be understood to represent a return to "unfinished business," reconnecting to older discussions after a period in which, rightly or wrongly, such orientations had seemed unviable, either theoretically or politically. Yet in another sense what we are witnessing is not simply a return of the repressed, or the dusting off of old clothes as the fickle cycle of theoretical fashions comes full circle. The specific nature of the challenges that contemporary movements confront, the specific configuration of opposing forces, and the specific terms in which themes from these old debates are consequently reposed today, are such that that we are not dealing with a mere formalist repetition but a genuine case of transformative inheritance under the pressure of our changed conditions.

For the question of the state today is not posed in the abstract, according to any of the now canonical definitions in modern political theory, whether as instance of sovereign decision, successful claimant to the use of legitimate violence, or committee for managing the common affairs of the bourgeoisie. Nor can it be reduced to the more recent, but no less abstract, conceptions of biopolitical machinations

or governmental logics. Rather, the question of the state is instead
posed in terms of the specific reconfigurations that state power has
assumed not simply over the last 50 years (since the end of the so-
called postwar boom and the first stages of the so-called neoliberal revolution), but after over two centuries of its contestation by so many
popular demands and struggles.

Contemporary capitalist states, that is, are not merely repositories
of an ahistorical "sovereignty" of which they are merely a recent "incarnation." Nor can their distinctive features be comprehended
through the adoption of any of the variants of the always oxymoronic
figure of "popular sovereignty." The state today, in its regional variety
but above all in its international unity, is constituted as the condensation and transformation of the subaltern politics that have for so
long contested it. It was these struggles that have "forced" capitalist
states, often in a literal sense through militant industrial and political
struggle, to take on roles, tasks, and responsibilities that are not immediately reducible to their classical repressive or ideological functions.
The "transformist" accommodation, deformation, and overcoding of
popular demands is the fundamental motor of the modern state's development, even and especially in its most "representative" and "democratic" forms.[5]

When contemporary movements relate to the state today, they are
thus not simply relating to an external antagonist, however much that
appears to be the case in the thick of concrete struggles over particular
issues. In ways that are not always immediately apparent, they are also
relating to the generalized, sublated forms of their own pasts, that is,
to the "statalization" of the demands and aspirations of previous popular movements. It is these movements, and not some sovereign ideal,
which have been ossified into the peculiar "alien power" of the bourgeois state form whose distinctive characteristic is that it can appear
to stand over society while simultaneously investing it from within
"microporously."

To think the latest transformations in this longer-term process of
statalization in terms of neoliberalism's "depoliticization" of society by
means of "economization" or even "governmentalization" fundamentally miscomprehends how they have occurred. Far from being un-
political, they have expressed a pre-eminently and classically political

logic of class power, as the neoliberal order's chief practitioners and theorists have sometimes not been too coy to acknowledge.[6] For if the notoriously nebulous term *neoliberalism* means anything at all, it surely designates the concerted attempt by elites over the last 50 years to dominate decisive sectors of the state in which its capacity for quotidian, structural violence is condensed: the fiscal and monetary policies that affirm and regulate private property of the means of production. Whatever dissimulating rhetoric was once employed, the ruling class offensive since the end of the 1970s was from the outset premised on an almost military style occupation of key offices and sectors in the broader state apparatus in order to secure the continuing implementation of economic policies as openly political and disciplinary procedures.[7]

In this sense, it has not been primarily leftist theory that has engaged in "economic reductionism," as has so often been charged. Rather, it is the ruling elites who have implemented a calculated strategy to reduce the parameters of political engagement entirely within the logic of an instrumentally reduced conception of the economic.[8] As a key instance of decision, implementation, and enforcement of such "capillary" policies and literally "biopolitical powers," the contemporary capitalist state can only be understood as simultaneously economic and political; or in classical terms, as an institutional condensation of the "political economy" of the ruling class. Recent radical social and political movements, particularly protests aimed against the logic of economic austerity policies, have thus not been able to avoid the question of the state. It constitutes both their immediate challenge and ultimate horizon.[9]

Viewed from this perspective, we can identify some important elective affinities between the challenges of today and those that were posed at the end of the cycle of struggles of the "long 1960s." Despite all the undoubted differences between these historical periods, there nevertheless are features and arguably even a common problematic informing both. Like the movements of the early twenty-first century, the end of the postwar boom witnessed mobilizations that were predominantly extra-parliamentary in their early phases, at varying degrees of "distance" from the state. In a variety of forms in different countries, the anti-systemic movements of the New Left sooner or later found themselves posing the question of how the specificity of the types of states that had emerged in the postwar period might be comprehended, opposed, or even harnessed in the interests of a politics of the left. It was precisely this problematic that determined the development of movements against the war in Vietnam, or the transition from industrial militancy in the 1960s, to projects such as "Eurocommunism" and its derivates in the 1970s.

This "institutional turn" was not always a case of calculating subjective caprice, as sails were trimmed down to fit the governing winds; the sheer range of forms of strategic theorizing in relation to questions of political power throughout the 1970s in particular, and in some cases still into the early 1980s, suggests that this tendency is not usefully comprehended according to the all too available narrative of a juvenile radicalism grown world weary. Rather, it was the dynamic of the growth of the movements themselves that pushed at least some currents of radical political thought in those years to look for ways in which engagement with the state might constitute an enabling rather than exhausting resource for emancipatory politics. As the long postwar capitalist boom gave way to deepening domestic and international crises, movements that began in oppositional protest and contestation were increasingly forced into formulating alternative proposals.[10]

Rather than a failure of political will or the irresistible rewards of renegacy, it was instead "economics" that here determined the appeal to the view that the "commanding heights" of the state might permit at least a perspective from which to glimpse potential resolutions to a phase of protracted, structural crisis. "Politicism" emerged from, rather than being opposed to, an excess of "economism." It was, that is, the question of the capacity of a political program to exert control over the logic of capitalist economic development that was ultimately the litmus test for the movements of the long 1960s. If history now records an overwhelmingly negative judgment of the proposals that gained significant support in the 1960s and 1970s before suffering almost total defeats with the rise of neoliberalism in the 1980s, the ways in which at least some of these positions were developed might nevertheless have something to say to a period such as our own that is experiencing similar tensions and tendencies.

From the Autonomy of the Political
to Eurocommunism

Although still not as widely known internationally as other experiences
from the end of the New Left, Mario Tronti's turn from his youthful
"workerism" in the late 1950s and early 1960s to the theorization of
an "autonomy of the political" in the 1970s might be taken as emblematic of both the motivations and pitfalls of such an "economistic-
politicist" approach. In his most famous book, *Workers and Capital*
[*Operai e capitale*], a collection of "occasional" texts from the early
1960s, Tronti had famously argued for a "strategy of refusal" of capitalist productive and social relations. It was a theoretical intervention
premised on the seemingly inexorable increase in militant industrial
struggle that marked the underside of the "Italian miracle."[11] Early
workerism, inspired by the increasingly militant industrial struggles
in Italy in the 1950s and early 1960s, aimed to valorize the capacity for
self-organization of the working class movement, beyond the forms
of institutional-political mediation that had captured them since the
foundation of the postwar Italian republic.

Capitalist development and workers' struggles were opposed in this
formulation as an absolute concrete antagonism. According to Tronti's
brand of "heretical" Marxism, it was the primacy of workers struggles,
and not the development of the means of production, that drove capitalist development forward.[12] It was workers' struggles that forced capital to innovate in the technical organization of production in order,
on the one hand, to harness the almost primordial force of workers'
militancy to its own ends, and, on the other, to institute mechanisms of
control and containment at the political level.

However, this analysis decisively changed with Tronti's perception of
a decline in industrial militancy from the mid-1960s onward. Already
in the "Postscript" to the second edition of *Workers and Capital* (1971),
Tronti began to transform his guiding thesis by means of a reflection
on the culture of the crisis of bourgeois society and its state form. He
now argued that fundamental transformations introduced into the regime of capitalist accumulation in the 1930s by Keynesianism in the
West, Fascism and Nazism in southern and central Europe, and the
command economy in the Soviet Union in the East had prepared the

way for a changed terrain of political struggle.[13] In the 1960s, Tronti had pursued the primacy of relations of production to the extreme, positing an unmediated irruption into the political of what he later came to describe somewhat ironically as a "rough pagan race" [*rude razza pagana*].[14] In the 1970s, he bent the stick violently back in the other direction. Politics was now put "in command."

Tronti announced the thesis of a possible "autonomy of the political" in late 1972 at a seminar hosted by Norberto Bobbio in Turin.[15] This perspective was further elaborated by Tronti and his close collaborators (particularly Massimo Cacciari) throughout the decade, although not always in ways consistent with its initial formulation. Unlike many other reflections on the political that presuppose a distinction between "politics" and "the political," Tronti's use of the proper noun referred not to a metaphysical distinction between merely "empirical" political facts and a determining conceptual cause. More mundanely, in line with modes of expression common within the distinctive political culture of the Italian "first republic," Tronti explicitly argued that "the political" was to be understood merely as a shorthand formulation to indicate all those institutions, practices, and relations traditionally comprehended as apparatuses of governance or state power.[16] The gambit of Tronti's notion of the autonomy of the political consisted in the attempt to valorize such an institutional ensemble as a terrain of struggle, reforging it into an instrument that would allow the working class movement to achieve an explicitly *political* hegemony over capitalist economic development and innovation.[17]

Decisive in this transition was a revaluation of the notion of "development" in non-economistic terms. Tronti now spoke not of an opposition between "originary" workers struggles and a derivative capitalist development, as he had done in his "Copernican revolution" in the early 1960s.[18] Rather, his argument in the early 1970s was for a possible "political development," one furthermore premised on the non-contemporaneity of politics and economics. This was not, however, a supposedly "traditional" Marxist argument regarding the temporal primacy of economic struggle as first and material cause of the political, which always arrives "too late." This was the perspective shared by Kautskyian orthodoxy, Lenin's often misquoted notion of politics as the "concentrated expression of the economic," and the "first" Tronti's workerism (in this precise sense, "classical" workerism was in fact far more "orthodoxly" Marxist than is today sometimes supposed).

Tronti instead proposed the non-contemporaneity of economics and politics in a reverse fashion, with the latter seemingly assuming the role of formal and final cause of the former. Sometimes politics lags behind economics, Tronti suggested; this seemed to have been in the case in Italy in the 1960s. Equally, however, sometimes politics could run "ahead" of economics, in what appears to be an argument for a voluntaristic "forcing" of what nevertheless remains a classically stagist sequential development.[19] Historically, Tronti argued, it had been politics' advance and not its delay that had been decisive for the formation of the state form most appropriate to the capitalist mode of production. Prefiguring arguments that would later be developed in a very different context independently by so-called political Marxism, he argued that capitalist markets could only emerge on the basis of the prior establishment of its legitimating politico-juridical framework.[20]

In Italy in the 1960s, economics had outstripped politics; but in the changed conjuncture of the 1970s, the time of the political had come. While the capitalist class had exploited the delay of politics in the 1960s in order to disorganize workers' struggles at the industrial level (which were thus dissipated rather than consolidated into a properly political hegemony), in the 1970s, the Italian bourgeoisie was attempting to make politics run ahead of economic development in order to achieve pre-emptive mastery of it. The Italian workers' movement, and particularly what Tronti now regarded as its pre-eminent political expression in the PCI (Italian Communist Party), needed to respond by anticipating this acceleration of the political. It needed, in short, to recognize the ensemble of existing political institutions and practices as the privileged terrain of struggle in this distinctive conjuncture, and assume the responsibilities of its autonomy. The state, that is, was assumed as the necessary terrain of workers' explicitly *political* struggle.

The curious coincidence of this minoritarian proposal with the PCI leadership's contemporaneous move toward a "historical compromise" aiming to bolster its credentials as a party of order and good governance did not escape Tronti's critics, many of them his former workerist comrades from the 1960s.[21] The subsequent tragic

conclusion to the long Italian sixties seemed to suggest that any ostensible "leftist" motivations behind Tronti's gambit had been, at best,
naively misguided, when not complicit with the savage state repression
that crushed the movements in the late 1970s. At the theoretical level,
the thesis of the autonomy of the political oscillated between a strongly
deterministic philosophy of history and an increasingly mystical metaphysics in which the political constituted an ever-receding destiny, ultimately in an explicitly Weberian sense.[22]

In its historical moment, and despite its deleterious political
consequences, Tronti's proposal nevertheless represented a novel revitalization of Marxist theorizations of the relations between economics
and politics. Tronti aimed to theorize the conditions in which political engagement with the state might be conceived not in terms of the
known narratives of accommodation and compromise but as a "ruse"
by means of which ostensibly leftist political forces might be able to
stem the lust of the capitalist Moloch. It is therefore doubly ironic that
this perspective did not seem to notice that it thereby fell for the ruse of
the bourgeois Leviathan's constitutive politicism, its incessant drive to
incorporate all social instances within the integrative and neutralizing
logic of its instrumentally reduced political forms.

The most widely discussed turn toward the question of
the state in the 1970s, however, was the season of so-called
Eurocommunism. According to a commonly accepted historical narrative, Eurocommunism slowly emerged in the wake of the years 1968
(Prague) and 1973 (Chile) as an alternative to traditional social democracy and the Soviet model. It was consolidated in the mid-1970s
into an identifiable current actively promoted throughout the communist movement, not only in the prominent cases of Italy and Spain but
with an important resonance elsewhere in Europe, and indeed, internationally. Briefly flourishing and seemingly rapidly "compromised," it
then slowly declined as a credible political force with the onset of the
massive shifts to the right in the 1980s and the final eclipse of all things
communist in 1989.

In reality, Eurocommunism was based in experiences much less
unitary in intention or consequences than is often remembered. Its use
of institutional engagement within the state as a means of furthering
leftist politics, for instance, was based in older and more complicated

historical experiences. This was particularly evident in the case of Italy, given the PCI's earlier enthusiastic participation in the constitutional formation of the post-Fascist Italian Republic. Similarly, it was much less "European" in its reach than the moniker suggests, in terms of its inspirations, interlocutors, and reverberations in the international communist movement. Eurocommunist themes, for instance, played an important role in orienting leftist forces in the so-called transition to democracy in Latin America in the 1980s and beyond.[23]

Eurocommunism today has taken on almost mythical dimensions in some areas of radical politics, frequently invoked as a foreboding warning of the contradictions into which contemporary movements may fall, or just as frequently championed as an enabling resource from which we might learn. Whatever the assessment of its historical significance, however, it seems clear that that this season of debate has now regained a surprising actuality: as one of the metaphors by means of which contemporary emancipatory politics is attempting to understand its own challenges and even itself.

A "Poulantzian–Gramscian" Tradition?

Perhaps the most significant theoretical reflection to have emerged from this season was the work of Nicos Poulantzas. In many respects, particularly if judged in terms of the ongoing productive research projects his thought has continued to nourish, Poulantzas's work still remains a highpoint of consciously Marxist attempts to theorize the nature of the modern, representative parliamentary state. Even more significantly, it remains one of the most sophisticated attempts to think about how emancipatory movements might engage with the state in order to further their own ends.[24]

In its historical context, Poulantzas's work was shaped by his response (more or less explicitly) to two of the most innovative politico-theoretical interventions of the 1970s, radically different in their presuppositions and focus but united in the shared assumption of a superannuation of the Marxist tradition. One the one hand, in the context of French intellectual life, Poulantzas's emphasis on the centrality of the state for any oppositional politics worthy of the name responded to Foucault's polemical claims against state theory *tout court*, whether Marxist or not. In Foucault's notorious formulation, "in political thought and analysis, we still have not cut off the head of the king."[25] On the other hand, in the context of the international communist movement, Poulantzas's work can be regarded as a refutation of Norberto Bobbio's even more polemically charged claim that Marxism did not possess a viable theory of the state, particularly in terms of accounting for its institutional instances and procedures.[26]

Through the anti- and post-Marxist 1980s and 1990s, Poulantzas was often treated as superannuated by subsequent theoretical and political developments. With some notable exceptions, he was maligned for his supposed "structuralism" or "Althusserianism" when those paradigms fell from grace (particularly in the anglophone world, influenced by the structuralist excesses of the framing of the famous Poulantzas–Miliband debate), or more generally consigned to a prehistory of a post-Marxist present.[27] Yet for some time now, in halting forms in different national contexts, there has been a rediscovery and revival of Poulantzas's work among a new generation of theorists seeking forms of enabling anxious influence.[28] Even more significantly, Poulantzas's thought has been invoked by some of the most prominent movements of the last decade, either explicitly (such as occurred in the rise of *SYRIZA* in Greece) or more often, implicitly, in the widespread advocacy of a key Poulantzian theme of the articulation of electoral politics with work in social movements (particularly notable in the decisive phase of the institutional consolidation of *Podemos* in Spain).[29] Unexpectedly, Poulantzas can now be regarded as one of the major theorists of our own conjuncture.

This process of generational rediscovery reveals another elective affinity between our own times and the debates of the 1970s. For just as Poulantzas is beginning to be considered today as a type of potential "future-past," so too was his own work nourished by a productive dialogue with previous key moments in the history of Marxist theory. Foremost among these was his fraught relationship with the thought of Antonio Gramsci. Like many others in the 1970s, Poulantzas identified Gramsci as one of the most advanced developments of Marxism as a political theory, with which it was thus necessary to settle his accounts.

Engagement with themes often regarded as "Gramscian" stand at the center of Poulantzas's distinctive theoretical proposals regarding both the nature of the capitalist state and the potential for participation in its structures to empower popular movements. It would be therefore tempting to think of these affinities in terms of a (retrospectively constructed) "Poulantzian–Gramscian" selective tradition—if such a formulation were not misleading regarding the motivation and goal of Poulantzas's evolving project. For it was not the ambition to inherit Gramsci's thought that drove Poulantzas's development. On the contrary, it was his repeated, anxious attempts to take a conscious distance from Gramsci that characterized the distinctive pattern of his thought, in all of its phases.

To a much greater extent than is sometimes recognized, the unresolved and perhaps unresolvable questions raised in Poulantzas's work, particularly in its final phases—the relative levels and "depths" of the state as a condensation of class struggle, the historical superannuation of a Leninist strategy of "dual power," the articulation of participatory and representative democracy, the viability of a "democratic road to socialism"—emerged directly from his critique of the "author" of the *Prison Notebooks*. Poulantzas's most innovative analyses and programmatic proposals—precisely the reasons that his thought is enjoying a revival in appeal today—arose directly from this confrontation. Even more presciently for us today, they were also explicitly formulated in terms of an opposition between strategies that take a distance from the state, or those that seek to navigate through its treacherous waters.

Poulantzas's evolving reading of Gramsci is marked by recurring ambivalences that are not easily ranked under the label of either affiliation or repudiation. Perceptive readers had noted early on that, despite his growing "structuralist" reputation, there seemed to be important similarities between the projects of Poulantzas and Gramsci.[30] Poulantzas himself, however, seemed less convinced in his early works. Particularly in the pathbreaking *Political Power and Social Classes* of 1968, he often deployed rhetorical strategies almost identical to those operative in Althusser's famous critique from the early 1960s in *Reading Capital* of Gramsci's "historicism."[31] In both cases, rapprochement and praise for the intelligence and fertility of the researches contained in the *Prison Notebooks* was rapidly followed by qualification and distancing from what were taken to be Gramsci's substantive theses.

Poulantzas spoke, for instance, of a Gramsci "whose political analyses, though always valuable, are often tainted by the historicism of Croce and Labriola."[32] At another moment, he argued that 'on the one hand Gramsci, with amazing acuteness, perceived the problems posed by the political functioning of bourgeois ideology in a capitalist formation; on the other hand, though his analyses are distinct from the typical historicist conception of ideologies as presented, for example, by Lukács, because of the historicist problematic which essentially governs his work, they demonstrate very clearly the impasses and errors to which this problematic of ideology leads.'[33]

Formulating a critique that enjoyed relatively wide diffusion in the 1970s and continues to shape some readings even today, Poulantzas argued that in Gramsci there is "a confusion of the areas in which hegemony is exercised . . . according to which force is exercised by the state in 'political society', hegemony in 'civil society.' "[34] Without providing a deeper engagement with the *Prison Notebooks* in order to determine if such a "distinction between force and hegemony" can indeed be found there, Poulantzas concluded that the origins of this confusion lay in "the historicist conception of [the] relation" of the "economic and political spheres," according to which the political would be a motor of "the 'economic laws' conceived in a mechanistic fashion."[35] The Althusserian critique of Gramsci's historicism thus essentially "governs" Poulantzas's work at this stage, foreclosing any more sustained engagement with the state theory developed in the *Prison Notebooks*.

Wars of position and wars of maneuver

In his final works, however, Poulantzas elaborates a reading of Gramsci that is in many respects diametrically opposed to his earlier Althusserian inflected perspective. For Althusser in *Reading Capital*, Gramsci's chief failing was that he had ultimately failed to break with the theoretical presuppositions of the Second International. For the Poulantzas of *State, Power, Socialism* (1978), on the other hand,

Gramsci's reflections on the state had instead remained all too indebted to concepts and strategies derived from the Third International.[36] Poulantzas thereby proposed an image of Gramsci that is very different from two other readings that were current on much of the international Left in the 1970s, and whose legacy is still operative today. Both of these readings focused on the famous couplet of "war of position" versus "war of maneuver" (frequently erroneously claimed to be of Gramsci's coinage), claiming that the former was both qualitatively distinct from and "preferable" to the latter. Equally, both readings claimed that such a war of position primarily occurs on only one of the "terrains" of civil society or the state, though their assessments regarding which particular terrain constituted the decisive theater of battle in contemporary capitalist societies differed radically.

According to the first of these interpretations (prominent in both libertarian and social democratic perspectives in the New Left in the 1970s), the privileged terrain of the war of position is "civil society." In a way not incompatible with the liberal tradition, civil society was here conceived as a geographical zone in the social formation lying outside the clutches of state reason. Rather than structured by the force of the state, civil society was instead taken to consist in the reciprocity of the ethical, the contingency of the social, or even simply by the indeterminacy of the non-political. A war of position on this terrain therefore needed to involve a strategy of slow and laborious accumulation of forces at such a distance from the state apparatus that the question of a definitive settling of accounts with it is effectively deferred to a suitably indeterminate future. Decisive instead would be the patient construction of a "counter-power" in the interstices of civil society in the hope that it might one day grow so strong as to throw off the impositions of its dominant other.

War of position was in this conception defined in contradistinction to a war of maneuver, which was understood to signify the desire for an immediate confrontation with the state. Such an impatience was furthermore argued to constitute the core of a "Leninist" or "classical Marxist" theory of politics. The latter strategy could only be successfully implemented by the Bolsheviks in the East in the early twentieth century, it was claimed, due to the relative immaturity of Russian civil society at the time. This understanding of war of position ultimately advocated a process of political development involving not, as is some-times thought, the confrontation of two powers—civil society versus the state—but instead the eclipse of the state, as a force of repression, by the freedom embodied in civil society's non-political constitution. The existing state was literally to be bypassed in the process of constructing an alternative form of social organization.

The second interpretation was proposed by what could be characterized as a "Eurocommunism of the right" (many of whose themes have been rediscovered spontaneously or consciously in var-iously modulated forms by "progressive" governmental programs today). According to this interpretation, Gramsci's war of position may commence in mobilizations in civil society, or draw on them for initial logistic support. Ultimately, however, it must make the transition to conducting its campaign within the state itself, given its importance as a final instance of decision and enactment of political command. War of position is thus understood as a proposal for a "long march through the institutions" of the bourgeois state, both those at its "core" (the state apparatus strictly conceived, in the form of sovereign legislative and executive bodies and their direct agencies of enforcement and repres-sion) and those constituting its periphery (in the sense of the broader array of organizational forces theorized in the eighteenth century by cameralism and *Polizeiwissenschaft*).[37]

The state in this vision is conceived as the sum of its individual com-ponent parts (civil society + state apparatus = state). It is this divisibility that permits a strategy based on the war of position to aim gradually to occupy individual institutional outposts, subtracting them from bourgeois political domination and adding them to its own conquered territory, until the sheer force of numbers of a simple arithmetical pro-gression forces open the inner sanctum of the state apparatus. Unlike a war of maneuver modeled—purportedly—on the "Jacobin imaginary," such a strategy does not attempt immediately to storm the citadel in a great set-piece battle. It instead involves a patient subversiveness, undermining the bourgeois state from within.

War of maneuver in Russia in October 1917 had been feasible, ac-cording to this reading, due to a relative immaturity not of civil society but of the state. The extension and complexification of the state (par-ticularly in the so-called West) in the intervening period had made such a strategy not only undesirable but unviable. This strategy thus interpreted Gramsci as a proponent of the thesis of the increasing "singularization" of the sources of political power. If, by the 1970s, the state had come to represent the sole locus of the effective reality of political power, it was there, within the state and not outside it in civil society, that offensive trenches now needed to be built.

Poulantzas's reading of these metaphors in *State, Power, Socialism* proposes a very different understanding of their strategic significance. Rather than opposing them, he posits a continuity between war of position and war of maneuver. In particular, war of position is understood to involve the traversing of the ostensible divisions between civil society and the state rather than remaining internal to one or the other. Poulantzas continues to regard Gramsci's civil society as a type of "lowland" encircling the fortified "citadel" of the state. This terrain of civil society, however, is defined by the quality and intensity of its relationship to the state rather than as a separate and qualitatively distinct territory. War of position is thus read not according to simplistic binary oppositions, either of strategies internal to one of the terrains or in terms of an incommensurability of war of position and maneuver. It becomes instead a question of a tactical decision within an overarching strategic perspective.

Poulantzas argues that the distinction between Gramsci's metaphors consists in their differential temporalities: proletarian "war of position," "essentially conceived" as an "encirclement of a fortress State," or "the application of Lenin's model/strategy to the 'different concrete conditions' of the West," is in effect presented by Poulantzas's reading as a type of war of maneuver "in slow time."[38] It is a strategy of "encircling" the state through the progressive consolidation and expansion of extra-statal strongholds. It may initially occur outside, not within, the state apparatus strictly conceived, on the battle plain of civil society; but it has an immediate relation to state power insofar as the purpose of positioning these trenches in the state's hinterland is to use them to prepare for an assault on the citadel-state itself. Poulantzas therefore distinguishes this understanding of war of position from the supposedly all-out confrontation urged by the war of maneuver, not in terms of strategy but in terms of tactics, tempo, and logistics.

Unlike other images of Gramsci current in the 1970s that regarded him as a more libertarian alternative to the supposed authoritarian excesses of Lenin, this is the depiction of a politician who had thoroughly internalized the Leninist strategy of "dual power"—indeed, perhaps even *too* thoroughly. Despite all the sophistication of his theory of the state, Gramsci remained, according to Poulantzas, a prisoner to the topographical metaphors of the tradition of the Third International. Poulantzas claimed that

> All Lenin's analyses and actions are traversed by the following *leitmotif*: the State must be entirely destroyed through frontal attack in a situation of *dual power*, to be replaced by a second power—soviets—which will no longer be a State in the proper sense of the term, since it will already have begun to wither away.[39]

Poulantzas was quick to acknowledge the difference between this revolutionary strategic perspective and its later degeneration under Stalinism. Nevertheless, he was equally as quick to argue that there was a line of continuity between the perspectives that had redefined the Bolsheviks' practice in 1917 and the state theory that was taken to define the international communist movement throughout much of the twentieth century.

This theory consisted, according to Poulantzas, in four fundamental presuppositions regarding the *nature* of social and political power, the *location* of political struggle, the *means* of this struggle, and its *goal*. First, the nature of political power was understood to be a "quantifiable substance" presently sequestered by the bourgeoisie, which could be expropriated by proletarian forces and wielded for their own ends. Second, the location of "the struggle of the popular masses for state power" was argued to lie outside the state, in a civil society defined in a negative fashion, as that which the state is not. Third, the means of this struggle consisted in the "creation of a situation of dual power." Fourth and finally, the goal of such a strategy was seen to consist in the capture and destruction of the fortress State, to be replaced "by the second power (soviets) constituted as a State of a new type."[40]

These were the perspectives that Poulantzas argued were also to be found in Gramsci's *Prison Notebooks*. Cognizant with Poulantzas's earlier Althusserian mode of faintly damning praise, *State, Power, Socialism* presented an unwaveringly ambiguous argumentative line.

> Of course, there is no disputing Gramsci's considerable theoretical political contributions, and we know the distance he took from the Stalinist experience. Still . . . the fact remains that Gramsci was also unable to pose the problem in all its amplitude. His famous analyses of the differences between war of movement (as waged by the Bolsheviks in Russia) and war of position are essentially conceived as the application of Lenin's model/strategy to the "different concrete conditions" of the West.[41]

Such Leninist residues were held to have had a decisive (and deleterious) impact on Gramsci's ability to theorize the State. Gramsci had not understood, Poulantzas argued, that "to take or capture state power is not simply to lay hands on part of the state machinery in order to replace it with a second power." He had remained enthralled by a notion of the State as "a fortress that may be penetrated by means of a wooden horse," or "a safe that may be cracked by burglary."[42] In the end, therefore, though more sophisticated and less prone to vulgar instrumentalism than either Stalinist or social democratic variants, Gramsci's proposal for the revolutionary working class movement in the West had remained within the problematic of the strategy of "dual power" insofar as "the decisive shift in the relationship of forces takes places not within the State but between the State and the masses outside."[43]

"A Copernican Revolution in Politics"

Ultimately, Poulantzas judged Gramsci's theorization of the state to be inadequate, not because of any conceptual inconsistency but because it failed to provide a theoretical structure with which to comprehend the historical advances in the forms of bourgeois state domination since the long post-WWII boom. It was a claim that he repeated in eloquent terms in what could well be considered his final political "testament," an interview (belatedly) entitled "A Copernican Revolution in Politics":[44]

Unlike Althusser, I was very influenced by Gramsci's thinking. But the more time passes, the more I am convinced that Gramsci does not represent, as I long believed, a completely new phase of theoretical reflection. Of course, Gramsci was certainly one of the first to identify a set of problems that are still ours: the expansion of the state, a very great sensitivity to civil society, the presence of the popular masses in the constitution of the state. . . . But he still reasons within a fundamentally Leninist conception, [and] his problem is to apply the Leninist strategy in the West. Even if it is no longer a war of movement, the state still remains to be conquered. [. . .] The problem of encirclement, of war of position, always rests on a double power. This is why I think—as others have already said—that there is not in Gramsci a positive theory of the exercise of power in the institutions of representative democracy, in the transition to democratic socialism . . . he remains dependent on the problems of his time and I believe that he cannot help us much in the unprecedented tasks that await us.

This was the "mature" Poulantzas's final contribution to Marxist theory. His insistence in 1979 that time had not been kind to Gramsci's theory of the state might appear to echo Althusser's dramatic declaration in Venice in 1977 of a "crisis of Marxism," as long cherished verities in the socialist movement were finally subjected to searching critique or even definitive refutation.[45] Yet the presuppositions of Poulantzas's critique of the tradition of dual power had already been formulated many years earlier; arguably, it can even be traced back to the strongly "humanistic" phase of Poulantzas's thought under the influence of Sartrean existentialism and phenomenology, before his encounter with the Althusserian paradigm.

Already in the early 1960s Poulantzas had argued that the contemporary capitalist state was not the object of (social or political) actions that occurred outside it, as if the state were merely one (administrative) instance alongside others in a homogenously stratified social formation. Rather, politics had come to constitute the very materiality of the state itself. The state was not "traversed" by class antagonisms and struggles (as if they originated elsewhere and only "passed through" the state), but was the concrete form in which those antagonisms and struggles always occurred. The topographical metaphor according to which there lay some place "beyond the State" in which the forces—whether ethical, economic, social, or political—for a future state could be mustered was thus rejected because the course of capitalist development had made the fields of politics and the state effectively co-extensive.

In effect, to adopt a variation of the famous Derridean formulation in its constitutive deconstructive ambiguity, Poulantzas claimed that *Il n'y a pas de hors-état* For this perspective, there was nothing "outside the state" [*hors-état*]; but even more fundamentally, no "outside-state," that is, no political practice that was not itself already "within and of" the state in an expansive sense. Throughout the 1970s, Poulantzas argued with increasing insistence that the state was instead to be comprehended immanently, as a "material condensation" of a power relation between classes.[46] Rather than transposition of a power relation already existing somewhere else, Poulantzas conceived this material condensation in terms of the intensification of the power relation between classes that is constitutive of the state as such. As pre-eminent institutional form, the state was thus ultimately thought of as an intensification of the power relation between classes *qua* power relation, as a doubling back of that relation on itself, or as its self-relating.

The outlines of this perspective were already central to the "young" Poulantzas. It is true that in this early period, Poulantzas seems to propose a structuralist-functionalist theory of the state as governing political instance of social practices that are still in some sense located beyond it, and that his notion of condensation seems largely reducible to the psychoanalytical emphasis on condensation as "representative" transformation. For instance, in 1968 in *Political Power and Social Classes*, he argued that the state "*has the particular function of constituting the factor of cohesion between the levels of a social formation*," or in an alternative formulation, that the state is "*the regulating factor of* [a social formation's] *global equilibrium as a system*."[47] Furthermore, when Poulantzas claims that the state is "also the structure in which the contradictions of the various levels of a formation are *condensed*," he seems to valorize precisely the metaphoric dimensions of condensation that were so strongly emphasized by Lacan's notoriously playful reading of Jakobson.[48]

By the time of *State, Power, Socialism* in 1978, however, the structuralist-functionalist residues have been entirely eclipsed by a more—and perhaps even *too* excessively—dialectical conception of the state's condensational efficacy. Poulantzas now argued that "once the State is admitted, we cannot imagine any social phenomenon (any knowledge, power, language, or writing) having a primitive, pre-political existence: all social phenomena always occur in relation to the state and class division."[49] The state was therefore not to be conceived, in a updated "Weberian" fashion, as that organization that claims—successfully—to condense within itself struggles that originated else-where; it was rather that process of condensation itself, permitting no appeal to forces that might arrive from "outside" to cut the Gordian knot of its contradictions.

Poulantzas here seemed spontaneously to rediscover the central insights of Hegel's *Philosophy of Right* regarding the constitutively political nature of modernity's ostensibly "merely" social relations (though Poulantzas himself never seems to have explored explicitly his elective affinities with Hegel).[50] For both Poulantzas and Hegel, seemingly merely "social" relations are always already "political" re-lations of power with a determinate relation to the state form. They are interpellated by and simultaneously constitutive of the state. Both ground and result of state formation, the dialectic between social and political relations here admits of no originary foundation but subsists only in their mutual co-constitution as reinforcing practices of socio-political organization.

By the late 1970s, Poulantzas's theoretical analysis of the capitalist state as a dynamically self-referential totality was consolidated into an explicit proposal for an alternative strategic perspective in the con-temporary communist movement: a "democratic road to socialism." As the processual nature of the metaphor suggests, Poulantzas un-derstood this strategy not simply as the articulation of a known "so-cialism" with the values of "democracy," generically conceived in terms of equality, liberty, individual rights, and so forth. Such appeals had been common among dissident currents in the international commu-nist movement particularly since 1956, growing in strength and ap-peal with each wave of Soviet backed repression. Nor was Poulantzas's reference to democracy simply indicative of a majoritarian emphasis, in the classical sense of the power of the demos set against that of elites.

The innovation of Poulantzas's proposal consisted in its attempt to give "democracy" a concretely historical and more precise institutional sense. On the one hand, democracy was understood not in the abstract, but as "actually existing democracy," as it had emerged from the ruins of WWII in Western Europe and beyond (frequently via the suppression of the anti-fascist partisan struggle) as the form of government of the self-characterized "free world." On the other hand, democracy as a terrain of struggle was also understood not generically but in terms of the forms and procedures by means of which the legitimacy of contemporary democratic regimes was secured. A "democratic road to socialism" was thus a proposal to progress toward socialism by means of, rather than in opposition to, the democratic processes of the modern, representative parliamentary state in the specific conjuncture of the fading *détente* of the Cold War.

This perspective was central to Poulantzas's argument that the strategy of dual power had been superannuated because it lacked a theory of transformation of the state apparatus. The Bolshevik tradition, he claimed, had simply opposed the supposedly "direct" democracy of the Soviets to the conventionally "representative" forms of the provisional government. Despite the appeal to immediacy as guarantee against temporal and substantial corruption, however, the Soviets thereby ended up effectively "mirroring" the existing state apparatus from without, rather than transforming it from within. The democratic road to socialism instead argued for an articulation rather than opposition of direct and representative democratic forms. This articulation was supposed to lead to the transformation of the state apparatus and thus seemingly also of the state itself. Poulantzas argued that "the long process of taking power" needed to involve "the spreading, development, reinforcement, coordination and direction of those diffuse centres of resistance which the masses always possess with the state networks, in such a way that they become the real centres of power on the strategic terrain of the State."[51]

The democratic road to socialism thus ultimately proposed what can be characterized as a "war of position" conducted within the existing state. It was a strategy to be pursued by means of struggles at varying levels of intensity and depth, some closer to the "center" of the state apparatus, others at a certain "distance" from it. By reinforcing representative democracy—as a guarantee of juridical equity—Poulantzas proposed to overcome the threat of degeneration into Stalinist autarchy. By strengthening the power of direct democracy—as the guarantee of an active participation of the masses—he proposed to overcome the risk of "traditional reformism" that he acknowledged was implicit in such a strategy.[52] Precisely what such a transformation of the state would involve, however, and whether it could lead to the *Absterben* [withering away] of the State as at least one prior Marxist tradition had hoped, remained enigmas that haunted all of Poulantzas's final texts.

A "Democratic" Road to Socialism?

This strategic proposal prompted a number of harsh criticisms at the time, predictably enough often focused on charges of "reformism" if not "renegacy."[53] It is undoubtable that Poulantzas's thinking about the state in the late 1970s, like that of so many others, was highly influenced by the events of Chile in 1973 and the later failure of the Portuguese Revolution. Yet it would be a mistake to dismiss his questioning of time-worn verities of the revolutionary Marxist tradition as merely an instance of (crypto-) apostasy overdetermined by the demands of the conjuncture. Poulantzas explicitly signaled that the democratic road to socialism, whatever risks of reformism lay along it, was avowedly a revolutionary strategic perspective, aiming to produce "real breaks" in the existing relation of class forces and "sweeping transformation" in the nature of state institutions.[54]

The real theoretical and practical difficulties of Poulantzas's strategic proposal derived from longer standing unresolved tensions in his basic theoretical presuppositions. Three of the most significant of these tensions emerge directly from the terms in which Poulantzas had framed his critique of Gramsci and by means of which he aimed to overcome the historical limitations of the tradition of the Third International: first, the thesis of the non-exteriority of the state; second, the conception of the state as a unitary condensation of political power;

and third, the notion of a strategic perspective beyond dual power. In each case, these tensions revolve around the difficulty of thinking a type of politics within and beyond the state.

Non-exteriority

Poulantzas conceived the unity of the state in terms of its non-exteriority. The state derived its consistency, that is, not in a negative relation to that which it is not, as in the various mythical moments preceding the properly political that have so fascinated modern political thought from Hobbes's state of nature onward. Rather, the state's consistency emerges from its relation to itself, in a virtuous circle of political power and state form mutually reinforcing each other. If the state is conceived in such totalized and totalizing terms, however, from where might it derive the dynamic that could drive its development, distinguish its component parts, and open it up to the possibility of radical transformation? Without an outside that limits and thereby determines the possibility of its internal structuring and unevenness (as precondition of movement), is it possible to provide an account of the nature of the relations within the state between, for instance, parties and movements, or between supposedly representative and direct forms of democracy—in short, between political form and content?

Whatever their other weaknesses, "instrumentalist" theories of the state can provide a clear answer to such questions. Due to the state's limitation to a specific institutional form (the state apparatus in the strict sense, as institution of governance and repression), only the first of the terms in these binary relations is properly "political," while the second is composed of the "non-political" objects that politics organizes and governs. Political form, that is, is conceived as "within" the state, or even as the state itself, while the content of politics is consigned to its exterior, as the other required by the state in order to demonstrate its own specificity and autonomy. These perspectives can thus provide a consistent account of the sense in which movements can be said to precede the parties that exceed them, or the way in which direct democracy might be regarded as a "primitive" form in need of sublation into the more mature institutions of representation. The social is tutored by the arrival of the political, just as content can only be defined as such when it is "contained" within a form.

Poulantzas's concrete analyses implicitly presuppose such distinctions and relations, given as they are to identifying the varying degrees of distance from the "core" of the state of particular forms and instances of political action. His explicit theoretical pronouncements, however, seems less capable of explaining how and on what basis the relations between these different moments either can or should be evaluated and coordinated, because they affirm that all politics is always already "condensed" by the state, even before it is "overcoded" by specific state institutions. In short, Poulantzas's strategic proposal confronts the following interrogative: Does the thesis that there is nothing outside the state not have the consequence of negating any strategic perspective that aims to produce a fundamental rupture with the current state form, insofar as it is not able to locate the Archimedean point from which such a transformation could be produced?

Unitary condensation

Poulantzas's argument that the state is "nothing but" a condensation of power relations opens up more difficulties that it at first sight seems to resolve. It presupposes an ultimately unitary conception of the nature of the political power that is generated within this condensation. This unitarian nature derives not from the singularization of a multiplicity of social forces during their condensation into the political form of the state—in other words, condensation conceived as reduction to a common denominator. Rather, the unitary nature of this condensation and the political power that results from it consists in the formalization of this multiplicity in terms of the specifically political forms of power embodied in the state. In this sense, the existing state and its institutions are effectively posited as the necessary appearance of an essence, in a circular and tautological relationship of affirmation.

In such relations of reflection between unitary political power and its unitary state, there would appear to be no space for the emergence of a type of political power that would be resistant, in principle, to its condensation in the existing state form. Does Poulantzas here come perilously close to a conception of political power as a type of "diagram" or "abstract machine" immanent to the state form and vice versa, similar to the conception that he claimed, under the influence of Deleuze, to be at work in the "neo-functionalism" of Foucault's "second order epistemological discourse" (as opposed to Foucault's more profound, "Marxist-compatible," concrete analyses)?[55] In short, does the theory of the state as a condensation of power relations run the risk of formulating a non-relational and formalist theory of political power in which political power becomes just the relating to itself of capitalist social relations?

Beyond dual power

For all the sophistication and forceful formulation of Poulantzas's vigorous critique of dual power as a political strategy, it is unclear if his alternative approach really does escape the limitations that he ascribed to this "third-internationalist" tradition—or even if his approach is not itself a theory of a type of dual power. His emphasis on the notion of social forces "traversing" the state at various levels, depths, and intensities, of a "center" of state power encircled by struggles on its "periphery," arguably leads him to repropose, implicitly, a theory of the "bifurcation" of a fundamentally unitary political power. Rather than an opposition between qualitatively different types of powers, however, the powers envisaged here are formally homogenous. They are distinguished not qualitatively, but merely quantitatively, in terms of their relative distance from an imprecisely defined center of state power.

In this perspective, power is "political" insofar as it is related to the state, and vice versa; it is the intensity of the relation to existing state institutions that determines the time and modality of transition from the merely social to the properly political. But is it possible to maintain the perspective of a radical rupture with existing forms of social and political order if the structural and necessary unity of *political* power as always *state* power is affirmed? While most theories of dual power from Lenin onward have posited a clear distinction between constituted state power and the revolutionary forces that aim to launch an assault on it, Poulantzas's insistence that contemporary capitalist state power must be seized from "within" seems to leave no possibility for the theorization of genuinely autonomous institutions of a "counter-power" of the subaltern classes and social groups. Can there ever be a politics beyond the state?

These unresolved tensions in Poulantzas's thought also continue to define many of the challenges that radical movements over the last 30 years have confronted. What is the most enabling relationship between parties and movements in the context of emancipatory politics? If the former are not redundant, what role can they play in reinforcing and extending the latter? How is power to be conceived both within the state and within movements aiming at its transformation, and how should their opposition and difference be understood? What would it mean to "take power" in contemporary societies characterized by the biopolitical diffusion of disciplinary technologies? Above all, what are the possible forms and spaces of dual power today, amidst the crisis of a "financialized state" in which economic and political power seem to be functionally fused? How is it possible to take the "distance" from the state required for the construction of a counter-power when decisive dimensions of the contemporary crisis, particularly in terms of state fiscal policy for social services, seem to demand not the pure act of separation from the state but the impure assumption of responsibility for resolving their most immediate and deleterious effects?

In other words, many of the debates currently animating contemporary social and political movements can be characterized as participating in the problematic "democratic road to socialism," with all its risks and opportunities. In this sense, Poulantzas should be regarded as one of the major theorists of the contemporary conjuncture, outlining a horizon of problems that emancipatory politics today is rediscovering in changed but not radically dissimilar conditions.

Given that the democratic road to socialism was proposed as an attempted superannuation of the supposedly lingering Leninist residues that compromised Gramsci's attempts to break with an instrumentalist theory of the state, the legitimacy of Poulantzas's proposal as a strategic perspective, and its contemporary utility, can be judged, at least in part, according to the accuracy of its characterization of the theory against which it sought to define itself. Poulantzas's reading of

Gramsci can therefore today be understood as an exemplary case study of the strengths and limits of Marxist state theory for confronting the central political challenges of contemporary emancipatory politics and its relation to the state.

Three seemingly merely philological questions can help to clarify the nature of these challenges:

- First, did Gramsci really posit a terrain outside the state on which a new political power could emerge, which could then go on to capture the state (apparatus) and replace it? Or was he instead a theorist of the "integral state" as dialectical "identity-distinction" of civil and political societies?
- Second, do the *Prison Notebooks* conceive of political power as a univocal "quantifiable substance" possessed by one particular class, and therefore able to be opposed by another "quantity" of power in the possession of another class? Or do they aim to theorize a type of political power "of a completely different type"?
- Third, is Gramsci's war of position really merely a more sophisticated variant of the strategy of dual power, in its fundamental presuppositions, still open to the same criticisms that Poulantzas directed at its Leninist, Third Internationalist and social democratic versions? Or can Gramsci instead be regarded as having elaborated a novel conception of the "duality of dual power"?

In each case, Poulantzas's reading anxiously misapprehended the nature of Gramsci's theory, which we can now read in terms much closer to the positions outlined by Poulantzas himself than he suspected. Even more significantly, in each case, this misapprehension helps to reveal significant dimensions of how emancipatory politics might be configured within, against, and beyond the state.

The Integral State

The most striking feature of Poulantzas's critique of Gramsci's state theory is that he did not discuss Gramsci's most distinctive contribution to state theory: the concept of the "integral 'state'," conceived as a dialectical "identity-distinction" of civil society and political society.[56] It is striking not because Poulantzas shares this neglect with many other readings of Gramsci from the late 1960s and early 1970s. Rather, it is striking because he was better placed than most to overcome this oversight, for at least two reasons. First, one of Poulantzas's closest collaborators, Christine Buci-Glucksmann, was among the first to direct attention to the importance of Gramsci's "general concept of the State" for comprehending the novel articulation of these concepts in the *Prison Notebooks*.[57] Second, as the early discussions of the concept of the integral state in the late 1970s had begun to discern, Gramsci perhaps goes the furthest of all prior Marxist theoreticians before Poulantzas toward breaking definitively with a exclusively instrumentalist conception of the state. The fact that Poulantzas does not even note the presence of this concept in the *Prison Notebooks*, let alone its specificity, might therefore be regarded as something of a symptomatic oversight, almost as if Poulantzas could not see that which was too threateningly close to him.

Following Buci-Glucksmann's pioneering interpretation, early discussions of the integral state in the 1970s tended to understand it as a euphemism for a historical process of "expansion" or "extension" of the state, or as it became widely known, the "extended state" [*stato allargato*].[58] Buci-Glucksmann here focused in particular on the political context of the 1920s and 1930s, with its increasing state protagonism and intervention into civil society, as a decisive influence on Gramsci's thought. The notion of the extended state was thus read as a variant of the contemporary theorization of the transformation of the state's role by Austromarxist theorists, among others. It was in these "stagist" terms that Gramsci's state theory was debated in Italy in the 1970s, with a particular focus on the notion of "transition." This debate exerted a strong influence on discussions at the time in Latin America, where the notion of an extended state arguably received its most sophisticated elaboration, and most far-reaching political consequences, as it was translated into the developmentalist debates and theorizations of democracy as a response to the dictatorships of those years.[59]

According to this reading, Gramsci's concept represents a variation of a well-known narrative, shared to a greater or lesser extent and recounted with enthusiasm or (more often) resignation, by such un-likely fellow travelers as Max Weber, Carl Schmitt, Jürgen Habermas, Mario Tronti, Michel Foucault, Quentin Skinner, Gianfranco Poggi, Norbert Elias, Pierre Bourdieu, Ranajit Guha, Michael Mann, Francis Fukuyama, and Giorgio Agamben—in other words, almost every sig-nificant current of twentieth-century political theory.[60] This narrative describes the increasing "statalization" of modern societies as a once territorially limited and demographically exclusionary organizational apparatus progressively increased its reach across an entire geograph-ical region, "colonizing" it and affirming its legitimacy as a general instance of deliberation and decision-making—and executor of legit-imate and legal violence. In other words, this is the story of how a par-ticular *Stand* (estate) managed to affirm itself as universal *Staat* (state), invading previously autonomous domains and subjecting them to in-creasingly intense supervisory and disciplinary control. Ultimately, this account is premised on the notion of a progressive "becoming po-litical" of the non-political, in a repetition of the myth of the apolitical foundations of society at the origins of modern contract theory.

In its different declinations, this narrative ultimately coincides with the thesis of modernity as a process of rationalization if not of secu-larization. This thesis envisages the emergence of a distinctive form of "impersonal power," embodied in the "artificial person" of the state, and a concomitant expansion of impersonal forms of bureaucratic reg-ulation of social life as an inherent and inexorable tendency in political modernity. From Nietzsche's chilling apprehension of the state as the "coldest of all cold monsters," to Weber's fear that the future belonged to soulless bureaucrats, to Habermas's pleas against the "colonization" of the lifeworld, to Foucault's reflections on the governmentalization of political power, such analyses have long fueled fears of the growing "totalitarian" dimensions of the modern state.[61]

The readings of Gramsci in 1970s that focused on the theme of an extension of the state inscribed the *Prison Notebooks* in this tra-dition. Understood in these terms, Gramsci's analysis of the emer-gence of a bourgeois "integral state" could be seen as primarily and ultimately a temporal theory of the process by means of which the modern state has aggressively sought to submit previously autono-mous social instances to its calculating and totalizing logic. Gramsci's political strategy could then be understood as an attempt to mobilize the last remaining residues of an "untainted" civil society against the encroaching corruptions of the state, as the organic asserting of its rights over the artificial, as the social reclaiming of its rightful primacy against the usurpation of the political: in short, as the recovery of all those forms of "authenticity" that have been lost in the unfolding of political modernity.

If the foregoing narrative constitutes a tragic perception of modern politics, a very different perspective tells the same tale in a seemingly more comedic fashion. For the notion of political modernity as a process of progressive rationalization of its pre-modern raw materials has also sometimes been thought to indicate a potential modernizing path for socialist projects. For this vision, the extension of the primacy of "politics" over the entire social formation represents the flooding of light into those dark corners of privilege lurking in the still merely "social." Conceived as the transparency of the public against the obscurity of the private, politics in this sense is affirmed as a fortunate destiny, or as the very definition of modernity itself, as transparent, self-reflexive, and consciously regulated organization of social life. "Socialism" is then represented not as an anarchic negation of the state but as its valorization; it replaces the "classical" bourgeois state form in the sense of sublating it, extending the political logic of the state beyond the state, or rather, universalizing its particularist limitations. Gramsci has also sometimes been read in these terms, and prominent theorists today who claim Gramscian inspiration have proposed variants of this comedic narrative.[62]

Both tragic and comedic tales have their attractions, and both have found their partisans in different eras of the history of modern political thought; and traces of each of them can certainly be found in different citations from the *Prison Notebooks*, particularly when they are read out of context. These narratives, however, are not Gramsci's most innovative contribution, just as the "extended state" is a term that is alien to the *Prison Notebooks*.[63] Gramsci does indeed develop the concept of the integral state by means of extensive historical analyses; and the *Prison Notebooks* do provide a distinctive account of the emergence, consolidation, and complexification of modern state power, including the intimate relationship between the development of civil society and the modern state. But he also outlines an alternative perspective on the political significance of this process, a perspective that is ultimately starkly at odds with both the presuppositions and consequences of the tale of the state's civilizing mission.

As it emerges in the *Prison Notebooks*, the notion of the integral state was an attempt to analyze the specificity of the modern state as an organizational form of bourgeois class power: the dialectical identity-distinction of state and society, or of the political and the social.[64] Explicitly affiliating his reflections to the Hegelian tradition of state theory, Gramsci aimed to analyze the mutual interpenetration and reinforcement of "political society" and "civil society" within a unified and indivisible state form. According to this concept, the state in its integral form is not to be limited to the machinery of government and legal institutions (the state understood in a limited or instrumental sense, as a state apparatus in opposition to civil society). Rather, the concept of the integral state posits a dialectical unity that is not conceived topographically, like the unity that a map imposes on the diverse terrains that fall within it. Rather, the unity of the integral state is conceived in terms of the subsistence of a relation, as the mutual dependence of particularity and universality. Gramsci therefore argued in a famous formulation that

> the general notion of the State includes elements which need to be referred back to the notion of civil society (in the sense that one might say that the State = political society + civil society, in other words, hegemony armored with coercion).[65]

Or in an even more significant formulation, capturing the strongly relational focus of Gramsci's theorization, "the State is the entire complex of practical and theoretical activities with which the ruling class not only justifies and maintains its dominance, but manages to win the active consent of those over whom it rules."[66]

Civil society in this vision is not a terrain beyond or outside the State from which a "counter-power" might emerge. Rather, civil society is a rough and ready amalgam of particularities "in search of a master," to use the phrase with which Lacan mocked the radical students of 1968.[67] In other words, civil society both is and is not the state: its institutions and practices are called on to "act" as the context of the state's regulatory project, and thus to concretize it. At the same time, however, like in the structure of an abusive relationship, it is unremittingly reminded of its own lowly status, as mere agent of the realization of an intention elaborated elsewhere. Civil society "occurs" whenever subaltern relations are constituted by the overdetermining power of political society, which claims for itself the right to be the "voice" that civil society is always constitutively denied.

In a similar fashion, political society also should not be understood merely as a euphemism for the state apparatus, as a geographically determinate location. In Gramsci's most innovative usages of the term, *political society* both includes and goes beyond the state apparatus in either a strict sense (in Weber's terms, the monopoly of legitimate violence) or broader sense (for Althusser, both repressive state apparatuses and ideological state apparatuses). "Political society," conceived as a relation, comprises not simply institutional arrangements but all activities of deliberation, decision, and command diffused throughout the social formation as instances of ordering universality. Like the panther to which Dante compared his "illustrious vernacular," political society's "scent" is everywhere, and not only in those places where it is to be seen.[68] "Spiritual orders" moving between the realms of the visible and invisible, civil society and political society are locked in an endless struggle as the two fundamental ways in which political action within the modern state occurs. The modern state is thus properly characterized as a curious "mixed constitution" of simultaneously particular and universal instances, each of which is only constituted in relation to that which it is not.

We can glimpse here a distinctive account of the emergence and consolidation of modern state power. It is not a tale of teleological progression but of formalist repetition of the modern state's fundamental logic. The dialectical reinforcement of civil and political moments in the degeneration of the Jacobin project in the extended French revolutionary process reached its "formal perfection" in the parliamentary regimes tenuously affirmed throughout the nineteenth century—a "perfection" and not betrayal of an original promise. The onset of what Gramsci describes as "passive revolutions" in the second half of the nineteenth century should thus not be understood as a counterrevolutionary antithesis of an originally "good" integral state, as if a bourgeoisie grown complacent had forgotten its heroic origins. On the contrary, those passive revolutions were the working out of the full consequences of the identity distinction of the social and political on which the bourgeois integral state was premised, within its Jacobin class "limits."[69]

According to Gramsci, those limits were first clearly revealed in the Chapelier law of June 14, 1791, which effectively repressed workers' autonomous organization. The distinctiveness of Gramsci's mature analysis of Jacobinism in the *Prison Notebooks*—distinct from his earlier position, and even from Marx's nuanced account—consists in his recognition of its dialectical complexity and contradiction as a practical ideological formation. He is thus able to acknowledge Jacobinism's historical strengths (as *faber* of the terrain of the national-popular on which a real unity of intellectuals and the people could be constructed) as simultaneously the source of its structural weaknesses for any genuinely self-emancipatory politics (insofar as the national-popular terrain is constitutively structured by relations of subalternity between the rulers and the ruled, between the organizers and the associated, between intellectuals and the *semplice* [simple]). The organic crisis of the post-WWI period that culminated in the rise of Fascism was thus not simply an "actual form" of passive revolution but rather the "perfection" of this primal logic of the integral state itself.[70]

Whether at the origins of Jacobinism in the late eighteenth century or the organic crisis of its legacy in the early twentieth century, political society's claim to universality was structurally premised on the consignment of the particularity of civil society to a subaltern role, the mere "object" of political society's comprehension and calculation. The emergence of the modern state for this perspective was not therefore a process of increasing "politicization." The fundamental presuppositions of modern state life were always already political in themselves, in the very act of institution of the "intimate separation" between the political and the civil. Political modernity is therefore conceived not as a process of "statalization" of social life, or an extension of the state into previously non-statal domains. It is instead better understood as the repetition of a primary—or "primal," in a Freudian sense—neutralization that inheres in the modern state, not as a "destiny" to be realized or feared but as its formal structure and basic mode of functioning.[71]

This is not a tale of the colonizing expansion of statal instances onto still unravished terrains, or the progressive becoming political of the non-political. Rather, it is the history of the intensification of the integral state as a machine for the production of "subalternity," that specific perverted, "pseudo-hegemonic" dynamic generated within the passive revolutionary dimensions of the bourgeois integral state.[72] The main theme of this narrative is not the expansion of political society, as enfranchisement is conceded to an increasingly larger portion of the population, according to the self-consciously self-congratulatory claims of liberalism's post-WWII selective tradition.[73] On the contrary, it is a tale told of the structural restriction of political society, which requires the continual production of its subaltern other in civil society.

Political society is "perfected" not at the end of a long road to liberation when it englobes all social elements and terrains within its beneficent "condensation" of claims to universality. Its elaboration consists in the repetition of its foundational gesture of constituting the particularities of civil society in the neutralized form of the supposedly non-political. Political society's claim, *qua* political society, has always and everywhere been to embody such an instance of universality, defined in opposition to the particularity that the "merely civil" is forced to assume. As the "administration of (persons as) things," it is doubtful that such an integral state could represent any type of possible "transition to socialism"—at least not if the latter is understood in the sense of a fundamental rupture with the logic and forms that have dominated political modernity.

Poulantzas's claim that Gramsci posits a terrain "lying wholly outside the state" perhaps reflects more the terms of debate in the 1970s than it does the potentials of perspectives sketched out in the *Prison Notebooks* in the 1930s.[74] There is no terrain outside the state for Gramsci, whether this "outside" is thought in the classically liberal terms of a properly "civil" society as a realm of (individual) freedom or the recent biopolitical reformulation of natural law's ideological foundation in the notion of a "bare life" that precedes and exceeds the state's "capture." For such a focus on the modern state as a political relation of subalternity does not comprehend the state as a "terrain" in any sense.

The state is instead conceived as a "non-place," or rather, as a political relation, the unitary formal synthesis of the multiple relations of force that both structure and subsist in processes of subalternization and their contestation.

Political Power "of a Completely Different Type"

Poulantzas's critique of a unitary conception of political power in *State, Power, Socialism* was conducted on two fronts, each marked by the transposition of contradictions derived from the other. On the one hand, Poulantzas criticized what he took to be a unitary and self-referential conception of power in (the early and middle) Foucault. He insisted on the need for a Marxist reformulation of the notion of disciplinary power in terms of the displacement and condensation of relations of class struggle, and questioned the theoretical presuppositions of Foucault's resistance to theoretical and political engagement within the state.[75] On the other hand, Poulantzas also argued against what he suggested was a curiously unacknowledged alliance between a formalist conceptualization of power and those currents in third internationalist Marxism, including Gramsci, that thought of power in terms of a "quantifiable substance." Currently sequestered by the existing state apparatus, such a quantity could either be expropriated by social and political forces "outside" the state or opposed by another quantity of power, in an effective reduction of politics to arithmetical calculation.

As has only been fully appreciated more recently, there was a frustratingly incomplete encounter between the development of Poulantzas and Foucault's work, particularly their texts from the second half of the 1970s.[76] Foucault's thought turned increasingly throughout the late 1970s to a consideration of the ways in which a manifold of powers is shaped, regulated, and systemized into unitary, albeit always contingent and unstable, systems. In the same period, Poulantzas instead attempted to deepen his conception of the pluri-relational dimensions of the political power condensed in the contemporary capitalist state as a terrain and structure of struggle. Their incomplete encounter may have been due to differences in their political and theoretical traditions, but precisely for that reason a fuller retrospective dialogue between their positions may help to illuminate that which was unthought in each of their works.

Yet there was also a missed encounter between Poulantzas's strategic approach to political power and that of Gramsci, a failure even more remarkable given how close their positions were in many other respects. Rather than a representative of a tendency in Marxism to think power in quantitative, formalist, and instrumentalist terms—in other words, as fundamentally compatible with the dominant modern conception of sovereignty as exhaustive, singular, and indivisible—Gramsci's exploration of the varied forms and modalities of hegemony instead can be understood as a significant early attempt within the Marxist tradition consciously to think political power outside and beyond such a souverainist frame.[77]

In the 1970s (and even sometimes still today), this was admittedly not a common reading of Gramsci, who was more often understood as a thoroughly state-centric theorist. Poulantzas in this sense again appears simply to have followed the accepted vulgate of his time, even as his intuitions can be seen to problematize its presuppositions. To many readers in those years, it seemed that the *Prison Notebooks* offered a general, unitary theory of political power. Indeed, one of the reasons for Gramsci's immense international popularity in this phase of the "post-New Left" was that he seemed to offer a sophisticated Marxist political theory that, in its comprehensiveness, could feasibly be presented as a Marxist candidate for inclusion in the pantheon of the "classics" of Western political philosophy, thereby countering claims that Marxism was characterized by an irremediable "deficit" of political reason.

At the center of this theory, according to these readings, stood the notion of "hegemony," understood as a structured system of power based on an almost arithmetic combination of different quantities of coercion and consent.[78] In effect, this reading interpreted hegemony as an "antechamber" to sovereignty, or as a stage on the way to its realization. Gramsci's often-quoted claim that there can and should be "a political hegemony" before the assumption of governmental power (originally formulated in relation to a specific aspect of the Italian Risorgimento, but frequently read as a generic maxim of a normative political science) would seem to offer a prime example of such a conception of political power as a quantity or instrument that can be appropriated and deployed by a variety of social and political forces, interests, and organizations.[79]

Similarly, Gramsci's later argument that there is always a struggle between "two hegemonies" seems to imply that we are dealing with two competing systems of power, opposed to each other but by no means incommensurable, insofar as each aspires to become a total sovereign system—which was precisely the reason for their clash.[80] According to these readings, hegemony might even be interpreted as the name for a certain "quantity" of political power that has been forged into an instrument of domination, available in principle for appropriation by different social and political forces.

Other passages in the *Prison Notebooks*, however, distinguish much more clearly between different types of hegemony, between the different hegemonic practices that imply and reinforce distinct types of political power.[81] The form of political power always depends on the specificity of the class forces and interests that it transforms. But it also depends, as some of Gramsci's reflections on varying hegemonic practices suggest, on the modality of this transformation, that is, the way in which power relations traverse the constitution of specific forms of political power. On the one hand, the type of hegemony that Gramsci analyzes in the emergence of the bourgeoisie as a ruling class in Europe during the long nineteenth century (primarily in his analyses of the Italian Risorgimento, but more generally in the elaboration of the notion of passive revolution) results in a form of political power that aims to constrain and limit the political expression of the popular classes. This form of hegemony could indeed be characterized, as some critics have recently begun to suggest, as a type of "sovereignty under another name."[82]

On the other hand, however, stands an entirely different practice of hegemonic politics, one closer to the Bolshevik model that inspired Gramsci's original engagement with the term of hegemony and the reality it sought to comprehend, as a political organizer and leader of the Italian Communist Party. Rather than a force of repression or domination, this sense of hegemony refers to the processes of leadership—of proposal, counter-proposal, example, guidance, correction, revision—involved in the learning process of the subalterns' struggle to "desubalternize" themselves. Passive revolutionary processes involve the relations of political society overdetermining those of civil society. This alternative practice of hegemony reverses the polarity. It is instead civil society that here asserts its potential autonomy from political society, thereby denying the legitimacy not only of existing political society as organizing instance, but also in a certain sense deconstructing itself, *qua* civil society, as a 'merely' associative instance.

In this conception, the specificity of political power is not thought in terms of an instrument or "quantifiable substance," but rather, in relational terms. Political power is here understood as the capacity, or incapacity, to act of one class or social group in relation to another. But just as crucially, it is also thought in terms of a class or group's ability to act in relation *to itself*. In other words, for Gramsci, political power is not immanent to the state as a condensation of a power relation between classes, for in Poulantzas's sense, such a condensation is possible only insofar as that power relation is itself already within, and therefore an expression of, the state form. Rather, in a perspective common to Gramsci and Lenin, political power is immanent to the hegemonic projects by means of which social classes or groups constitute themselves *as* classes in an integral and properly political sense, rather than remaining an incoherent mass of 'corporative' interests at the subaltern level of civil society.[83] It is the capacity of such hegemonic projects to transform those experiences of subalternity into institutions of self-organization that allows a class to elaborate its own distinctive forms and practices of politics, within but also potentially beyond the existing state.

In the assimilative form of an integral state reinforced by passive revolution, the European bourgeoisie in the nineteenth century had found a way to advance its own contradictory form of modernization. According to Gramsci's perspective in the early twentieth century, the state apparatus of the bourgeoisie could be neutralized only when the subaltern classes and social groups had deprived it of its "social basis" through the elaboration of an alternative hegemonic project, concretized in their own distinctive institutions or "hegemonic apparatuses."[84] Only in this way would the subalterns be able to exercise what Lenin had called a "power of a completely different type," or what Gramsci characterizes as exhaustion of the dyad political and civil society and the emergence instead of a "regulated society."[85]

Poulantzas was thus mistaken to claim that Gramsci had paid insufficient attention to the specificity of political power within the modern state. On the contrary, the *Prison Notebooks* advance a novel thesis regarding state power's active and continual constitution by means of a dynamic developmental dialectic between associative and organizational instances. Rather than an acceptance of the (ultimately political-theological) representation of political power as exhausted in the singular figure of sovereignty, Gramsci instead aimed, in ways not dissimilar to those of Poulantzas—and in different ways, also those of Foucault, Deleuze, Guattari, and Derrida—to provide an analytics of power beyond the abstraction of sovereignty—that is, to delineate the mechanisms, techniques, and means by which sovereignty is continually constituted and reconstituted as a "functional fiction." Gramsci's elaboration of the problematic of hegemony, both in terms of the deformed dynamics of bourgeois passive revolution and the unprecedented practices of subaltern self-emancipation, was precisely an attempt "to cut off the head" of this fairy tale of the modern state's self-assurance.

The Duality of Dual Power

Poulantzas's critiques of Gramsci's conception of the state and of political power cannot be sustained today, particularly not when the *Prison Notebooks* are read through the lenses of the debates of contemporary politics. Those critiques nevertheless remain significant and symptomatically revealing of unresolved tensions in Poulantzas's own thought and, by extension, of a season of debate that produced a political language that is still important for us today. Poulantzas's third critique of Gramsci, however—that is, the argument that the notion of war of position presupposed a variant of the Leninist strategy of "dual power"—was correct, though not for the reasons that Poulantzas supposed. For the notion of dual power, at its origins and in the complexity of its elaboration, represented a more sophisticated and contradictory political perspective than Poulantzas's polemic allowed him to recognize.

As originally elaborated by Lenin, dual power was not a matter of the choice of one strategic proposal over another. Nor did it involve a simple rejection of engagement with the existing state apparatus in favor of a "purer" power located elsewhere. Lenin in fact always argued that engagement with the state, including the mechanisms of parliamentary democracy, could be tactically useful for the revolutionary movement, in particular conjunctures and under certain precise political conditions.[86] *Pace* Poulantzas, "all Lenin's analyses and actions" are not "traversed" by the "*leitmotif*" of "dual power."[87] Indeed, the term "dual power" [*dvoevlastie*] is not to be found in Lenin's voluminous writings before the Russian Revolution of 1917. The thesis of dual power in fact only emerges explicitly in Lenin's political vocabulary in the very specific moment of "interregnum" between the two revolutions of February and October 1917.[88]

Arguably present "in a practical state" in the *April Theses* composed during Lenin's journey to the Finland Station, explicitly formulated in an article published in *Pravda* on April 9, 1917, and most famously presented in *The Task of the Proletariat in our Revolution* (written a day later on April 10, but not published until September), the thesis of dual power was an attempt to comprehend the entirely unexpected "*interlocking of two* dictatorships," Soviets ranged against the Provisional Government. In the article in *Pravda*, Lenin explicitly notes that "*Nobody* previously thought, or could have thought, of a dual power."[89] The type of political power embodied in the Soviets emerged outside but alongside the existing state apparatus, an apparatus that had been severely weakened in both legitimacy and functioning by a major social and political crisis. Dual power was here configured not as pure versus impure powers. Rather, it represented an unstable type of "mixed government" of the competing claims of "political society" (organization) and of "civil society" (association) at the moment of the destabilizing of their normal hierarchies.

The social bases of these two "governments" or "dictatorships," however, were entirely different. The Provisional Government was a "State in the proper sense of the term," that is, a state apparatus founded on "law" and ultimately the rights of private property. The Soviets, on the other hand, represented a "special type of State" that recalled, for Lenin, the defining features of the Paris Commune. Both the Commune and the Soviets were founded on and functioned as popular initiative (in particular, the replacement of the police and army by the arming of the people itself, direct popular control of officialdom and bureaucracy). These two governments were, in the strictest sense, mutually incompatible political powers, founded on entirely different presuppositions regarding the nature and functioning of political institutions and politics itself. Their antagonism had to end in the disappearance of one or the other. Lenin insisted on the exceptional and necessarily temporary nature of this conjuncture: "There is not the slightest doubt that such an 'interlocking' cannot last long. Two powers *cannot exist* in a state," he argued. "Dual power merely expresses a *transitional* phase in the revolution's development."[90]

The notion of dual power also represents a transitional phase in Lenin's thought, as he attempted to comprehend the unprecedented configurations thrown up in 1917. It is a phase that traverses the highs and lows of the Summer of 1917, which reached its programmatic conclusion in Lenin's reflections on Marx's writings on the Paris Commune in *The State and Revolution*, a work that can legitimately be inscribed amongst the great "unfinished works" of the materialist tradition.[91] Begun during the almost Machiavellian solitude of Lenin's time as an outlaw in a haystack, it was a work that he happily "abandoned" (in Valéry's sense) when the revolutionary upsurge returned in the early Autumn 1917. Just as Spinoza's *Tractatus politicus* symptomatically breaks off just as the discussion of the nature of democracy begins, so Lenin's treatise on Revolution "interrupts" itself precisely at that moment when it sets out to recount the history of the Russian revolutions of 1905 and 1917 in a comparative perspective. "It is more pleasant and useful to go through the 'experience of revolution' than to write about it," Lenin famously dryly remarked after the insurrection of October 1917.[92]

"Dual power" was also itself interrupted by the events of late 1917. The term largely disappeared from Lenin's writings as the state of exception of 1917 was resolved and the revolutionary government was forced to confront very different political contexts. First civil war and then, the counterrevolutionary tide seemingly stemmed, the hesitant construction of a socialist order under the NEP, saw the Bolsheviks grappling with, and ultimately being defeated by, the challenges of occupying the "commanding heights" of administrative authority in the absence of a powerful social movement from below. The invocation of the potentials and pitfalls of dual power in Lenin's writings thereby became an anomaly without precedents or successors. It was in this sense less a finished concept than a genial intuition still marked by potentially productive ambiguities. It was an insight never fully elaborated at the time of its emergence, which thus remained particularly open to endless revisitations and reinterpretations by the subsequent Marxist traditions.[93]

How might such a perspective to be reconstructed and actualized today? Significant currents of contemporary radical thought have comprehended this "power of a completely different type" as the moment of the re-irruption of an originary constituent power, as it breaks out of the constricting constitutional form cruel history had imposed on its molten, titanic force.[94] A situation of dual power, that is, is regarded as the re-assertion of a qualitatively distinct type of creative power that lies at the foundation of every constitutional order, a power that may be repressed or distorted but can never be exhausted or eradicated. As primordial force of innovation, constituent power in this vision functions as a once present but now absent cause, passing into the new constitutional order its innovation has called forth, like the "hidden God" that disappears into his creation. Yet insofar as ontologically primary, constituent power nevertheless subsists within the form over whose birth it had presided, as a latent threat of renewed innovation at the moment when the constitutional order sooner or later passes over into corruption.[95] Understood in this way, dual power seems to represent the fusion of a Marxist theory of the singularity of revolutionary crisis (always a novel overdetermination of overdeterminations) with the fundamental presupposition of the natural law tradition, namely, the ultimately generic and ontological foundation of political action and power.

While conceiving a situation of dual power in terms of an originary constituent power may secure its temporal and ontological primacy, however, it also destines it to dying soon after the day of its birth. For as Lenin claimed, "such an 'interlocking'' of powers 'cannot last long." A situation of dual power is by definition an exception to the normal functioning of sovereignty. As tempting as the

notion of a prolonged situation of "permanent dual power" may be—
that is, autonomous institutions of popular political organization
subsisting alongside established forms of state power over a longer
period of a protracted structural crisis, intermittently harassing it
in guerilla-like skirmishes—it does not resolve one of the fundamental paradoxes that lies at the heart of the notion of constituent
power itself.[96] This is the paradox that constituent power can only be
configured as such—and crucially, can only be recognized *as* constituent power—through reference to its formal and temporal difference from the constituted power at whose origins it is thought
to lie.[97] In a situation of enduring dual power, the weakly emergent
constituent power would remain structurally subaltern to the established order. The longer such a situation of "low intensity dual
power" were to endure, the more opportunities constituted power
would have to reassert itself as sole organizing political instance.
The growth and decline of radical movements over the last 30 years
have provided ample evidence of this tragic dialectic, from the containment and slow exhaustion of the initial Zapatista uprising to the
dissipation of the radical movements in the squares that had fueled
the so-called Arab Spring and its reverberations once "normality"—
either authoritarian, as in Egypt, or parliamentary, as in Turkey—
was (re)imposed.

What such an ontological understanding of dual power also tends
to obscure, however, is not only Lenin's emphasis on the temporally
exceptional status of dual power but also the precise sense in which the
Soviets represented for Lenin a "power [*vlast'*] of a completely different
type." It was different not because incommensurable with the power
claimed by the Provisional Government; a common measure had been
imposed by the conjuncture. Neither the Soviets nor the Provisional
Government put themselves forward simply as generic forms of power
(in Weberian terms, as *Macht*, the mere capacity to act). Rather, both
made claims to function as the concrete sovereign authority in the
very particular concrete conjuncture of 1917—in Weberese, as the
Herrschaft [domination] that could constrain actions, or force them to
be undertaken even if "unwillingly."[98] If the Provisional Government's
decrees had been able both to gain at least a passive or tacit consent (in
the sense of not being actively opposed by strategically located sectors

of the population), the Soviets' pretensions to represent an alternative governmental power would not have been entertained for long.

The Soviets instead represented a power of a completely different type, both because of the way in which this power was produced and because of the way in which it functioned as a sovereign authority.

Regarding the *mode of production*, on the one hand, the Provisional Government's claims were made within the established paradigm of the production of modern sovereignty: legality guaranteed by the constitutional form within which legitimacy was produced by means of the "re-presentation" of the popular forces that the constitutional form had made absent. On the other hand, the Soviets inherited an old revolutionary tradition that insisted on the always revocable nature of political delegation. The continuous review of the implementation of the Soviets' decisions—that is, the articulation of executive, legislative, and administrative powers in an organic relation of mutual correction—constituted the basis for an always revisable form of political order, or in other words, of continuous re-ordering.

Regarding *function*, the Provisional Government's fragile claim to represent a sovereign authority aimed fundamentally to assert the primacy of political command and regulation over the social, and the permanence of order as goal of the exercise of political power. In other words, the *vlast'* of the Provisional Government aimed to maintain the existing order and its foundation in the "right" to private property as structuring principle of the public realm. The Soviets were instead conceived in Lenin's argument not as a variant of the (modern representative) "state in the proper sense of the term," but a nascent rupture with its fundamental logic. Their assertion of sovereign authority was in this sense nothing more than a negation of their opponent's competing claim to it. It was a refusal to recognize that there could be any higher power impeding the institutionalization of re-ordering that the Soviets continuously enacted in the very nature of their functioning.

The difference between the types of powers represented by the Provisional Government and the Soviets was therefore neither a case of the incommensurability of two qualitatively distinct powers, nor a simple opposition of one power set against another in a symmetrical antagonistic confrontation, on which a mere excess of force could decide. Rather, the difference resided in the very nature and function of the type of sovereign authority that they represented. Varying a formulation of René Zavaleta Mercado, I propose to characterize this difference as the "duality of dual power."[99]

Zavaleta preferred to use the notion of a "duality of powers" [*dualidad de poderes*], rather than "dual power" [*poder dual*] or "double power" [*doble poder*], in order to emphasize that the revolutionary situation theorized by Lenin (and following him, Trotsky) did not involve the bifurcation of a "single, classically unique power," but instead the emergence of "two powers, two types of state," which were fundamentally incompatible.[100] It was a theorization influenced in particular by the experiences and discussions of dual power situations in the early 1970s in the Popular Assembly in Bolivia and the brief season of Popular Unity in Chile—reflected tragically in the postface that Zavaleta appended to the original edition after the events of the "first 9/11."

With the notion of a "duality of dual power," I instead seek to emphasize the disequilibrium between the two powers contending to occupy the place of sovereign authority. One power—the Provisional Government—sought sovereign power in order to maintain it; it was, to use the terminology of both Zavaleta and Poulantzas, a "unitary power" that aimed to "condense" within itself, and thereby to regulate, all social conflict. The other power embodied in the Soviets, on the other hand, did indeed seek to occupy the "normal" place of sovereignty in the seizure of the Winter Palace; but the goal of this seizure was not that of "taking power" in order to maintain the existing sovereign system.[101] It was instead a seizure undertaken in order to disable the normal functioning of not only the Provisional Government but of sovereign authority as such, and thereby to permit the already functioning power of the Soviets to expand, dissolving the "place" of sovereign power into the non-place of a political relation of continual sociopolitical reordering. It was in this precise sense that Lenin's slogan, "All power [*vlast'*] to the Soviets!," had a historically concrete and explosive meaning.

Janus-faced, the Soviets both did and did not participate in the paradigm of modern sovereignty. But therein lay the Bolsheviks' terrifying gambit. By insisting that the time was right to assume governmental

responsibility with the insurrection of October 1917 and the dissolution
of even the formality of the Provisional Government, the Bolsheviks
were gambling that the political relationality and immediacy of popular expression in the Soviets (as a "working government" of the Paris
Commune type, according to Lenin) would sustain the continuance of
a deconstructive dissolution of sovereignty. Throughout the setbacks
and reversals that quickly followed October 1917, through the civil
war to the institution of the NEP and the politics of the United Front as
an attempted "cultural revolution," the Russian revolutionary process
was marked by the increasingly frantic attempts to recapture that
fragile utopian vision and experience—before being swept away definitively by the restoration of the naked, absolutist sovereignty of Stalin's
counterrevolution.

Like other revolutionaries of his generation, Gramsci inherited this
utopian vision of the duality of the situation of dual power, of the opportunity it represented for the emergence of a power of a completely
different type that occupies the center of sovereign power in order to
deconstruct it. The creativity of the particular way he inherited it is
evident in his analysis of the contradictory constitution of the bourgeois integral state and his emphasis on the distinction between
the limits of bourgeois passive revolution and the expansive hegemonic politics of the subaltern social groups and classes. Above all,
it receives its clearest expression in his proposal of the possibility
of a post-statal "regulated society." Historically, the bourgeoisie's
ascendance to the status of a ruling class had been marked by the institution of a structural divide between subaltern associational and
ruling organizational instances in civil and political societies; passive revolution consisted precisely in maintaining the dominance of
the latter over the former, and preventing a mass transition from one
to the other. The "desubalternization" of the subalterns could not involve a mere reversal of fortunes, or the assertion of a formerly civil
society finally become political. Rather, the institution of a "regulated
society" necessitated the dissolution of those relations: the abolition
of civil society *qua* experience of subalternity and the valorization of
the self-organizational capacities of association; but just as crucially,
the immanent deconstruction of political society itself as separate
organizing instance.

Isolated in the "commanding heights" of sovereign state power, the original experience of the duality of dual power in the Russian Revolution proved unable to prevent the return of political society— that is, the reaffirmation of the primacy of organization over associa- tion. It was an experience repeated so often at the end of all the other great popular uprisings throughout the twentieth and twenty-first centuries that few today even consider the dissolution of political society as anything but utopian in a deleterious sense. How is such a seemingly inevitable return of the politics of the party of order to be resisted?

As we have been reminded so often over the last 30 years, any pol- itics that begins by taking a principled distance from the state sooner or later risks becoming little more than a descent down into the rag and bones shop of civil society, where all relations of subalternity start. Does this then mean that that state remains our destiny, a regrettable but necessary instrument, stage or goal for the construction of eman- cipatory political projects? Can we now only hope for the "democratic" transformation of political society, but not its dissolution, as so many contemporary theoretical and practical radical projects seem to have accepted? It may instead be by advancing forward into the lair of polit- ical society itself, into the mode of its production and the process of its material constitution, that we may still be able to glimpse the nature of a power of a completely different type.

2

Material Cause

The Constitution of the Political

The recurrent waves of emancipatory mobilization over the last 30 years have not infrequently been criticized for being well intentioned but ultimately utopian and ineffectual. According to this learned perspective, many contemporary movements lack the type of considered relation between determinate means and ends that is claimed to have characterized more robust oppositional cultures and practices in the past. While it is not surprising that such critiques are expressed by representatives of the party of order, it is more interesting to observe the way in which this general outlook has sometimes been internalized and reproduced within critical cultures on the Left, particularly in the tensions between different generational experiences and their contested forms of inheritance. Stated bluntly, the enthusiasms of much contemporary leftist practice and theory—from a focus on the inclusivity of mobilizing cultures and practices to experimentation in forms of direct democracy and consensus decision-making—have seemed to some schooled in older leftist traditions to be untutored naivety, when not a merely embarrassing recapitulation of already discredited illusions.

What such characterizations underestimate is the extent to which the ultimate meaning of any political movement—whether thought in terms of a singular event, a sequence of phases or stages, or an extended process—is only ever constituted retrospectively, as its contribution to a longer-term process of "primitive political accumulation" and institutional consolidation becomes clear. If few contemporary oppositional movements can be judged to have achieved decisive breakthroughs, always falling short of the supposedly higher standards bequeathed by previous political conjunctures, it might be worthwhile recalling that the normal condition of emancipatory politics is that of

Radical Politics. Peter D. Thomas, Oxford University Press. © Oxford University Press 2023.
DOI: 10.1093/oso/9780197528075.003.0003

the "unimportant failure." It is after all the daily, small defeats that constitute the reality within which such an "abnormal" politics becomes necessary in the first place.

Rather than being regretted, in a now all-too-common lamentation that thinks of itself as always born too late, it is more enabling to think of such lack of success as the paradoxical precondition for any decisive advance. As Rosa Luxemburg was well aware, it is the defeats of emancipatory politics that make of it a perpetually and productively open "learning process," a pedagogical experience of the discovery of specific solutions to concrete problems rather than application of already elaborated generic policies.[1] Emancipatory politics in this sense derives its strength, like Hercules's agonist Antaeus, from being thrown to the ground. Its successes are built on an accumulation of defeats—at least when they are neither romanticized nor merely lamented, but transformed into the initial, necessarily mistaken hypotheses that always precede the discovery of the solution to a problem.

Critiques of a lack of realism in contemporary leftist cultures, however, also fail to register the extent to which the cycle of movements over the last 30 years have cultivated a different relation to reality based on a different sense of the Real. For participants in these movements, it has not been their consciously utopian demands—for an alternative globalization, peace against war, people before profit, or public provision before private greed—that have seemed insubstantial. On the contrary, it has been the world against which these demands have been made that has seemed unrealistic, an undoing of the Real that deceivingly conceals something more substantial behind its murky forms.

For whether affirming itself as the only alternative (TINA: there is no alternative), *la pensée unique*, or the mundane neoliberal common sense of our times, the anxious need of the established order continually to emphasize its necessity (and the even more perverse need to make such necessity the basis of its claims to legitimacy) almost seems designed, in its preemption, to provoke dissenting voices. The possibility of alternatives seems, that is, to be suggested in the very act of denying their feasibility so vigorously from the outset. Rather than substantial shapes, our overly performative present thus appears to be made up more of flickering images, dazzling because fleeting in their

appearance; they arouse a desire for the substance that their incon-
stantly simulating forms can stimulate but not satisfy.

Inside the Cave

The shifting shapes of the contemporary order, in their performativity,
transience, and superficiality, have at least something in common
with the shadows projected onto the cave wall in Plato's famous allegory.[2] The images of the shadow puppets in that tale could be endowed
with the meaning of a "reality" only as long as the chained spectators
remained in a state of constrained ignorance, physically unable to discern the substance that was the cause of the merely apparent. The moment the spectators were able to turn around and become aware of
the techniques and arrangements that had produced those flickering
images—that is, the reality that literally lay behind both the spectators
and what they until then had thought to be the Real in itself—the
shadows upon the cave wall could be recognized for what they
were: simulacra, or imitations of the meanings their elaborate production was designed to prevent, in both senses of the word, as prohibition
and as deformed prefiguration.

The shadows on the wall of the Platonic cave were not in any sense
of the term "unreal"; they possessed a power to enchant and en-
trance with which citizens of a "theatrocracy" were all too familiar.[3]
They could be made to *become* unreal, however, in the process and as
a consequence of the prisoners' self-emancipation. The shadows' "reality"—in the Marxian sense of their *Wirklichkeit*, or the Machiavellian
sense of their "effective truth" [*verità effetuale*]—had depended on the
chained spectators' incapacity to envisage the conditions of their own
liberation, in the tense of the future perfect.[4] In a metaphorical sense,
Plato's cave was not, as a still influential tradition of interpretation of
The Republic claims, a lost state of "natural" ignorance, conceived as
mere privation, as an absence of knowledge.[5] Rather, the cave was precisely the type of pseudo-knowledge that is generated by the political
combination of constraint and the internalization of the subjection
that results from it: the pacification of incapacity in general and the incapacity to discern the production of the apparent in particular.

The cycle of political struggles in the early twenty-first century could be characterized as repeated attempts to break the mind-forged manacles that have allowed the new world order to present itself to so many as just such a substantial and constraining shape. Here, however, the analogy with Plato's analogy breaks down, as all good mimetic impostures eventually must. The famous little morality tale that punctuates the narrative flow of *The Republic* highlights both the difficulty of the ascent out of the cave as well as the risks of descending back down into its enveloping darkness once the light of the supposed Real had been glimpsed. The fate of the Enlightened one who returns to the cave in order to inform his former fellow prisoners of the paucity of their captive situation stands in this sense as merely the first in a long tradition of fantasies in which intellectual distinction is presented as a cure, however unwelcome, for the pathologies of the present.

It has not been this opposition between a zone of truth and space of delusion that has constituted the fundamental challenge for contemporary movements. Participants in these movements have exhibited few illusions in the claims of the ruling order, and the condemnation of its injustices has not for the most part even been presented as news. Our challenge has instead been to understand how a process of collective emancipation might be constructed from within the cave itself. While Plato was content to propose the figure of an individual's knowledge against the delusions of the masses, our movements have instead searched for the practice of a knowledge that expresses itself as a project of collective emancipation. Contemporary oppositional movements, that is, have not sought the Real outside the cave but have attempted to cast some light on the Real that is our contemporary cave. In their search for the mobilizing slogans, affective states, and intransigent orientations of collective empowerment of the subaltern social groups and classes, they have endeavored to comprehend the production and potential transformation of the simulacra of contemporary society from within its own terms.

What Is Emancipation?

The Real to which the diversity of the intersectional sociopolitical movements of today seem to have aspired, albeit in radically different forms and frequently in contradictory ways, could be characterized as a response to a starkly formulated question: "What is Genuinely Emancipatory Politics?" In the face of the continuing reduction of the ostensibly once vibrant political cultures of the post-WWII order in so many countries to merely technocratic administration—whether in fact, with suspensions of constitutional norms and conventions, or in spirit, with ideological homogenization around an "extreme" liberalizing consensus—oppositional movements over the last 30 years have often engaged in a (re)discovery of a type of "politics beyond politics," or in the Platonic metaphor earlier essayed, a "politics beyond the cave."

This imperative has taken varied forms, from the ultimately ethical forms of experimentation in "micropolitics," conceived as a prefigurative culture, to the valorization of the "truly" radical political act, thought as a redeeming instant. It has also been expressed in different organizational terms, from the skepticism regarding the relevance or efficacy of political parties expressed at the height of the alternative globalization movement at the turn of the century, to conceptions of movements' potential "occupation" of political parties in the wake of the post-2011 wave of Occupy.[6] What unites such otherwise opposed forms of political activity is the conviction that most of what today passes for "politics"—particularly in those institutional forms immediately shaped by engagement with the state—exists in a fallen state. It is regarded as a type of politics that is less than itself, or even as a mere word that falls short of its concept. "Real politics" is taken to be ever elsewhere; always in excess of its institutional appropriation; subsisting in reserve as a disposition; a way of saying, seeming, and being beyond the unreal limits of the actual.

The search for genuinely emancipatory politics thus seems to think of itself as a type of rose in the thorny cross of the present. In its claims to have located a source of purity beyond the corruptions of the present, this project could be characterized as a recapitulation of what Koselleck described as the tendency for the practice of certain type of *Kritik* to constitute a moralized space outside "official" politics, an outside engendered by the shifting boundaries between the public and private during the absolutist state's terminal crisis. In the eighteenth century, according to Koselleck, such a notion of *Kritik* aimed to present itself as a legitimate form of opposition to established power precisely on the basis of its asserted exteriority, even if such an assertion, as an illocutionary act, could only in reality be maintained within the confines of the existing order.[7]

Today, the notion that real politics exists in some zone beyond the corruptions of the established order is often presented as the foundation for properly oppositional politics—that is, the type of politics that represents a radical rupture with the present, rather than merely alternative policy proposals that seek to reform, modify, or ameliorate its most extreme injustices. The type of *Kritik* analyzed by Koselleck understood itself to represent an avant-garde of historical development, in the sense of ushering in a new age, as an excess of contemporaneity and the acceleration of the "new." Today, the notion of a genuinely emancipatory politics seems to be attractive for certain dispositions precisely because it claims to constitute a way of being more actual than what is supposed to be actuality itself.

The notion of genuinely emancipatory politics in this sense—as both exterior and radically opposed to existing institutional politics— is founded on at least two significant presuppositions, both fundamentally Platonic in their structure and consequences. First, the search for a *genuinely* emancipatory politics presupposes that what is commonly called "politics" today—the electoral competition between political elites organized in parties, parliaments, and state institutions—is but a corrupted imitation of a more substantial form of political action, a "real" politics whose manifestation, or "revelation," would finally and definitely make apparent the mimetic failure of the present. Second, placing the accent on the notion of *emancipatory* politics—and not merely politics as such—presupposes that it might be possible to think of the relationship between "emancipation" and "politics" in such a way that they are thought as each other's logical complements. A genuinely emancipatory politics, that is, would finally reveal the destiny of politics itself, as the realization of what it has always been in intention, even if rarely in concrete embodiment.

Understood in this way, the search for an authentic politics that has marked so many of recent oppositional movements can be seen to participate in a problematic that defined political theory—and particularly self-consciously radical political theory—throughout the twentieth century, but in increasingly intense ways in the wake of the global uprisings of 1968. This problematic can be characterized as the "anxiety of the autonomy of the political," declined in radically different ways, from Weber and Schmitt to Arendt and Badiou, to cite only a few representative names whose diversity already indicates the contested nature of this problematic. Its common center consists in an attempt to specify a distinctive feature, method, or function of properly "political" activity, understood as a condition to be valorized, both in itself as a virtuous condition and for the positive effects its clear delineation can exert on political development as such.

The focus of many recent political movements on forms of institutional experimentation—from variants of consensus-oriented politics, to networked forms of coordination, to new types of political parties—represents a particular form of operationalization of this more general problematic. It inherits the post-new-leftist expansion of the field of political engagement and comprehension. Frequently, this inheritance has been of a direct nature, as a post-68ist political vocabulary has achieved a diffusion and prominence in movements today that signals a significant distinction from previous political cultures, even those at not so great a temporal distance from the present. Notions of "micropolitics," of "governmentality" or "horizontalism" derived from Deleuze, Guattari, and Foucault, for instance, seem just as distant from the political culture of the early New Left in the late 1950s and early 1960s (in the writings of C. Wright Mills or the rhetoric of the Port Huron Statement) as they do from the popular-frontist and anti-fascist political languages of the 1930s. To the extent that such a vocabulary is now a shared resource of the radical left (also when it is contested or rejected), even those currents that declare a need to be done with the memorialization of (a selectively constructed memory of) "May 68" still continue to participate in a politico-theoretical problematic strongly marked by those events and their "archivization" in a distinctive political conceptuality.

Yet debates in radical political theory since the 1960s can also be seen to have prefigured many of the concerns of contemporary movements in a more general sense, less in terms of direct and explicit affiliation or citation, and more in terms of shared orientations or perspectives. For the "wake" (in both the sense of "that which comes after" and that of "celebratory mourning") of the politico-theoretical culture of the long 1960s continues to be strongly marked by the search for a theory of a more genuine form of "politics beyond politics." The ways in which this search has been undertaken has varied in different contexts, oscillating between investigations into the nature of "the Political," on the one hand, and an emphasis on dealing with the given reality of politics, or "real politics," on the other. What these diverse projects share, however, is a common presupposition: namely, the notion that an authentic experience of politics awaits us, as promise and unprecedented future.

On the Shores of the Political

The debates regarding the nature of politics in Italian Marxism in the 1970s can be understood as a type of "ground zero" for this type of politico-theoretical orientation, both in a literal and metaphorical sense. Literally, it was in the debates of theorists of the Italian Socialist and Communist Parties in this period that the theme of "the Political" was most forcefully posed in concrete terms as a strategic orientation toward the "real politics" of the time. It was not coincidental that the seminar at which Mario Tronti first announced the turn to the "autonomy of the political," discussed in the last chapter, was presided over by Norberto Bobbio. For it was Bobbio, undoubtedly one of the most internationally influential political theorists of the second half of the twentieth century, whose interventions in the 1970s had stimulated a wide-ranging debate in Italy in which the fundamental claims of Marxist political theory were put in question.[8] Bobbio's critical interrogative regarding the existence of a Marxist theory of the state, for instance, was paralleled at the time by Lucio Colletti's skepticism regarding the existence of a Marxist theory of politics as such—a prelude to his later embrace in the 1990s of the politics of Bonapartist Berlusconism.[9]

Less well known outside Italy, a more significant response to this polemic was provided by Franco De Felice's seminal contributions to Gramscian studies in the 1970s, and in particular his focus on the category of passive revolution in Gramsci's *Prison Notebooks* as the outline of a novel theory of the formation of modern politics as a process of co-optation and deformation of popular struggles.[10] In one way or another, the debates of these years have continued to influence the development of significant currents of political theory in Italy ever since, from the very early turn (in comparison to other national cultures) to Carl Schmitt's thinking of the political, to the "metaphysicalization" of a broadly Trontian approach in different ways by Massimo Cacciari or Roberto Esposito.[11]

The terms this debate established have even exerted a strong influence on those who flatly rejected it. Negri, as previously noted, was scathing in his refusal both of Tronti's notion of an autonomy of the political and of Bobbio's ascription of the paucity of the PCI's state theory to Marxism *tout court*. His work from the 1970s onward, however, with its focus on developing a Marxist political theory centered on the creative dimensions of the multitude's constituent power and capacity of self-organization, can be read as effectively a continual rebuttal of both Tronti and Bobbio's claims.

While these debates in what has been retrospectively homogenized as "Italian theory" were, historically, of central importance not only in Italy but internationally, many later revisitations of these themes have tended to accord more attention to positions that had developed in France in the same years, sometimes in parallel and under the influence of the Italian discussion, and sometimes in relation to quite distinct initiatives and priorities. The early revivals of anti-Stalinist Marxism in France around *Socialisme ou Barbarie*, particularly in Cornelius Castoriadis's focus on the critique of bureaucracy, had already placed an emphasis on comprehending the political forms of modern society. This approach was developed further by Claude Lefort in subsequent years with his focus on political "institution," as both condition and process. The notion of the saving power of an authentically political experience later became one of the central themes in Philippe Lacoue-Labarthe and Jean-Luc Nancy's proposal to "retreat the political" and their work in the *Centre de Recherches Philosophiques sur la Politique* in the 1980s, which influenced in a not insignificant way Derrida's supposedly "ethico-political" turn in the 1990s, particularly in what arguably represents his most sustained contribution to political theory in a strict sense, the pathbreaking *The Politics of Friendship*.[12]

From a very different tradition in France, Daniel Bensaïd's entire work can be characterized as an attempt to think through the distinctive nature of revolutionary politics as both theoretical practice and practice of theory by means of a meta-theory of politics. For Bensaïd, revolutionary politics seems to subsist somewhere between the reading of the psychoanalytic symptom and the writing of a Geertzian "thick description."[13] It involves a deep immersion in particularities in order to explicate the generalities that govern them. Such a "sensuous" politics (in the Marxian sense of *sinnlich*) attends carefully to the murmurs of rebellion and resistance of the social and tries to guide them toward the forms of articulateness and coherence that they could be found, retrospectively, to have carried within them.

Central to these debates in France from the 1960s onward, overdetermining even those perspectives that were highly critical of it, was of course the experience of "Althusserianism" and its dissolution. "Post-Althusserianism"—understood as all those initiatives that have emerged in the wake of and reflected on the "classical" Althusserianism elaborated in *For Marx* and *Reading Capital*—can in effect be characterized as an extended mediation from different perspectives on the nature of politics and its forms of comprehension. The final phases of the public elaboration of Althusser's thought in the late 1970s, as he navigated between the declaration of Marxism's "crisis" and the defense of the dictatorship of the proletariat within the PCF, was marked by an urgently anxious attempt to specify the nature of genuinely revolutionary politics as that which supposedly should occur "within the party," but also as that which the party should be able to enact beyond its borders.[14] The evolution of some of Althusser's former students and collaborators can be understood as so many attempted responses to the unresolved ambivalence of this orientation.

Étienne Balibar, for instance, has suggested a partly typological, partly dialectical classification of different political modes, moving from an "autonomy" of politics linked to emancipation, to a "heteronomy" of politics related to transformation, and finally to the "heteronomy of heteronomy," an "other scene" of politics consisting in an ethical horizon of "civility."[15] Quite differently, Alain Badiou's notion of metapolitics moves in at least two, arguably incompatible, directions. On the one hand, he has explicitly thematized the nature of "politics as thought," to use the formulation of his collaborator Lazarus, that is, the capacity of politics to constitute its own rationality and thus to pose itself in distinction from philosophy.[16] On the other hand, he has also reflected on the way in which politics represents one of the conditions in and through which philosophy operates, in an effective reformulation of the "middle" Althusser's conception of the unification of different theoretical domains under the aegis of philosophy.[17]

Above all, however, it has been Althusser's most errant student, Jacques Rancière, who has proposed one of the most militant accounts of the specificity of genuinely radical politics, not in the terms of a (philosophical) theory of "the Political," but by means of a more sweeping redefinition of "politics" as such.[18] For Rancière, just as for Badiou, real politics is rare and fleeting. What is normally called politics is, for Rancière, not politics at all but merely the machinations of "the police." The police represents not the simple negation of politics, or an anti-politics, but on the contrary, its mimetic imposture. The police, that is, constitutes a simulacrum of a real politics that it seeks to render impossible—but by so doing, almost ensuring its intermittent irruption, as the occasional exception it requires in order to define the conditions of its enduring rule.

The novelty of Rancière's position depends on his understanding of "real politics" as not the regulation of a given unity—in his terms, a given "distribution of the sensible"—but the emergence, always forcefully, of the part that has no part in a social order, the purely egalitarian demands that are not "recognized" or "justified" within any given order but are precisely those excluded elements whose impossible presence constitutes the order's scandal. This approach is not simply distant from but ultimately fundamentally incompatible with the conception of politics explored in recent work by those claiming affiliation to the tradition of the Frankfurt School.[19] For Rancière defines politics itself, in its "authentic" sense, as precisely that which is constitutively unrecognizable and therefore unjustifiable within any order because an order, conceived as a concrete process of ordering, only arises in the first place by foreclosing such an authentic politics. In its emphasis on a purity of origins, one of contemporary philosophy's most militant anti-Platonists ironically ends up not very far away from Plato's cave, even and especially while thinking to escape it.

The Political and Real Politics

While there appears to have developed a broad consensus amongst otherwise conflicting positions concerning the priority of a search for political authenticity, there are nevertheless different proposals regarding how this search is to be undertaken. One current urges a return to foundations, or an expressly philosophical search for the essence of "the Political." Another current seems to bend the stick in precisely the opposite direction, eschewing theoretical constructions and proposing an almost hyper-empiricism that valorizes the facticity of "real politics." There is no simple opposition between these different camps, however. There has not only been exchange across different tendencies, but sometimes also the transformation of one position into the other, almost like a perspectival divergence within a convergence around a shared presupposition.

The almost canonical formulation of this unevenness can be found already in the very structure of the seductively phenomenologically charged opening arguments in Schmitt's *The Concept of the Political*.[20] In a first move, Schmitt begins by asserting the *autonomy* of the political, founded on its own distinctive structuring opposition (between friend and enemy), a seemingly classically metaphysical construction of opposition and non-identity that is symmetrical with oppositions on other terrains (the Aesthetic, the Economic, etc.). What I suggest should instead be characterized as the *specificity* of the Political, however, as that domain in which the claims of one group over and against another is paradigmatic (particularly in the form of existential threat and ultimately the possibility of violent death), immediately destabilizes this asserted autonomy. For insofar as it is the notion of concrete *grouping* that is central for Schmitt's perspective, above and beyond any merely formal opposition, the Political is driven to function less as a principle of distinction and more as an extreme state of intensity that can irrupt, literally, on any other terrain, in a process of the becoming political of the supposedly non-political. It results, that is, in a heteronomy of the Political, insofar as it is reliant on those other terrains of social action that are now seen to bear the Political within them as a latent threat.[21]

From its foundational status, therefore, the Schmittian Political soon disseminates throughout other seemingly "non-political" terrains as the threat of politicization by any grouping that embodies an authentic experience of the Political as existential opposition. In other words, "the Political" becomes not an origin of politics but the moment of its transcendental reordering—a reordering that occurs on the basis of the experience of the particular intensities of real instances of political action and opposition. In this sense, the very concept of the Political comes to rely on an empirical experience of "real politics," which both enacts and validates its now only retrospective comprehension in the concept of the Political.

From a seemingly entirely opposed perspective, Rancière attempts to avoid the lures of a metaphysically founded notion of the Political by means of a turn to a notion of politics as exceptional instance. He begins by expressly rejecting the abstractions of (the return of) political philosophy, positing instead the distinction between the police and politics as a distinction between norm and exception. But Rancière then concludes by according politics, precisely in its austere rarity ("always local and occasional"), an effective purity that would be the envy of any purely "philosophical" construction of either politics or the Political. Politics, he argues, is "rare," a "singular construction of cases of universality" in opposition to the mundanity and consistency of the "count" of the police order.[22] The reference to a "real" politics thus ultimately comes to be functionally indistinct from a reference to a foundational moment of the Political. In this sense, the Political and politics, despite their initial opposition, end up becoming synonymous in the concreteness of their abstraction.

A similar dynamic can be observed in the very different approaches of Raymond Geuss and Lois McNay. Geuss's rejection of contemporary Rawls-inspired liberalism's focus on abstract conceptions of rights and justice leads him to propose a non-Kantian, non-ideal, and surprisingly "neo-Leninist" theory that attends to the actual conditions in which politics occurs (in terms not dissimilar to those that motivated Koselleck's critique of *Kritik*). "Real politics"—however that is assessed in each instance by the craft/art of "political judgement"—thus takes the place of the Political as the determining criterion of effective political engagement. McNay's criticism of the abstraction inherent in a "misguided" search for the Political, on the other hand, proposes instead to a focus on the amelioration of real instances of embodied suffering and injustice as a more concrete form of political theorizing. Rather than rejecting the abstraction of the Political, however, this strategy runs the risk of only replacing it with an equally abstract anthropological construction in which an ethical disposition provides the basis for political engagement. In both cases, the notion of a more authentic politics arguably comes to play the same foundational role as that claimed by the most austere ontological versions of the autonomy of the Political.[23]

The real differences in the debate over the Political and real politics, therefore, do not consist in the propositional content of one camp or another, which tend to coincide with each other even in their opposition. It is rather in the way in which different theoretical initiatives have posed radical politics as a problem for thought that more significant distinctions can be found, that is, in the orientations, approaches, or "styles" of thinking that have been adopted in order imagine a mode of politics that might definitively break with the established order.[24] These styles are transversal to any fixed opposition between real politics and the Political, and reveal hidden alliances between only seemingly diametrically opposed approaches.

Viewed in this perspective, it is possible to distinguish between at least two significant ways in which contemporary radical thought has attempted its assent out of our own cave, two distinctive philosophical styles that are simultaneously modes of political orientation. One style seeks to discover a foundation from which politics can begin; the other seeks to (re)construct a utopia that political engagement should seek to realize. Between a return to origins and flights toward the future, therefore, I propose to call these two approaches contemporary radical thought's "Platonizing" and "reconstructive-transcendental" styles.

A "Platonizing" Style

One influential current of contemporary radical thought—arguably strengthened by its felicitous coincidence with the revival of

normativity in mainstream political philosophy, in both its openly liberal and avowedly critical variants—has sought to formalize the relationship between "politics" and a particular concept of "the Political" in
a foundational sense. The Political is posited as the ground or origin of
politics, "founding" the very possibility of politics in the sense in which
a normatively conceived constitution might be said to found a polity.
Determining the nature of this foundation is then seen as the necessary precondition for the elaboration of any particular political practice, precisely because politics is represented as but the conjunctural
instantiation of a structure of the Political that necessarily and always
precedes and exceeds it. For this perspective, the Political as foundation is not produced, constituted, or repressed by politics; rather, it is
productive and constituting of it, preceding it in both a temporal and
logical sense.

While by no means limited to it, the rediscovery of Carl Schmitt's
thought by leftist anglophone political philosophers and theorists over
the last 30 years can be taken as representative of this approach. Schmitt
has been argued to offer an intensely political characterization of the
Political, one not available in such clear theoretical terms elsewhere,
and particularly not in the Marxist tradition. Chantal Mouffe's evolution is exemplary in this sense. Following the emphasis on antagonism
and political institution in *Hegemony and Socialist Strategy*, in the
1990s, Mouffe turned to Schmitt in order to deepen her theorization of
an agonistic radical democracy, abandoning his existential claims and
valorizing the purely formalist oppositional logic.[25] The Political for
Mouffe, in its properly curated "agonistic" form, offers a way to think
conflictuality as a primary material or even anthropological substrate
of political action as such on which the institutional forms of any particular political order arise.[26] Recognition of this unvarying nature of
the Political and harnessing it institutionally in the service of progressive political aims thus becomes for Mouffe the fundamental challenge
of contemporary leftist politics. In its presupposition of an integral link
between representation and politics, it is a position more widely shared
than is commonly recognized.

Such positions can be characterized as a "Platonizing" style not
simply or even primarily because they seek to find an origin or foundation of politics in a generic conception of the Political. In other words,

it is not due to the "ontologization" of the Political that this style of philosophical reflection could be characterized in relation to the paradigmatic Academic tradition. Rather, it is the style of its argument that signals its affinity with some of the most strategic rhetorical devices that mark Plato's works, particularly the method of diairesis employed in the so-called late dialogues. *The Sophist*, for example, goes hunting for the sophist by progressively eliminating what he is not; the extensive use of comparison functions not in order to increase a spectrum of meaning but to reduce it.[27] In a similar fashion, the contemporary Platonizing style operates by means of a "comparative-subtractive" method: that which is political is repeatedly distinguished by comparing it to that which is asserted not to be political. At the end of this process, the notion of the Political steps forth in its impoverishment as a mere accumulation of those distinctions, the empty positive center of a set of negative differences.

Whatever claims are sometimes made regarding the gritty "realism" of such foundational conceptions of the Political, in reality, their generic nature participates in one of the most venerable and idealistic illusions of the Western metaphysical tradition: namely, the dogmatic assertion of a generic or universalistic moment that constitutes an essence both realized in and determining of specific or particular contingencies. The Political in this vision has a foundational role in relation to mere politics. In temporal terms, it could be said to lie at the "beginning" of politics, were it not presented as something akin to an atemporal logic, in the sense that it precedes any particular political action only insofar as it is not itself temporal. The quality of any particular instance of politics can be judged according to the extent that it expresses this foundational essence. It matters little if this essence is argued to consist in a primordial conflictuality (as in the case of Mouffe), or in novel experience of freedom (as in Arendt). What is important is that an intense, "hard core" of the Political governs the nature of politics, both in potential and in its always inadequate realization.

A certain type of political philosophy—the type that claims to think the distinct nature of the Political—purports to have a privileged access to this foundation. It presents its credentials as the art of symptomatically reading the traces of the Political whose nature is precisely to remain forever concealed as an essence within, but also before or beyond, the mundanity of concrete political activity. It is this symptomatic reading strategy that in fact distinguishes it as a political philosophy, unlike political science, which can only, according to this perspective, analyze "mere" politics, reading its surface phenomena but not penetrating into its true depths. To use the metaphors of *The Republic*, such a type of political philosophy offers a way out of the cave of politics into the light of the Political.

The claim, however, is tautological: insofar as such a concept of the Political is itself already a "metaphysical" construction (in the sense both of an atemporal formalism and an abstraction from any particular political content), a certain type of metaphysical philosophy, or the type of philosophy that presents itself as a theory of the generic, cannot but have privileged access to it, in a relationship of mutual confirmation. What remains unthought in this approach is both the material forms in which the Political achieves its dominance over politics and the way in which the production of the conceptual space of the Political its itself preeminently philosophical, bound up with the constitution of philosophy as a discourse of mastery, even and especially over the Political.

As much as such a style invokes the Political, in reality it champions the Philosophical. It is philosophy as a discourse of mastery that functions as the principle that founds the Political, which only then can assert its own claim to found politics. It is difficult to determine if this mimetic chain signifies the becoming philosophical of politics, or the becoming political of philosophy—or, indeed, if there is ultimately that much of a difference between them.

Transcendentalism redux

Against the flight back to origins, another style of contemporary radical thought has attempted instead to determine the conditions not of politics in general, but of radical politics in the specific conditions of the present. I propose to characterize this, in a deliberately paradoxical formulation, as radical political thought's "reconstructive-transcendental" style. While Kant's classical transcendental arguments necessarily posed their famous "conditions of possibility" in the present indicative, this transcendental style proceeds retrospectively, departing from memories of the past that are projected as conditions for a possible future. If classical transcendental arguments assume the givenness of a particular present situation in order to subsequently determine its formal causes—in the sense of the necessary and sufficient conditions for the constitution of that situation—this reconstructive variation instead posits the absence in the present of what is only dimly remembered in order to imagine the conditions necessary for its reconstitution. "Radical politics exists; how is it possible?," a classical transcendental style might ask. The "reconstructive-transcendental" question is instead, "radical political engagement once existed; how could it become possible again?." As a style, this approach can be characterized as "transcendental" because it focuses on the formalist determination of this generic possibility. It is "reconstructive" in the sense that it seeks to repropose—or perhaps more accurately, to "revivify"—a formerly present but now absent situation, an actuality that has retreated into potentiality.

The conceptual structure of the classical transcendental argument *à la* Kant is thus in a certain sense "historicized"; instead of aspiring to identify the conditions of any possible political action *ex ante*, it is reconfigured as a strategic decision and intervention into a specific conjuncture, an intervention whose conditions—both objective and subjective—are not given but must be actively reconstructed through recourse to the past. *À la recherche du politique perdu*, therefore; but with the conviction that such pasts can only be recovered because they remain, in however mutilated, repressed, or frustrated a form, latent in the present.

Ironically, Badiou's vehemently anti-historicist (and proudly "Platonist") notion of the temporal endurance of a "communist hypothesis" or "Idea" might be regarded as emblematic of such an eminently "historicist" project.[28] Badiou seems to posit the communist hypothesis as a transhistorical, if not ahistorical, constant, one that stretches from Spartacus's uprising in antiquity (though traces might already be found before in the communism of Plato's guardians), to its manifestation in the workers' movement in the nineteenth century, to its restless search for a contemporary form of embodiment.[29]

The history of these different instantiations of the communist Idea is conceived as a gallery of so many "images" of past radical politics, displayed for our contemporary consideration. They represent exemplars for imitation; studying their defining and essential characteristics might contribute to a more effective re-actualization of them in the present, in a contemporary re-embodiment of the strengths of the past.

While a foundational approach to the Political seems to founder on the tautology of its own self-assertion, the reconstructive dimensions of such a transcendental approach seem at first sight a more promising and productively open orientation. Yet such a "shy historicism" soon enough encounters its own limits as a type of formalist de-historicization and ultimately aestheticization. A reconstructive-transcendental style does indeed propose to learn from concrete instances of politics in the past rather than asserting an abstract standard of "politicity" that preceded and supersedes them; but it can only do so by reducing those exemplary instances from the past to the status of formal models. It is precisely this process of de-historicization by means of formalization that permits the "transmission" of the "model" from past to present.[30] At the same time, however, it dissolves the historicity of that past into an aestheticized conception of politics as a question of subjective preference for—or "fidelity" to—one model or another. If a Platonizing style in the first and not the last instance presupposes an abstract conception of the Political that is unable to account for the political nature of its own constitution, a reconstructive-transcendental style concludes in a politicism that empties the present out of any determinate relation to the past from which it emerged.

In Search of Authentic Politics

The contradictions that accompany both the Platonizing and reconstructive-transcendental styles may give rise to different consequences, but they stem from a common source: namely, the shared insistence of these styles on recovering an authentic experience of politics, of politics as it once was and should once again be. As with any reference to the authentic, these styles are defined by an acute sense of current privation. But it is a privation that is not simply non-presence, but an absence of what was once present, or in other words, an experience of lack. Lurking behind both these styles is thus one of the oldest and most common narratives: the myth of a fall from a state of plenitude into corruption. It is a myth that serves both to define the present as a degraded version of its past but also as a type on interregnum that precedes—it is hoped—the restoration of what has been lost.

Origin and goal are here fused into one self-referential narrative. The present is defined as the place where this fusion is to occur, as a zone of the simultaneous recovery of what has been lost, and of the fulfillment of what had been before only promised and thereby deferred. In short, both styles offer a narrative of the authentic experience of politics as one of a redeemed time, of a present in which politics would both recover its lost former grandeur and fulfill its infinitely deferred promise to be that which it really should be. Both styles promise, that is, revelation and redemption; they offer to reveal, finally, definitively, a politics beyond the cave.

It is precisely this emphasis on authenticity, revelation, and redemption that most strongly signals what these styles of theoretical reflection have in common with the structures of feeling that have been operative within movements of emancipatory politics over the last 25 years. For both theoretical and activist orientations, authentic politics has been imagined to be always elsewhere, repairing the damage done to its pure form by the contingencies and corruptions of our fallen present. A genuinely emancipatory politics, it is assumed in theoretical terms, would be synonymous with this authentic politics; in practical terms, the recovery and embodiment of this authenticity is then understood to represent a mode of opening to the future, or the act of emancipation itself.

Seductively combining nostalgia for the past and projection into the future, this practico-theoretical orientation is nevertheless vulnerable to a series of naïve, skeptical objections. What if politics has always already been precisely that which it is and that which it is supposed to be; and what if it will never be more authentically itself than it already is? What if it is precisely this plenitude of politics that is the problem to be confronted, not a golden age to be recovered or an ideal toward which we should strive? In other words, what if there is no authentic politics to recover, because any authenticity of politics has always consisted only in its inauthenticity, in its dissimulation of the existing order, as its practical apology and theoretical justification? What if, that is, there really is no "outside cave" at all?

Constitution and Deconstruction

Such skeptical questions provide the initial impulse for thinking of the possibility of a different "style" of conceptualization of the challenges of contemporary radical politics, one that could steer its way between the Scylla of a metaphysical foundationalism, on the one hand, and the Charybdis of an aestheticized transcendentalism, on the other. Instead of searching for the purity of origins, this style would aim to comprehend the constitutively impure nature of emancipatory politics, its constitutive division between the current situation and that which is to come, between the existing state of affairs and that which emancipatory politics aims to construct. Above all, such a style, by abandoning the nostalgia for origins or the search for authenticity, would enable us to think emancipatory politics not in terms of imitation or repetition but in the optic of a renewed critical sense of historical progress. My thesis is that at least some of the ways in which Gramsci's *Prison Notebooks* theorize the nature of politics in the modern state can be understood as such an alternative to both Platonizing and reconstructive-transcendental styles.

Despite recurrent attempts to present Gramsci as a participant in a supposedly perennial conversation regarding the nature of politics— or what today is characterized as a "normative" political theory—his most significant contribution did not consist in offering a "general theory" either of politics or the Political.[31] Given the specificity of so many analyses in the *Prison Notebooks*, it is unsurprising that Gramsci was not much tempted to establish an "ideal" notion of "real" politics against which the concrete politics of his own time—from international Communist revolutionary to Fascist counterrevolution—could be measured as instances of lack. Rather than aiming to formulate a generic theory, whether of the Political as ontological essence or real politics as ontic facticity, Gramsci's efforts might be better characterized as a deconstructive reading of the "constitution" of political action within modern societies, or what he characterizes in synthesis as "political society."

The notion of political society has long played a contentious role in the history of interpretations of the *Prison Notebooks*. It occupied a minor yet significant place in Norberto Bobbio's provocative reading of Gramsci's social and state theory in the 1960s, with its suggestion of a supposedly more Hegelian than Marxist matrix of Gramsci's thought, and Jacques Texier's prompt and devastating critique.[32] In the 1970s, it was invoked in even stronger terms by the effective inheritor of the methodological presuppositions of Bobbio's argument, Perry Anderson. According to *The Antinomies of Antonio Gramsci*, the ambiguities in the notion of "political society" were a symptom of Gramsci's increasing confusion regarding what Anderson characterized, in a Weberian fashion, as the sole effective criterion for defining the unitary nature of the capitalist state—that is, the supposed "last instance" of its monopoly of legitimate violence.[33]

More recently, Partha Chatterjee has undertaken an innovative appropriation and redeployment of this formulation, though as he himself admits, it is a loose appropriation that makes no claims to be a development of the meanings that Gramsci had associated with it.[34] For Chatterjee, political society signifies a political logic distinct from the rationality embodied in "civil society," taken to be characteristic of the "non-colonial." A terrain of populations rather than citizens, subject to biopolitical forms of governance and excluded from a regime of rights, political society is used by Chatterjee as a periodizing category in order to designate the difference of the postcolonial conditions of popular politics "in most of the world" from a supposedly normative, traditional, and ultimately occidental and metropolitan understanding of the modern state.[35]

These interpretations and rhetorical appropriations were elaborated at varying distances from Gramsci's own texts. More recent readings of the *Prison Notebooks*, attentive to their historical context and the "rhythm" of their development, have enabled us to appreciate the specificity and novelty of the argument that Gramsci develops under this heading. "Political society" in Gramsci's most innovative usage is conceived not as a discrete zone or institutional terrain, and is expressly not limited to "official politics." It serves instead to designate the organizational instances generated over and against associative practices by the inner logic of political modernity as a form of "limited manumission seasoned by constraint." Conceived as a synthesis of all relations of organization, regulation, and coordination in modern societies, political society describes a distinct sociopolitical relationality, dialectically implicated with, and constituted by, the subaltern, associational relationality "performed" in the guise of "civil society." The development of the complex conception of passive revolution in order to denominate that specific nature of bourgeois hegemony and its processes of subalternization is one of the ways in which Gramsci analyzed the historical fusion and separation of these civil and political societies—not only in Western Europe but as a characteristic of political society as such.[36]

It was by means of his research on passive revolution that Gramsci attempted to register the ways in which historically identifiable political practices—the social relations of communication, coordination, and organization of the project of the bourgeois class as a ruling class—came to define the nature of "politics" as such within political modernity. In this sense, Gramsci's notion of the constitution of political society by passive revolutionary dynamics can be understood as an attempt to think the very problems highlighted by more recent theories of the Political (i.e., the foundation of politics) or of real politics (i.e., the "successful failure" of politics ever to correspond to its presumed "essence"). Rather than positing either of these hypostases as exhaustive, however, the notion of political society attempts to think them deconstructively in terms of their "constitution," that is, in terms of the sociopolitical relations that they both produce and that they seek to regulate.

A significant contribution to state theory in itself, what is particularly relevant for the argument of this chapter is the style that Gramsci employs in the elaboration of this line of research. It is a style that can be characterized as simultaneously "constitutive" and "deconstructive," registering the distinction in identity of both the reality and nonreality of politics, that is, both its inevitability and also its impossibility. It is this style that enables Gramsci to draw on and to synthesize a range of seemingly unrelated themes from across the *Prison Notebooks* in his formulation of the notion of political society not as the resolution of political modernity's contradictions but as their most consummate expression and institutionalization.

"Constitution" is intended here in both a material and active sense. On the one hand, it refers to those properties traditionally associated with the juridical sense of the word, indicating the foundation, structures, and shaping powers of a given political order, but conceiving them in the material sense of an ongoing process of "constitutionalization."[37] In this sense, political society represents the ensemble of formal and informal institutions that are both productive and restrictive of political action, the practical forms in which "official politics" within the modern state occurs and by means of which it is frustrated. On the other hand, however, my use of the notion of the constitution of political society also gestures toward an active sense of the word derived from critical appropriations of the phenomenological tradition.[38] This meaning is concerned with both political society and its dialectical complement of civil society not as given "things" but as active relations. Both political society and civil society are continually (re)produced as a synthesis of the relations of hegemony and subalternization within the integral state. Their constitution is in this sense always provisional, retrospective—and always the object of contestation.

On the other hand, this style can be characterized as "deconstructive"—but only if this overused adjective is understood in its most productive and philosophically coherent sense, that is, as a critical inheritance of the dialectical tradition's emphasis on the primacy of relationality and consequent negation of foundations.[39] It posits the necessity of political society while simultaneously denying the possibility of its coherent self-affirmation. Political society is both a real structuring principle of modern societies and at the same time its own self-deception. The theme of the constitution of political society thus functions as a perspective from which to think of the possibility of a type of political action that would work to deconstruct rather than ratify its own formal conditions of possibility in the dialectic of the integral state. It is, in other words, an attempt to think of a type of politics that would work to undo itself as a simulacrum.

Three general lines of research in the overall project of the *Prison Notebooks* can be seen as contributing to this argument, with the latter synthesizing and sublating the perspectives of the former two. The first line consists in a non-essentialist theory of "translatability." This perspective enables Gramsci to think social and political relations beyond foundationalism, that is, as constituted solely in and by the dialectical interchange between the different moments that subsist as such only in their relation. The second line develops as a critique of the "speculative mode of production"—not only philosophical speculation but also the speculative social and political relations that structure civil and political societies as antagonistic but mutually dependent modes of association and organization. Finally, the third line of research can be summarized in the notion of "subalternization" as the fusion of the relations of translatability and speculation between civil and political society in the overall dynamic of the bourgeois integral state. Taken in their totality and in their dialectical interaction, these three lines of research flow together into an alternative way of thinking of "politics" as a sociopolitical relation in which the "cave" of bourgeois political modernity is continually affirmed—and contested. It is precisely for this reason that neither the Political nor real politics can be simply rejected or embraced. Rather, they can only be deconstructed by means of the always impure forms of their practical and concrete critique.

Translatability without foundations

At first sight, "translatability" may not appear to be the most pressing strategic concern for leader of a clandestine communist party imprisoned by the world's first Fascist regime. Unsurprisingly, then, the early publication and discussion of Gramsci's carceral writings largely excluded his own translations and dedicated relatively little attention to his theoretical reflections on the theme of translation.[40] It has only been more recently that attention has turned to Gramsci's elaboration of a distinctive conception of translatability—perhaps equally unsurprising given that this has also been a period characterized by a multiplicity of intersecting radical claims and movements and the translations between them.[41] Indeed, we are now in a position to recognize translatability not as simply one among many themes explored in the *Prison Notebooks*, but as one of—if not *the*—central perspectives and methodological orientations that unites all of his disparate fields of research.

Gramsci was inspired to elaborate a theory of translatability in the first instance by Lenin's remark to the Fourth Congress of the Third International in 1922. Speaking in defense of the newly minted policy of the "United Front," Lenin argued that the Russian Revolution had not yet been able to "translate" its language into the Western European languages.[42] Formerly trained as a historical linguist, and already sensitive to linguistic difference due to his own multifaceted cultural background, Gramsci explored the significance of this enigmatic statement in a variety of contexts, not least of all in his comparative analysis of the non-derivative relations between dialects and national languages.[43]

As Gramsci's repeated recollection of Lenin's comments evidence, what interested him most was not the purely linguistic problem of the transfer of "content" from one language to another (itself an impoverished and ultimately positivistic conception of translation), but the broader problem of the role of particularity even and especially in moments of supposed universality. Translation for Gramsci in this sense is fundamentally a question of the constitutive relation between difference and unity in the formation and transformation of sociopolitical realities.

Translatability is also central to Gramsci's theory of the relationship between philosophy, politics, and history as the major representative forms in which a wider range of social relations are "condensed." After having criticized at length Croce's attempt to posit a "non-political" (in the sense of "non-ideological") or purely "philosophical-conceptual" foundation for philosophy, Gramsci argues that "we arrive thus at the equality of, or equation between, 'philosophy and politics,' thought and action . . . the only 'philosophy' is history in action."[44] The notion of the potential equation of different discursive and affective regimes—that is, not their sameness but the active construction of equality as a relation, or equalization—is central to Gramsci's distinctive conception of translation as a productive and even "creative" activity, rather than merely mimetic repetition.

Here he was intervening in one of the debates that had marked the central division that emerged in the "post-Marxist" development of Italian neo-idealism: the debate about the possibility of translation between the erstwhile comrades-in-arms Benedetto Croce (liberal philosopher of the history of freedom) and Giovanni Gentile (state philosopher of the Fascist regime). Croce's indebtedness to a broadly neo-Kantian conception of historical singularity led him to insist on the untranslatability of "genuine" poetry, as the paradigmatic case of the non-iterable because absolutely singular expression of pure unified intuition. Gentile, on the other hand, had pointed to the historical reality of translation as simultaneously impossible and inevitable, as the mode in which the unity of the spiritual act is continually reaffirmed within and despite temporal differentiation.[45]

The decisive innovation represented by Gramsci's theory is the notion of reciprocal translatability, or of what might be called "translatability without foundations." Significantly, this perspective is not present from the outset of the *Prison Notebooks*, but emerges in the course of their development, in both theoretical and political terms. In his earliest notes on translation, Gramsci seems to understand translation in terms of a paradigm of purification, or as he phrases it, a "reduction" from one linguistic register to another.[46] Furthermore, in this period he seems to advocate what can be understood as a "realist" conception of translation as the mode of articulation in different linguistic registers of "the same thing." Translation here appears to be thought in the classically Platonic terms of a foundational paradigm, with linguistic expression constituting a sort of contingent and arbitrary "superstructure" in relation to a "base" of socio-historical reality that both precedes and exceeds its variable expressions.[47]

Later notes, however, particularly those written or revised in the wake of the elaboration of the philosophy of praxis in 1932 as a distinct conception and practice of philosophy, place a greater emphasis on translation as a relational dynamic.[48] For this reason, Gramsci stresses that "the translatable" is a critical potential that inheres in any social practice insofar as being always open to resignification through struggles over its meaning and value. He also argues, however, that the philosophy of praxis is particularly well placed in comparison to other inheritances of the philosophical tradition to highlight this potential translatability, insofar as the philosophy of praxis alone, according to Gramsci, adequately registers the constitutively practical dimension of social life. Translation here is not understood as a type of "decoding" of a hieroglyphic "original" text in order to reveal an even more "originary" meaning or truth in which original and copy can then be seen, retrospectively, to participate. It is instead seen as the fundamental mode of the production of all meaning, or the metaphoric displacement of meanings that characterizes communication and human sociality as such.

Unlike Croce's conception (among many other theories of translation in the twentieth century), this theory of translatability does not rely on the positing of an authentic "original" from which subsequent departures could be measured in terms of corruption, diminution, or inadequacy. Rather than the reductive or derivative forms of a hierarchical causation, or of an external articulation or even overdetermination of distinct and autonomous realms governed by their own logic, Gramsci posits relations of translatability as a dialectical relationship of simultaneous identity and distinction. The equation of philosophy and politics, thought and action, for instance, is not posited as a function of an originary unity ("the same thing") that is "expressed" and thereby "realized" in different terrestrial forms, at sequentially linked temporal moments. This, in effect, is a Platonic theory of translation that has curiously continued to mark much post-Romantic reflection on the nature and form of translation as an essentially mimetic practice, even while theories of the imagination as productive and expressive faculty have reshaped reflection on all other literary practices and genres.[49]

Gramsci instead conceives of the identity of philosophy and politics as an active relation of ongoing translation between different organizational levels and forms of a social group's activities. Philosophy and politics can be equated in this model only in the sense of being actively "equalized," that is, continually confronted the one with the other as alternative and competing modes of comprehension and transformation of any social practice. There is thus no *Ursprache* for Gramsci, just as little as there is a *telos* of immediate comprehensibility, in the type of homogenizing *Esperanto* popular in some currents of the early twentieth century socialist movement, and against which the young Gramsci had so forcefully polemicized.[50] It is the potentiality of translatability, rather than the actualization of the (un)translated, that signals the always unfinished and therefore transformable nature of relations of communication between different social and political practices.

This theory of non-foundational translatability has a profound impact on the way in which Gramsci conceives the relations between civil and political societies. According to an influential interpretive tradition of the young Marx's critique of Hegel's state theory, political society should be understood as an artificial mimetic failure to capture the vibrancy and "true reality" of civil society (conceived in Feuerbachian fashion). For another reading drawing from the (in)famous metaphors of Marx's 1859 "Preface" to the *Contribution to the Critique of Political Economy*, a similarly foundational status is accorded as the "economic structure" on which arises a political (and juridical, religious, etc.) "superstructure." In both cases, political society is viewed as secondary, derivative, and ultimately, "unreal."

The Prison Notebooks propose a different approach. To use the terminology of much recent translation theory, political society is not posited as a "target text" derived from the more or less successful imitation of the "source text" of civil society.[51] There is instead a reciprocal interchange without originary or foundational priority of either instance. Political society and civil society are both in this sense "translations" of each other, or variable forms of the dynamic of translatability without foundations. If political society "translates" the contradictions of civil society into its own institutional forms and practices, it is equally the case that civil society in its turn translates those same institutional forms and practices into its own contradictory idiom. It is this variability that, for Gramsci, lies at the heart of the political relation, as the constitutive mode in which political society relates to what it is not, which thereby defines the inherent instability and heteronomy of politics itself.

The Speculative Mode of Production

The non-essentialist notion of translatability is also at work in Gramsci's critique of "speculation."[52] Speculation is intended here not simply as a particular mode of philosophical activity (associated with the transhistorical claims of a certain type of "metaphysics," understood as a science of the generic) but conceived in a more expansive sense. I propose to characterize this as a critique of the "speculative mode of production," a mode that is simultaneously philosophical, social, and political.

The initial stimulus for this development was provided by Gramsci's engagement with the rigorously philosophical terms of Benedetto Croce's critique of Marx—arguably, the most rigorously philosophical critique of Marxism ever developed. The most objectionable element of the Marxist tradition for Croce was not its purported "materialism" (or non-philosophy), but on the contrary, what he argued were its all too naively metaphysical presuppositions.[53] Marx's notion of the "economic structure" of a social formation was for Croce not a historically dynamic conception of an ensemble of active social relations, institutions, and changing causal forms. It was instead nothing more than a static foundation of a dual-world metaphysics. Elaborating the philosophical coordinates that would later be exploited, often unknowingly, by various seasons of "post-Marxism," Croce proposed a critique of Marx's thought as both metaphysical and essentialist: Marx accorded full reality, Croce argued, only to the economic structure, leaving the superstructure to be grasped as secondary appearance (in a Kantian "phenomenal" sense), or worse, as mere mimetic failure (along the lines of Feuerbach's critique of Hegel's "inauthenticity").

In effect, and ironically, the former Marxist Croce applied to Marx's thought that particular version of the more general nineteenth-century critique of metaphysics as abstract, unreal, and dissimulating that had been developed by the young Marx himself. This critique was initially elaborated largely in texts that remained unpublished in Marx's own lifetime (above all, the manuscripts that would later become known as *The German Ideology*, the so-called *1844 Manuscripts*, and Marx's notes on Feuerbach from 1845). It was a critique that was later influentially developed by Engels in his extended commentary on the latter Marxian text, *Ludwig Feuerbach and the End of Classical German Philosophy*—alongside *Anti-Dühring*, the text in which "Marxism" as a distinct doctrinal system was most influentially elaborated. It was this version of "Marxism" that Croce rejected by turning its own anti-metaphysical claims against it. It was, in a sense, an attempt to "out-Marx Marx."

Yet Croce's critique of Marxism's supposed metaphysics, like so many similar critiques that followed it, relied on its own metaphysical foundation. The Crocean system posited an unbridgeable distinction between historical events and the conceptuality used to comprehend them. For Croce, the structure of genuine thought in the form of philosophical concepts necessarily remains unsullied by historical development, and thought's structure is not fundamentally changed by the contexts of its deployment. Genuine concepts are rigorously and qualitatively opposed to the merely "pseudo-concepts" operative in practical action.[54] They are not particular words that can be distinguished from other words on the basis of the intensity of the history of their repetition, the rhetorical force with which they are deployed, or their decisive role in particular argumentative structures or strategies (such as is the case for Reinhart Koselleck's nuanced understanding of the "über-wordly" nature of fundamental concepts [Grundbegriffe].[55] Rather, just as the genuinely philosophical is distinguished by Croce from the merely ideological, so are concepts qualitatively distinct from the words that may express but not exhaust them. The Crocean "concept of the concept" in fact engages in an open restoration of precisely that type of dual-world metaphysics that Croce had so forcefully condemned in Marx.

This orientation is "speculative" in Gramsci's sense because it presupposes the transcendental constitution of a contemplating (and in this sense, "speculating") subject [Subjekt] that stands over and against the object of its gaze; the "object" [Objekt] is in this sense only constituted as an object by the speculative relation, which simultaneously constitutes the subject as subject, in a relation of mutual formalistic dependence.[56] This critique of speculation thus implies and presupposes a critique of the philosophical grammar of subject–object relations, and thus of any philosophical anthropology, including that of the so-called political subject.[57]

It is this identification of "speculation" as the hard core of metaphysics that perhaps constitutes the most original feature of Gramsci's critique of metaphysics, in comparison to both the prior Marxist tradition and his contemporaries, Marxist or otherwise. It distinguishes his approach from objections that focus on metaphysics' "abstraction" from reality (in an ironically mimetic paradigm), its "idealism" (in the sense of ascribing causal power to the ideal), or its "transhistoricism" (in the sense of a claim to validity in diverse historical periods). The rejection of speculation is also not limited to the purely philosophical. Rather, it is motivated by a precise analysis of the role that a speculative logic plays on the "ethico-political" terrain, to use one of the key terms that Gramsci appropriated from the Italian neo-idealist vocabulary. Speculation is here understood as an orientation fundamentally rooted in the experience of sociopolitical passivity and objectification. The speculative mode of production that generates metaphysical concepts is also operative in the relations of subalternization that structure the modern state.

Ultimately, Gramsci extends this insight into the project of deciphering this speculative disposition as an index of the political development of a class project, or what he calls the resolution of "speculation into its real terms [as] ideology."[58] Rather than being definitive of philosophy as such, the speculative metaphysical form of philosophy is thereby recognized as a particular phase in the historical development of an ideological formation. It is symptomatic of a phase of achieved social and political hegemony that seeks to insure itself against dissolution and disaggregation by means of ideal refinement and conceptual perfection. Insofar as philosophy is defined as a practical social relation alongside others, the way is open to think the transformation of philosophy by the social relations it seeks to comprehend, or in other words, the status of thought itself as a social relation of communication, coordination, and organization. It is along this line of research that one of the most powerful dimensions of Gramsci's "philosophy of praxis" is elaborated as an entirely new way of posing the so-called fundamental questions of philosophy as themselves instruments of practical action.

Speculation is this sense represents a failure of translation, or the hierarchization of relations of translatability. Speculation "occurs" when there is a blockage in these relations, and instead of co-constitution and reciprocity between instances one relation lays claim to a foundational status. It is the speculative relation that enables one instance to present itself, and be accepted as, a "source text" (*Subjekt*) to which another moment—the "target text" (*Objekt*)—is then seen as derivative and subordinate. Such "mistranslations" are essential to the hierarchized relations that emerge, for instance, between (national) languages and "their" dialects, or between an "authorized" text and the fragments of its "interpretations," or the textual performances that are judged only to "approximate" the former's supposedly originary unity.

Political society represents precisely such a hierarchization of relations of translatability. It emerges as a speculative comprehension of a civil society that is constituted in its particularity precisely by political society's claim to be an instance of organizing universality. Rather than the continual translation between organizing and associative instances, with each constitutively requiring the other in order to be itself, the speculative relation at the heart of "political society" represents a stillborn dialectic, one that ends in a hypostatization because it begins in one.

In one version of this relation (the thesis of the "primacy of politics"), political society is posited as the target text that "improves" on the deficiencies of the source text in civil society. It claims to be a regulative instance that resolves the chaotic tendencies of civil society into a higher and more coherent unity. Translation in this sense functions as emendation, and as the dominance of form over content. In another and even more insidious version of this relation (the "autonomy of the Political"), political society instead posits itself as the hitherto poorly translated source text. Civil society, as the target text that fails to comprehend its source text adequately, thereby stands condemned of being a "bad" translation. Only if the speculative subject focuses its gaze on and valorizes the traces of its own rationality deposited in disjointed form in its object, enforcing a proper comprehension of itself, can this failure be overcome. In both cases, the result is the same one-sidedness: speculative command displaces the dynamic of co-constitution at the heart of non-essentialist relations of translatability.

Subalternization

Gramsci's reflections on translatability and speculation are concretized in his theory of the constitution of political society as a process of "subalternization." Since the *Subaltern Studies* collective first directed international attention to the theme of subalternity in the 1980s, and increasingly after Gayatri Spivak's influential intervention focused on the singular figure of "the subaltern," subalternity has frequently been understood as a condition of disempowerment, subjugation, and oppression.[59] Subalternity, that is, has been thought to be equivalent to that condition of subjection to an alien power that Max Weber characterized with his distinctive notion of "domination" (*Herrschaft*).[60]

For Weber, domination is not simply power (*Macht*) writ large but constitutes its almost direct antithesis. Domination can be characterized as a "vicariousness" of power, in at least two senses. On the one hand, domination is vicarious in the sense that, under its reign, power is experienced not as a capacity to act of a purposive agent but only in terms of the capacity to impose such purpose on another. On the other hand, domination is also vicarious in relation to power in the sense that it is the form in which power is experienced after it has been made absent. While power here refers to an agent's capacity (in the sense of unrealized potency) to undertake their "own" (intended, purposive) action (conceived as externalization of a previously interior state of consciousness), domination consists in the fact of the external imposition of intentions onto other agents, who accept them as if they were their own and accordingly act to realize them.

Power in this sense refers to the ability to act in a way that is proper to an empowered member of a political community, or what is often understood today (particularly in "neo-Republican" traditions) as a quality of the "citizen" as a deliberate and deliberative actor. Domination, on the other hand, indicates the specular opposite, or the condition of the non-citizen, reduced not simply to passivity or instrumentality (i.e., in Kantian terms, posited as a means to another's end) but excluded from the political realm in which the powers of deliberation and decision can be meaningfully exercised. The subaltern has come to be understood in contemporary critical theory as just such a submission to an alien will, condition of incapacity, and experience of exclusion. It is a destitution that is simultaneously political, economic, ethical, and even (and perhaps especially) aesthetic, conceived in the sense of a lack of access to and participation in the order of "the sensible" in all senses of the word.

Such an understanding of the subaltern as the product of relations of domination is not entirely consistent with Ranajit Guha's emphasis in the early volumes of *Subaltern Studies* on an originary autonomous history and life of the subaltern classes in colonial India.[61] For Guha in the early 1980s, the subaltern was precisely a figure that was not produced, whether by relations of domination or the exercise of public (administrative) power. Unlike the "citizens" interpellated by the relations of the modern (non-colonial, hegemonic, or "European") state, the colonial subaltern existed in a space separate from and independent of the realm of "politics" in an official sense. Guha's later characterization of the colonial state as a "dominance without hegemony," on the other hand, suggested a more immediate relation between subalternity and domination, whereby dominance was called on to account for the experiences of colonial subalterns in a way formally similar to that in which hegemony was argued to be constitutive of citizenship in the imperial centers.[62]

The subaltern as a figure of the type of destitution produced by domination has certainly become the most widely accepted understanding of the term in the wake of Gayatri Spivak's "Can the Subaltern Speak?" (which influenced Guha himself).[63] In this influential essay, the subaltern represents such a complete removal "from all lines of social mobility" that it effectively becomes a vanishing signifier, constrained to represent what is unrepresentable in the current political but also aesthetic order; to adopt once again Rancière's terminology, it is the part that continues to have no part even at the moment of its impossible revolt.[64]

While this interpretation has gained a wide currency, giving rise to an entire scholarly archive exploring the subaltern's incapacity, it is a reading for which limited textual support can be found in Gramsci's *Prison Notebooks*.[65] Studies of the *Prison Notebooks* in the wake of *Subaltern Studies* have instead drawn attention to the ways in which Gramsci's notion of subalternity not only cannot be reduced to such a figure of exclusion, but on the contrary, represents almost its direct antithesis. Subalternity for Gramsci does not represent a state of removal from the structures of the modern state, but their most consummate realization. Conceived in an active sense, as subalternization, it represents the ways in which the modern state actively seeks to mobilize—and in so doing, to domesticate—the rebellious energies of subaltern social groups.[66] As such a process, subalternization is realized and continually renewed in the dialectic between civil and political societies, particularly in the moments when the latter seeks speculatively to comprehend the former.

Subalternization, understood in this sense, is a function of the process of the material constitution of the modern state itself. Unlike so-called pre-modern political orders, the modern bourgeois integral state does not understand itself to be given as a natural datum, but instead acknowledges its always contingent and provisional nature. Its distinctiveness consists in the way in represents itself as the institutional embodiment of a historical process and promise of the popular (or "democratic") refoundation of the political field, no longer conceived in terms of regulation, but, as Max Weber was all too anxiously aware, of legitimation. Similarly, unlike the older ruling classes from which it continually feels the need to distinguish itself, the bourgeoise is not able to enwrap itself in the comfort of a claim to autonomy. It instead constitutively acknowledges its relational and thus heteronomous character.[67] In other words, unlike the elites of previous political orders, the bourgeoisie must permanently place its own position in question in order then to be continually reaffirmed and renewed. It is by means of the continually renewed subalternization of the popular classes that the ruling classes in the bourgeois integral state are able to maintain themselves as ruling classes in a qualitatively new and "modern" way. They need the subaltern classes in order "to become" themselves.

This relational dynamic has important implications for the way in which Gramsci understands the constitution and capacities of the subaltern classes and social groups. Unlike the widely defused notion of the subaltern as a figure of destitution, this approach emphasizes the active dimensions of subalternity, even and especially when this occurs in passive and pacifying forms. Far from being unrepresentable, subaltern social groups in the *Prison Notebooks* are depicted as the product of elaborate representative and self-representative strategies; instead of being unable to speak, Gramsci's historical and cultural analyses emphasize the extent to which the subaltern continually makes its voice heard and its presence felt in contradictory and complex cultural, social, and political forms. No exceptional or marginal case, subalternization for Gramsci is all too quotidian and central; it describes the basic structuring conditions of political modernity in all of its contradictory forms.

Conceived in these terms, there is an important difference between Gramsci's conception of the modern state as a relation of subalternization and the notion of the modern state as a regime of domination. From Weber and Schmitt to Althusser and Mann, the modern state was frequently understood throughout the twentieth century as a political apparatus, machine, or dispositive in which domination is "produced" as a regulative instance, and as excess of force, coercion, or violence.[68] This excessive product is then "applied" to a separate (civil) society deficient in its own self-regulating features, thereby achieving an equilibrium between the state's organizational capacities and society's associative nature. The state dominates society, just as the political seeks to dominate the social. Central to this notion of domination is the claim of an originary autonomy of dominating and dominated instances. State and society, the political and the social, may later enter into more or less conflictual relations; but at their origin—so the story goes—they are properly understood as distinct, and generated by their own immanent principles, rather than in the interaction between them. It is only from within the terms of this narrative that the state's power over society can be characterized as domination by an "alien power."

The notion of subalternization, on the other hand, highlights not the state's separation from society but its deep and constitutive implication in its foundation, functioning, and daily renewal. Neither political society nor civil society, as forms of political relationality, are given in their separation but are instead only mutually constituted by means of their interaction. For this reason, the relation between civil society and political society is not conceived in terms of the domination of the former by the latter, for such a conception assumes the self-sufficiency of the dominant position, which asserts its legitimacy in terms of its relationship to itself and not in terms of its relationship to the dominated. Unlike the relation of domination, which involves a structural "passivation" of the dominated elements, the relation of subalternization is one of simultaneous mobilization and domestication, of activation of social forces and their immediate containment. In this precise sense, the notion of subalternization constitutes a politically focused corelate of the "mature" Marx's theory of proletarianization as a relation of exploitation (surplus value expropriation) only made possible by according "liberty" to those who bear labor power to commodify themselves; indeed, subalternization is a formal cause or explanation (*aitía*) for proletarianization, accompanying it wherever it may go. The type of bourgeois state power signified by the notion of political society for Gramsci is thus not merely oppressive but productive; it may censure, but it does so in the process of cultivating; it disciplines, but in order to reward the achievement of its own ends.

This distinction between subalternization and domination is crucial for grasping the nature of political society not as a place but as the "non-place" of a mobile political relation. Political society is not the originary location of a "will to dominate" that then emanates "down" to a subordinate civil society. Rather, political society is thought of in these relational terms as one of the forms that generates subalternization as a heteronomous relation. On the one hand, subalternization, as a process of mobilizing domestication, is founded on political society's claim to represent an organizational instance that supplements (in the sense of fulfilling a lack within) the "merely associative" instance of civil society. Civil society is thereby subalternized in relation to political society to the extent that the latter claims (with success) the monopoly of the legitimate use of organization, ordinance, and ordering in a given sociopolitical formation. On the other hand, however, subalternization does not occur by mere decree, as if political society were an autonomous source of sovereign power capable of subjugating those drawn within its sphere of influence. Rather, subalternization depends on the active participation of civil society in the ratification of political society's claims to organizational priority; associative civil society must "recognize" political society as a source of legitimate organization in order for both to come into being. Civil society in this sense "performs" its own subalternization, or is precisely the form in which this subalternization is realized as enduring social and political relations that are incorporated in concrete institutions and practices.[69]

The Constitution of Political Society

This tripartite deconstructive analysis of the constitution of political society represents a distinctive theory of the nature of the modern state as a political relation. It is a perspective that is irreducible to the broadly neo-Kantian presuppositions of mainstream liberal political theory throughout the twentieth century and its contemporary continuation in the guise of those normative theories that begin by presupposing the legitimation of an already given order as the fundamental problem of political theory. For emancipatory politics, instead, what must be explained is not order but the process of *ordering* by means of which the political field in modern societies, with its regularities, tendencies, and institutions, is produced out of the contradictions, conflicts, and contingencies of the "merely" social. Order in this sense is only ever a retroactive speculative construction imposed on conflicts that it can banish but not vanquish.

This approach, however, also gives the lie to those caricatures of Marxian and Marxist state theory that assert it to be an anti-political theoretical tradition. The *Prison Notebooks* instead attempt to develop a theory of the constitution of political society as an active process that is central to the constitution of modern society as such—including and especially its supposedly non-political forms, which are always in reality politically overdetermined. This is not merely a question of the political institution of the social, acutely discerned by Laclau and Mouffe. It is also a case of the political institution of the Political itself, that is, of the active production of the Political as a distinct relationality specific to political modernity and not one grounded in a transhistorical condition (e.g., a "generic antagonism") or philosophical anthropology.[70] The dialectical interaction between translatability, speculation, and subalternization in the constitution of political order can in this sense be understood as a critical redimensioning of three central features of the young Marx's critique of politics, and particularly the way in which the young Marx engaged with the strengths and weaknesses of Hegel's state theory.

In terms of translatability, Gramsci's insistence on the reciprocal relations between civil society and political society provides a corrective to Marx's (Feuerbachian-inspired) assertion of the primacy of an extra-political foundation over the "merely" political (in Marx's early works, in the notion of civil society; in his "mature" texts, in the notion of an "economic structure" subtending civil society itself).[71] The *Prison Notebooks* here recover a critical potential of Hegel's state theory that was ironically submerged in Marx's too hasty critique, namely, the emphasis on the political constitution of the social—which itself is overdetermined by the social constitution of the political, in a dialectic without beginning or end.

In terms of speculation, the analysis of political society's mode of relating to civil society as a speculative relation both extends and specifies Marx's critique of the hypostatization at the heart of the modern state, or the way in which it elevates the contradictions of civil society into structuring principles of the political realm. Yet whereas the young Marx's analysis of the metaphysics of the modern state at times might appear to represent it in terms of a unidirectional relation (from the corporeality of civil society to its inadequate comprehension in political society), Gramsci's emphasis on speculation's practical function also recognizes the extent to which this political overdetermination is not simply oppressive of civil society but productive of its meanings, values, and practices. Political society, that is, is not a parasitic addition to a civil society that precedes it. It instead actively intervenes to shape civil society into what can then be presented as an antechamber to itself.

In terms of subalternization, the *Prison Notebooks* highlight the way in which the modern state attempts to capture and direct the popular political energies that its contradictions have cultivated. Unlike young Marx's negation of the existing political institutions as an illusory comprehension of civil society's reality (in this sense, merely reversing the polarity of valorization from organization to association), Gramsci acknowledges the constitution of political society as a real dynamic at work within association itself. The popular will generated within and by the modern state is not merely a formalistic illusion but the real political overdetermination of associative practices by instances of organization that remain structurally separate from them. The modern state, that is, tries to call forth "the people" that would be adequate to its own designs; or in Brechtian terms, the modern state sets out to "elect" the people it feels it deserves. It is precisely in the production of such a people as constitutional object that political society affirms its own necessity as the form in which the subaltern social classes and groups can seek redress for their "own" inadequacies. What remains constitutively disavowed in this construction, however, is precisely the extent to which political society itself, as failed translation, speculative relation, and subalternizing process, produces those very inadequacies, and thereby its own—contingent, constructed—restorative "necessity."

Beyond the Authenticity of "Pure" Politics

This deconstructive reading of the constitution of political society constitutes a fundamental critique of what I have defined as the "Platonizing" style of contemporary radical political thought that is oriented toward an origin to which emancipatory politics could return in an act of purification or "de-corruption." Against this thoroughly traditional metaphysical construction of a hierarchical relationship between generality and particularity, a theory of the constitution of political society seeks to demonstrate how the political relations of the bourgeois integral state have been historically constituted in precise institutional terms. It is not that politics has been subjected to processes of neutralization or depoliticization, leaving behind the merely technical or administrative organization of the social—or what appears to some critics to be even worse, the "economization" of both. A once and future real politics has not been dissolved into the unreality of our insubstantial present. Rather, politics itself just is and always has been precisely the sum of those neutralizations of the conflicts and struggles that constitute the fabric of the modern state, the conflicts that the modern state calls forth in order immediately to suppress. For this reason, the search for the "genuinely political," whether undertaken historically, normatively, or anthropologically, will always be disappointed—because what it will discover is always yet another shadow on yet another cave's wall.

The notion of the constitution of political society, however, also provides a critical perspective on what I have referred to as a "reconstructive-transcendental" style. Rather than a model of a pure, real, or more authentic politics to be found in the past in order then to be reproposed or actualized in the present, such a perspective emphasizes the inherent formalism of political society as a concrete institutional relation structuring political modernity since its inception. "There is no outside-politics" might be taken as a slogan for this approach: just as civil society is not a "pre-political" stage exterior to political society, so there is no real politics lurking in the shadows of the past to which we might return. It is politics as such, as a distinct relationality of (mis)translation, speculation, and subalternization that is the focus of this critique. In other words, just as there is no uncontaminated space from which an external assault on existing political society could be launched, so there is no moment in the past, before the fall, when *potentia* was free from a parasitic *potestas*. There can be no "natural history" of constituent power because it is always constitutionally overdetermined, even and especially in rebellions against existing orders.[72]

Existing political society in the bourgeois integral state—in other words, politics as we know it—is not a mere illusion that could be wished away, or replaced by a more amenable formalist variation of its fundamentally self-same logic. Rather, it is a real abstraction produced by the speculative relation it establishes in order to subalternize civil society. It can therefore not be a question of subtracting the supposed deformations or corruption of the existing political society in order to reveal a hard core of the Real, whether that be understood as traditional social democracy's civil society or one or another form of "purer" antagonism, such as those championed by post-68 micro-, infra-, im- or metapolitical approaches. On the contrary, insofar as the hypostatized forms of political society really do determine the conceptual space in which politics in the bourgeois integral state can occur—not only official" institutional or parliamentary politics, but politics as such, as the conflict over the relation between association and organization—it is much more a case of determining the particular forms of practice, even and especially in their conditions of subalternity to existing political society, that would be capable of deconstructing its material constitution from within.

It is a question, then, not of seeking a type of politics purified of those features of the present that are held to be responsible for its corruption or fall from itself. Rather, any truly radical engagement with actually existing political society is more likely to achieve its own distinctive ends if it begins by acknowledging the constitutive impurity of politics itself as the problem to be overcome and not the solution to be sought. How can such a self-negating intervention be undertaken? In other words, is there a type of politics that simultaneously seeks to undermine itself *as* politics? Is it even worth posing such a question in a period in which one of the main challenges for radical movements is understanding how their initial rebellions might be able to become "more political," in both a limited and expansive sense?

If there are no guarantees at the beginning or end of politics, at the level of a fundamental ontology of the Political or that of the ontic facticity of real politics, it may be instead in the midst of "doing" emancipatory politics itself, conceived as a distinctive method of de-subalternization, that these questions can be posed in more concrete terms.

3

Efficient Cause

Hegemony as a Method of Political Work

At the center of the synthesis of nineteenth-century radicalisms that retrospectively came to be known all too homogeneously as "classical Marxism" there stood the notion of self-emancipation. The most radical element of this perspective consisted not in that claim that emancipation represented an achieved condition of freedom or liberty, however that idea was defined: as freedom from or freedom for, as the absence of constraint or presence of non-domination, as incapacity of external determination or ability for self-direction. Rather, the notion of the self-emancipation of the popular classes emphasized the active and ongoing process of removing oneself from servitude, in all of its various forms. Resistance to the existing order was conceived as itself a process of construction of an alternative order. It was an act that was no longer defined by the coordinates of the present but was already, in its active and processual nature, a mode of production of the future.

Viewed in this light, the declaration in the *Manifesto of the Communist Party* that the workers have "no country" (*kein Vaterland*) can be understood not as a condition of destitution, but on the contrary, an expression of strength.[1] It was by means of subtraction from the lures of the patria and its abstract communitarianism that the proletariat was constituted as a political force simultaneously within and beyond the given situation, the moment of the immanent rupture of that situation. Similarly, the rousing rejection of any redemptive figure in *The Internationale*—"there are no supreme saviors, neither God, nor Caesar, nor tribune"—emphasized the radical nature of the type of self-emancipation that the early workers' movement aimed to inherit from the great slave revolts that had defined the most radical expression of "the Age of Revolution."

Radical Politics. Peter D. Thomas, Oxford University Press. © Oxford University Press 2023.
DOI: 10.1093/oso/9780197528075.003.0004

Henceforth, emancipation could no longer be equated with the extension of privileges to those who had previously been denied them, according to a model of the inclusion of the formerly excluded. This had been the "levelling up" implicit in the Third Estate's demand (as ventriloquized by Sieyès) to become the "something" in the political order that it deserved to be.[2] By positing itself as the object of its own action, however, the self-emancipation of the popular classes instead signified the abolition of the possibility of privilege as such. For privilege is always conditional on those who grant it and only has meaning insofar as the order from which it derives ensures that there remain those who are denied it. Self-emancipation, however, is self-authorized, and by definition is open to all those who engage in it on their own terms, without comparison to the conditions of others. In this sense, the notion of self-emancipation that developed in the radical movements of the eighteenth and nineteenth centuries was a plebeian "levelling down" of the existing political order in a fundamental sense; that is, levelling down conceived not as reduction to a common denominator but as the demolition of the divisions and distinctions that structured the existing political order.[3]

The notion of self-emancipation signaled a reconfiguration of the entire political field that had emerged out of the bourgeois revolutions and has come to define our political modernity. For unlike the demands, claims, and appeals for emancipation that have been perennially addressed by the subjugated to those claiming to hold or exercise power, and which thereby performatively confirm the very preeminence that they claim to contest, the act of self-emancipation begins with a refusal to recognize not simply the legitimacy but the very existence of a given order; indeed, the fundamental fact of self-emancipation is the refusal to recognize the master as master. Self-emancipation in this sense represents not primarily an emancipation "from" a negative state, whether that negative state is conceived as slavery, domination, exploitation, or some other form of injustice or injury. It is an emancipation "for" emancipation itself, an emancipation from the given and an emancipation for the construction of a new social order. Self-emancipation, thus conceived as the immanence of emancipatory politics to itself, does not seek recognition from any higher instance; it presupposes and produces itself as an emancipation from the politics of the established order.

Self-emancipation within political modernity, however, has proven to be as difficult as it is rare. At each moment of its re-emergence over the last few centuries, it has immediately been confronted by attempts to domesticate it, to neutralize it, to reshape it into forms that are compatible with the existing order, whether that order be conceived under the classical watchwords of "Freedom, Equality, Property and Bentham" or our contemporary updated formulation of "Liberty, Human Rights, Citizenship, and Rawls."[4] In each case, there has been an attempted reduction of self-emancipation to those types of freedom that can be granted within the limits of the existing order, that is, the benevolence of a manumission that is always conditional. It is thus easy to understand how the very notion of self-emancipation can seem impossibly utopian and ephemeral. It may momentarily flare up in the overthrow of an old order, but then just as quickly it fades away when a new order seemingly inevitably is affirmed; it is the sparrow that does not make a spring.

This is not to say, however, that there is any inevitability of self-emancipation's defeat. The counterrevolutionary negation of self-emancipatory politics must be actively organized, as a defensive and reactive move against the growth of popular movements in potential and strength. In response to such reconfigurations of the political terrain, the ruling order proposes its own deliberate and conscious "structural adjustments," which actively seek to reduce aspirations to and possibilities of self-emancipation. One of the dimensions of Gramsci's concept of passive revolution was designed precisely in order to comprehend the ways in which popular strivings for freedom had contributed, not only in their defeats, to a transformation of the constituent elements of the ruling order. Indeed, sometimes even the popular classes' victories had contributed to the consolidation of the established order's dominance.

Is it possible to practice emancipatory politics in such a way that prevents its incorporation, corruption, or neutralization by the existing political order? In other words, is there a "method" of self-emancipatory politics that distinguishes it from the types of politics that are not only compatible with the existing order but ultimately,

EFFICIENT CAUSE   131

actively, albeit unintentionally, reinforce it? This has been a fundamental problem that has traversed the history of the struggles of popular classes and social groups on a global scale throughout political
modernity. It haunted all the classical debates on the opposition between "reform" and "revolution" in the late nineteenth and early twentieth centuries, just as much as it continued to animate disputes in the
1960s and 1970s New Left and its aftermath over the possibility of a
politics without "dirty hands."

This problem has been reposed for movements over the last 30 years,
in their waves of extra-governmental mobilization, partial electoral
successes, institutional consolidation, and seemingly inevitable decline. Time and again, powerful social movements have "encountered"
state power and found themselves unable to resist its lures and logic,
regardless of their prior ideological preparation. The involution of the
Partido dos Trabalhadores (*PT*) in Brazil might be taken as the contemporary paradigm of such a process of "sovereigntization" of movements
of resistance. The *PT* emerged as a regrouping of progressive and often
explicitly revolutionary forces in post-dictatorship Brazil, witnessing a
spectacularly rapid growth on social and political terrains throughout
the 1990s and the early years of the current century. But electoral success soon enough proved to be poisoned chalice, as the *PT* saw itself
reshaped within the structures of state sovereignty and reduced to the
passive basis of a regime of uneven regulation and amelioration of capitalist property relations, before the reassertion with a vengeance of the
representatives of the party of order with Bolsonaro's administration.
The same dynamic has been replicated on a larger or smaller scale(s)
in many other experiences in the Latin American "pink tide," but also
in Europe, with the most prominent and significant example being the
neutralization of the movement that led to the election of *SYRIZA* in
Greece in 2015.[5]

In each of these cases, the radical wings of the movements from
which these governmental experiments emerged were confronted
with the challenge of thinking and practicing a form of politics that
would be resilient to co-optation. Yet good intentions, appeals to
the popular democratic will, or even "sheltering" in revolutionary
traditions were not enough. They ultimately proved unable to elaborate an alternative perspective that could constitute a viable path

of political development on anything approaching the scale of mass politics. They thus soon found themselves confined to a minoritarian corner, repeating time-worn verities of the radical tradition's condemnation of reformism and renegacy—perhaps entirely justifiably and correctly, but not for all that any less impotently. Given the steady accumulation of these defeats in recent years, precisely in the context of the mobilizations that had seemed the most dynamic and promising, is it still possible today to imagine some method that might allow our intersectional sociopolitical movements to break out of the deadlock between recurrent mobilizations and revolts from below, followed by stabilization and administration from above, whether by "governments of the Left" or the rush to the right that now seems to follow them?

The Seasons of Hegemony

Since the postwar New Left, one of the most widely discussed candidates internationally for such a method of genuinely emancipatory politics has been the notion of hegemony. It has frequently been understood as a distinctively "democratic" practice of politics, both a precondition for radical change (in its emphasis on a plurality of mass movements) and as a means by which to achieve it (as a way of bringing those movements together in the pursuit of a common goal). It has seemed, that is, a way of making the transition from "mere" emancipation, conceived as removal of a suffered servitude, to self-emancipation, experienced as political actors' involvement in the construction of their own liberation.

If the preeminence of this notion in radical political cultures over the last 60 years has inevitably seen it regularly subjected to partial and total critiques, it has also prompted its reformulation in different conjunctures. In the period under consideration in this book, skepticism about the continuing relevance of hegemony at the turn of the millennium has given way to its conscious revival and extension over the last decade. A particular conception of hegemony played a central role in the debates around the rise of *Podemos* in the 2010s, for instance, just as it is currently championed as a potential leftist antidote to the poison of authoritarian, right-wing populism. Given its enduring presence in such a wide range of political cultures and periods, hegemony can function today as something like a litmus test for understanding transformations in the notion of emancipatory politics over the longer term—and how it might be transformed by and within movements today.

So deeply has hegemony entered into the everyday language of contemporary politics, in both its radical and mainstream variants, that it is sometimes difficult to remember that the prominence of hegemony is a relatively recent phenomenon, closely tied to the fate of the posthumous publication of Gramsci's *Prison Notebooks* in postwar Italy and their later international reception. Indeed, the frequency with which hegemony is invoked in English today is directly linked to the translation of Gramsci's carceral writings in the early 1970s, after which the word witnessed a veritable explosion in both usage and range of contested interpretations.[6]

In the 1970s, the notion of hegemony as a strategy of the accumulation of a nebulous "consent," as the foundation for the legitimacy of a socialist political program or even governmental participation, was one of the tendencies explored by what became known as "Eurocommunism." While that political movement was widely criticized and soon faded away, hegemony did not die with it. On the contrary, if anything, hegemony's prestige increased with the proliferation of different theoretical versions of it throughout the 1980s and 1990s. There is now a remarkably wide range of meanings associated with the word, frequently directly conflicting with each other. It is nevertheless possible to thematize at least four significant interpretations that have historically been associated with Gramsci's use of the term, in different overlapping seasons of interpretation.

According to the first influential reading, hegemony involves a leading social group securing the (active or passive) "consent" of other social strata, rather than unilaterally imposing its decrees on unwilling subjects. It relies more on subtle mechanisms of ideological integration, cultural influence, or even psychological dependency than on the threat of censure. In this version, hegemony-consent is conceived as the opposite of domination-coercion, according to presuppositions that effectively reduce hegemonic politics to an unmediated ethical relationship that precedes the foundation of the properly political in institutions of (potential or realized) violence.

This reading has accompanied the reception of the *Prison Notebooks* almost since the moment of their first publication in post-Fascist Italy. It was a particularly prominent perspective during the early discussion of hegemony in the Italian Communist Party in the 1950s and went on to strongly mark the terms in which Gramscian hegemony began to be discussed more widely in the English-speaking world in the 1970s.[7] This interpretation now constitutes a sort of "beginner's guide" to the meaning of hegemony, both in general political discourse and in a wide range of academic disciplines, ranging from cultural and literary studies to sociology, anthropology, and postcolonial studies. The most sophisticated formulation of this interpretation is arguably provided by Ranajit Guha's notion of a "dominance without hegemony" in which hegemonic consent is regarded as supplementary to the "mature" forms of dominance proper to the modern (imperial) state, but absent or weaker in its colonial satellites.[8]

A second interpretation regards hegemony as fundamentally a theory of the formation of a unified social and political order. Hegemony here is understood to signify the path leading from the disaggregation of the social to the consistency of the political. This version effectively posits Gramsci's concept in relation to radical-liberal traditions of the collective political agent, whether that agent is conceived as groups, class, caste, or, most frequently, "the people." In this sense, this version of hegemony can be regarded as a "bridge" between those traditions and the many contemporary theories that see the main task of radical politics as fundamentally one of promoting a unifying process, or the articulation of heterogeneity into some form of more or less stable consistency, as the basis for engaging in meaningful political action.

Historically, this reading emerged from the encounter between communist and liberal thought in the Italian postwar constitutional process.[9] Particularly in the novel theorization of Gramsci's former comrade in arms and successor as head of the Italian Communist Party, Palmiro Togliatti, this perspective placed a particular emphasis on the "national-popular" as a terrain of ethico-political struggle. It envisaged the representative-democratic constitution of the people as both object and subject of sociopolitical development and as the goal of a hegemonic form of politics. References to hegemony today in political philosophy and political theory as a theory of the aggregation of a "political subject" draw on the legacy of this interpretation, often explicitly in terms of its development in the work of Ernesto Laclau and Chantel Mouffe.[10]

A third interpretation represents hegemony as a political technique proper to "civil society," as distinct from methods deemed to be appropriate within the state apparatus. This interpretation effectively synthesizes the presuppositions of the understandings of hegemony as consent and unity by first "spatializing" and then "temporalizing" them. In a first moment, hegemony-consent is assigned to the terrain of civil society, while the state is argued to be the locus of domination-coercion. In a second moment, the accumulation of hegemony-consent in civil society until it solidifies into a unified political subject is posited as the necessary precondition for any confrontation over the possession of the means of domination-coercion on the terrain of the state. In effect, this interpretation presents hegemony as "pre-political," that is, not properly or fully political in itself but the precondition without which politics (understood in statal terms) could not emerge.

Derived from readings of the New Left in the 1960s and 1970s, and strongly influenced by the ideological interventions of the Italian Socialist Party and its fellow travelers in this period, it was an interpretation that later came to exert a powerful influence on left-wing Eurocommunism's reformist program of the gradualist capture of the representative state by means of a prior steady accumulation of social forces. It is a version of hegemony that continues to be operative today in discussions in political science and political theory, not only among currents that could be regarded as the revivification of Eurocommunist perspectives but also among more seemingly radical movementist approaches.[11]

Finally, a fourth interpretation understands hegemony in what is sometimes asserted to be its "conventional" sense, that is, as a characterization of the varieties of power that define the geopolitical relations between sovereign states. While this version often claims a lineage for itself dating back to Thucydides, the particular emphases of its contemporary formulation undoubtedly owes much to the general reformulation of anglophone political science discourses during the Cold War.[12] Hegemony is here configured at the level of a now open, now hidden, struggle for influence and power between states, prior to but sometimes including the outright declaration of military hostilities. An emphasis on the presence of such geopolitical considerations in the *Prison Notebooks* effectively inscribes them as a critical perspective within a tradition of political realism that regards the state as the key political actor of modernity.

Precedents for a focus on this dimension of hegemony can be found in the discussions of the international situation in the Third International in the mid-1920s, with which Gramsci was obviously familiar, though this was arguably of less significance for his thinking than were the debates about hegemonic politics as a strategy of class leadership, with which he had directly engaged during his residence in the early Soviet state in 1922–1923. Today, this interpretation is often encountered as an established "image of Gramsci" in discussions in International Relations, particularly in those theories characterized as "neo-Gramscian."[13] Above all, however, it has perhaps been Giovanni Arrighi's work that has represented the most prominent project linking Gramsci's thought to these themes, particularly with his claim to reformulate the notion of imperialism in terms of shifts in global hegemony over the last 70 years.[14]

Hegemony and *Herrschaft*

Each of these four interpretations effectively reduces Gramsci's notion of hegemony to an already known figure or concept in the history of modern political thought: respectively, the concepts of order, unity, integration, and sovereignty.

> *Order*: The first interpretation depicts hegemony as what can be characterized as a type of "inverted Hobbesianism." For Hobbes, mythical mutual covenants mark the transition from the state of nature to a properly civil society; yet once instituted, it is the sovereign's decision "from above" that commands obedience and ensures the maintenance of the political order in which all social

phenomena find their meaning. In the reading of hegemony as consent, on the other hand, political order is provided with an ethical foundation that is repeatedly renewed, or contested, "from below." In both cases, hegemony-consent is conceived as subordinate to and ultimately a function of the political order in which it is exercised.

Unity: The second interpretation of hegemony as a process of aggregation rediscovers Rousseau's concern with a unity of interests as a foundational feature of modern political societies. For Rousseau, it is the genuinely "general will," as opposed to a mere sum of individual wills, that provides the common denominator on which such unity can be constructed. The notion that hegemonic politics aims to produce a collective body inherits this approach. Hegemony is here thought in terms of an intersubjective mechanism for effecting the transition from Rousseau's "will of all" to the "general will," a unity that is simultaneously result and presupposition of political aggregation.[15]

Integration: The third interpretation of hegemony as a practice proper to a civil society opposed to the state presents it as a "stunted Hegelianism." Rather than civil society finally discovering that it relied all along on the always already present rationality of the state, this reading posits the apparent diversity and richness of existing civil society as autonomous and therefore as the potential foundation for an alternative mode of socialization. It is the role of hegemony within civil society to act as an integrating agent or "social cement" that binds together these atomistic elements, thereby making possible a future sociopolitical order that replaces the old one.

Sovereignty: The fourth interpretation of hegemony views it as a "modest" variant of the modern theory and reality of sovereign state power, projected onto the geopolitical stage. While sovereignty lays claim to be the ultimate moment of decision in any given political community, this notion of hegemony offers to measure the relative "weights" of distinct sovereign projects, without thereby annulling any of their individual, geographically delimited claims. Influence rather than supremacy, hegemony in this vision is seen as the most that a political actor can attain when sovereignty itself is out of reach, or a type of "sovereignty-lite."

It is the combination of these four interpretations that yields what is today the most widespread "synthetic" understanding of hegemony. This perspective understands the politics of hegemony to involve, first, the securing of consent of a significant proportion of political actors in a given social formation; second, the construction of their unity as a collective "political subject"; third, the engagement of this newly constituted political subject in a struggle against another such subject formed by a similar process, each seeking to enlarge their occupation of the "peripheral territory" of civil society until they possess sufficient forces to launch an assault on the "center" of the state apparatus; and, in a final moment, the clash of hegemonically constructed states in competition on the international terrain in a geopolitical repetition of the originary domestic process. The primary significance of hegemony, that is, is thought to be the way it provides a description of the organic emergence of modern state sovereignty and its geopolitical consequences.[16]

What enables these four very different interpretations to be synthesized into a total theory in this way, despite their very different theoretical antecedents, histories, and disciplinary locations, are three presuppositions that they share, with varying degrees of emphasis:

- First, each interpretation supposes that one of Gramsci's major projects in the *Prison Notebooks* can be characterized as the development of a more or less coherent "concept" of hegemony, that is, a relatively stable definition of what hegemony "really means."
- Second, these four readings are united in the (explicit or implicit) claim that this concept provides the foundation for a general theory of the functioning of modern political power, one that could, in principle, be valid for the analysis of a wide variety of specific political actions and actors, across the ideological spectrum and in diverse geographical locations.
- Third, these understandings of hegemony suppose that such a general theory is founded on a distinctive historical narrative of the emergence and development of the modern state, which

is viewed as the instantiation and elaboration of the concept's originary logic, in a virtuous circle of mutual confirmation.

Once posited, such a concept, general theory, and historical narrative can then be put to work for very different ends. On the one hand, they could be deployed in order to delineate the preconditions of the legitimation of already established power relations and structures; or, on the other hand, in an almost mirror-image inversion, they could be used in order to contest the existing state of affairs. In the first case, Gramsci is asked to step forward as a curious type of "Weber of the Proletariat" (to modify a famous Crocean phrase), explaining to the subaltern classes the historical roots of their subjugation as a seemingly unavoidable "destiny." In the second case, Gramsci appears as something akin to a forerunner of Foucault, that is, as a critical "genealogist" of the forms of political power in the modern state who seeks to make it possible to think the history of the present "differently."

In both cases, hegemony effectively comes to denote the means by which the stability, integration, and legitimation of a given political order is secured. In other words, hegemony is inscribed within a "typology of domination" of broadly Weberian dimensions.[17] When hegemony is characterized as a type of "political leadership based on the consent of the led," for instance, or when "political leadership" is itself understood in terms of sovereign authority, they are effectively represented as a type of "domination based upon the will of the ruled" (*Wille der Beherrschten*). It was precisely such a type of "democratic domination" that Weber had belatedly hypothesized as a fourth type of domination alongside his classic trio of charismatic, traditional, and legal-bureaucratic legitimate *Herrschaft*.[18]

Understood in this way, hegemony can then be regarded as an *Aufhebung* of the pre- and early-modern techniques of the political embodied in the notions of charisma (as self-anointing), tradition (as self-perpetuating), and bureaucracy (as self-regarding). It synthesizes the respective strengths of these modes and transforms their institutional externality into the interior life of the conscience of each individual will in its act of consent. Hegemony in this optic can thus finally appear as a qualitatively new political practice and even distinctively modern "logic" of the political. The discovery of this logic, it is thought

by some, is a precondition for meaningful emancipatory political engagement. For others, the elaboration of this logic leads to the consolidation and completion of the liberal democratic order as a system of
political integration of individuals and equilibrium of interests: a form
finally found in which to work out the "bourgeoisification" of the world.

Lineages of Hegemony

These four understandings of hegemony and their synthesis were in
their main lines elaborated on the basis of the thematic publication of
Gramsci's prison writings in Italian in the immediate postwar years
under the editorship of Felice Platone, assisted by Palmiro Togliatti. In
what has been accurately described as a veritable politico-theoretical
"operation," this edition's rearrangement of Gramsci's chronolog-
ically dispersed notes into coherent thematic topics—the particular emphases implicit in its organization and the explicit priorities
highlighted by its editorial apparatus—established the general terms
in which Gramsci was established as a major theorist of twentieth
century political thought.[19] Even after the publication of Gerratana's
critical edition in 1975, this interpretative tradition has continued
to influence profoundly the ways in which the *Prison Notebooks* are
usually read. Indeed, such has been the success of the earlier edition
and the translations that were made on the basis of it (including the
most widely diffused volume in English, *Selections from the Prison
Notebooks*) that many influential interpretations of Gramsci should
properly be called readings of the composite "author": "Gramsci–
Platone–Togliatti." This is particularly the case for what is today often
assumed to be Gramsci's "signature concept" of hegemony.

Hegemony is today so widely identified with Gramsci's name—
indeed, it is still sometimes even erroneously thought to be a concept
of his own coinage—that it is an experience similar to a Brechtian
Verfremdungseffekt (alienation effect) to conceive of readings of the
Prison Notebooks that do not accord it a prominent role. Yet the early
reception of Gramsci's carceral writing in the immediate postwar years
in Italy was not at all organized by what would later be characterized as
the "hegemony of hegemony." Much more significant for the discussion

of Gramsci's legacy in the Italian Communist Party in the late 1940s and early 1950s was instead his analysis of the role of intellectuals in the organization of (national-popular) culture, his reflections on Italian history, or the selective tradition of the classics of Italian political thought that ran from Machiavelli's "new Prince" to Gramsci's (and the PCI's) "modern Prince."[20]

It was not coincidental that 1956 witnessed the beginning of an increasing emphasis on hegemony as a distinctive conception of politics. For as the international Communist movement went into crisis in the wake of Khrushchev's denunciation of Stalin's legacy, the leadership of the Italian Communist Party—then the largest Communist Party in Western Europe—found itself constrained to elaborate a political strategy that could be credibly claimed to represent an independent policy to that dictated from the Soviet center. Hegemony was thus quickly valorized as both a "red thread" running through the complex and often elusive *Prison Notebooks* and as a distinctive theory of political action, one particularly suitable for addressing the tasks awaiting the party on the long "Italian Road to Socialism."[21] The journalist and professional revolutionary of the 1920s and 1930s thus became much better known posthumously, in the very different conjuncture of the 1950s, as the theorist of a distinctive concept of hegemony.

It was not long before the focus on hegemony as a concept led to readings that saw it as the foundation for a distinctive theory of modern politics in general. A notable feature of this early phase of reception in the 1960s and into the 1970s was the emphasis placed on hegemony as a way of rethinking the popular foundations of sovereignty. Central here was the attention given to Gramsci's use of the formula of "force and consent,"—a formula of generic Machiavellian lineage but in the *Prison Notebooks* one that was refracted through the specific debate in 1920s Italy between Fascist, liberal, and communist appropriations of the Florentine Secretary's heritage.[22] Indeed, although the couplet has no exact equivalent in the Russian debates on hegemony that had so stimulated Gramsci's explorations, the combination of force and consent was quickly understood to be a succinct definition of hegemony as such. In this way, hegemony could now be understood as a general theory of the nature and constraints of political action, relevant in different ways to a variety of particular cases. It was this reading that formed the basis for the initial international diffusion of hegemony in the first wave of translations and interpretations of Gramsci's writings outside Italy. It is remarkable the extent to which early non-Italian readings either were directly influenced by the main coordinates of the Italian debate, or spontaneously rediscovered them, enriching their insights with a wealth of empirical material drawn from reflections on other national traditions.[23]

The full development of hegemony as a general theory of political power, legitimacy, domination, and sovereignty, however, only occurred much later, in the 1970s. It was the emergence of a particular understanding of the role of the (until then, largely neglected) formula of "passive revolution" in the conceptual architecture of the *Prison Notebooks* that strengthened the tendency to think hegemony not simply as a general theory but more specifically as a theory founded on a sophisticated historical narrative of the emergence of the distinctive forms of power that characterize political modernity. The history of the reception of passive revolution in some ways represents a repetition of the reception of hegemony; in both cases, initial neglect gave way to valorization and sometimes even unilateral expansion and overextension. Thus, while passive revolution was largely ignored during the first 25 years of Gramsci's postwar fame, since the 1970s, the concept has assumed an increasing importance and visibility, arguably even surpassing that of hegemony itself in some quarters.

Passive revolution has since then become a central point of reference for philological studies that seek to navigate their way through the labyrinth of the *Prison Notebooks*—perhaps unexpectedly, given its previous neglect, but viewed retrospectively, unsurprisingly, given the fact that it represents Gramsci's genuinely novel addition to the Marxist vocabulary, much more than hegemony.[24] Even more significantly, it is also now one of the most influential of concepts derived from the various Marxist traditions in wider historical and contemporary scholarship. It has been productively employed, for instance, to analyze state formation and popular rebellion in such diverse cases as the contradictions of modernization in Wilhelmine Germany, the (post) colonial Indian State, revolutionary Mexico and its aftermaths, the "pink tide" in Latin America and its aftermath, the rise of Islamism in Turkey, post-Apartheid South Africa, the Egyptian Revolution, and the wider Arab Spring. Both neoliberalism since the 1980s and the contemporary rise of populist politics on a global scale, it has been argued, should also be understood as passive revolutions.[25]

The initial valorization of passive revolution, however, occurred in a very different conjuncture and focused in the first instance on the particular dilemmas confronted by the Italian Communist movement in the 1970s. It was a conjuncture defined, politically, by the PCI's search, after 9/11/1973, for a "historic compromise" and the emergence of "Eurocommunism"; while theoretically, Bobbio's provocative denial of the existence of a Marxist theory of the state prompted creative new readings of the Marxist tradition. Following Franco de Felice and Christine Buci-Glucksmann's pioneering readings of Gerratana's critical edition of the *Prison Notebooks*, passive revolution played a central role in the Istituto Gramsci conference of 1977, "Politics and History in Gramsci."[26] Here, and increasingly in the following years, the concept of passive revolution was used to theorize the conditions frustrating potential democratic "transitions" to a nebulously defined "post-capitalist" society. Gramsci's reflections from the early 1930s were thereby read through the lenses of the debates of the communist movement in the 1970s, not only in Western Europe but increasingly on an international scale.[27]

Even more significantly, the focus on passive revolution fundamentally transformed the terms in which hegemony was understood. Rather than an autonomous strategic perspective, hegemony was increasingly conceived in terms that subordinated it to the historiographical paradigm of passive revolution, in effect positing the particular dynamics of passive revolutionary processes as constitutive of hegemonic politics as such.[28] It led to a reading of hegemony, in Fabio Frosini's words, "in the light of the *primacy of stability over instability*."[29] In this way, Gramsci's thought could be re-inscribed in the main currents of modern political thought, with their overwhelming focus on the stabilization of political *order*—and not its *transformation*—as the fundamental problem of modern politics.[30]

Passive revolution thus became another description of the unfolding of political modernity as the construction of an increasingly rationalized and bureaucratic Weberian "iron cage"; hegemony in its turn became "a mere occasion for the transformation of the parties of the workers' movement into parties of government."[31] This reading not only provided a particular systematization of the debates over the meaning of hegemony from the 1950s through to the 1970s that had focused on its coherence as a concept, or its capacity to reformulate the claims of theories of modern sovereignty. It also constituted the theoretical foundations of many of the readings of Gramsci that came to prominence throughout the 1980s and early 1990s, on an international scale.

Among the most innovative of these "translations" of passive revolution in a Latin America preparing for transition from military dictatorships was that produced by Juan Carlos Portantiero. In the anglophone world, Stuart Hall's approach had a profound impact on the formation of cultural studies, and it later played a politically significant role in its impact on the tendency of Communist Party members and fellow travelers affiliated with *Marxism Today* in the United Kingdom who paved the way for the formulation of the British Labour Party's purported "Third Way" under Blair. Ranajit Guha's approach, on the other hand, was foundational for the Subaltern Studies collective and the wide variety of initiatives in South Asian history and postcolonial theory more broadly that have followed in its wake.[32] Just as the international reception of Gramsci's thought from the early 1960s onward sometimes consciously but more often unwittingly reproposed the terms pioneered earlier in the Italian discussion of hegemony, so too from the late 1970s onward paradigms of hegemony understood in terms of passive revolution that had first been explored in Italy were internationalized, producing very different consequences in diverse linguistic and national zones.

Passive Revolution and Socialist Strategy

Arguably, however, the most theoretically ambitious conceptualization of hegemony that emerged from this season was proposed by Ernesto Laclau and Chantal Mouffe in their influential *Hegemony and Socialist Strategy: Towards a Radical Democratic Politics*, published in 1985. For Laclau and Mouffe sought not only to use a received notion of hegemony for their own ends but to reformulate it directly in relation to the central concepts of modern political thought, and with explicit reference to its relevance for comprehending what some regarded as the "new social movements" of those years. The success of their initiative can be observed in the fact that for significant currents in contemporary radical thought, the concept of hegemony itself is now primarily associated with the names of Laclau and Mouffe, while Gramsci has assumed the role of their distant ancestor.

In many respects, however, their approach can be regarded as an ingenious synthesis of earlier understandings of hegemony, from the focus on the national-popular in the late 1950s and 1960s to the presentation of hegemony as a generic theory of power in the debate on passive revolution in the 1970s. The significance of *Hegemony and Socialist Strategy* is thus not merely "conjunctural," in the sense of responding to the immediate events and debates of the period in which it was elaborated. Rather, as its subsequent influence testifies, it has an enduring theoretical importance as a distinctive reformulation and combination of significant traditions of reflection on the role of hegemony in Gramsci's thought.

Laclau and Mouffe argued that the "concept" (if not yet the "word") of hegemony in Marxism had its origins in a crisis of the notion of "historical necessity" in Second International Marxism, particularly as it migrated from German social democracy to the Russian revolutionary movement in the late-nineteenth and early-twentieth centuries.[33] It emerged as the classical tradition's "faith" in the revolutionary subject of the working class was shaken by the concrete political events in which the proletariat had not proved up to the level of its ascribed historical tasks. What Laclau and Mouffe retrospectively identified as the first stirrings of hegemonic politics was thought to be fundamentally the search for a new potential revolutionary "subject," conceived not as any single class but as a "composite body" of disparate interests and groups.

The notion that hegemony consisted in an alliance of social forces grouped around a "fundamental class" (conceived economistically, as an assigned position in the relations of production) nevertheless continued in the Bolshevik's explicit use of the notion of hegemony in the struggle against Tsarist autocracy, and even in Gramsci's later appropriation of it to theorize the tasks of revolution in the West.[34] But these instances were argued to compromise the "hard core" of hegemony as a new type of political logic of contingent articulations and a theory of the political constitution of the social and the economic. Laclau and Mouffe's own theorization of the radical democratic potentials of the "new social movements" in the 1980s aimed to liberate this fundamental logic from the economistic deformations that they claimed had presided over its birth and growing pains.

Hegemonic struggle for Laclau and Mouffe thus ultimately came to signify not merely one mode of politics but the very possibility of the institution of "society," defined as a terrain traversed by claims that competed to represent the terrain's impossible closure. Insofar as the very notion of society is what distinguishes political modernity from its (real or imagined) precursors, Laclau and Mouffe's argument in this book presupposes that hegemony is valid only for those social formations structured by forms of popular sovereignty.[35] In other words, hegemony is understood as a type of shorthand to indicate the nature of modern political power and its institutionalization in the distinctively modern state. Popular sovereignty is thereby understood to be hegemonic in nature; while at the same time, in a relation of mutual confirmation, hegemony is defined as central to political modernity as such. Laclau and Mouffe's work thus emphasizes, to use a precise formulation, "the hegemonic constitution of modern sovereignty."[36]

Debates at the time of publication of *Hegemony and Socialist Strategy*—which had infelicitously coincided with an atmosphere of generalized sectarian recriminations amongst erstwhile comrades in arms from the final phases of the New Left—tended to focus on Laclau and Mouffe's provocative "delinking" of hegemony from any necessary reference to class, and more generally, their marginal suggestion that their work might be regarded as in some sense "post-Marxist." Their famed "chains of equivalence" of demands, for instance, was argued to present hegemony as a type of free-floating "stream of sociopolitical consciousness" oblivious to the hierarchies of primary and secondary instances that were presumed—by both Laclau and Mouffe and their critics alike—to have deformed the concept of hegemony before their salutary and corrective intervention.[37]

This "post-Marxist" dimension of their work, however, did not represent the real innovation of their theorization of hegemony, viewed in the historical perspective of the different meanings ascribed to the word throughout its contested history. Rather, their novel contribution instead consisted in the formalization of insights from earlier debates, consistently developing some of their politicist presuppositions into a sophisticated and coherent formalist theory. The articulation of this theory consisted in a series of three, sequential concepts: those of the formation of political unity, the embodiment of this unity in a political subject, and the consequent drive toward an always relative universalization.

In a first move, *Hegemony and Socialist Strategy* argued that hegemony operates by means of the building of equivalential chains between initially discrete demands. A diversity of interests, identities, and subject positions is offset by a tendency toward unification in hegemonic "composite bodies." As a "type of political relation," or a "dimension" or "form" of politics, hegemony appears as the mechanism by means of which such unexpected unity is produced politically, however provisionally, out of the logic of difference that they argue dominates the social.[38]

Second, for Laclau and Mouffe, hegemony fundamentally describes the process of unification as the "articulation" along this equivalential chain of the diversity of social struggles and demands into a political subject. If the constitution of this subject is always contingent and never predetermined by any foundational moment, once constituted, this political subject acts as the determining ground on which political action takes place. In their early collaborative work and in Mouffe's more recent sole-authored writings, the constitution of a unitary political subject was described in terms of the formation of a "collective will" (again, appropriating another concept from Gramsci).[39] In Laclau's later work, the goal of such unification most frequently appeared as a unitary "people," the formation of which was argued to constitute the "main task" of radical politics.[40]

Third, once stabilized in such a political subject, the very notion of hegemony as a distinctively modern form of politics implies the progressive expansion of this political subject in a synecdochal logic, of a part attempting to represent the whole. A particularity, that is, strives to stand in for the universal, or rather, to assume the absent place of a "universality" that is comprehended in starkly formalistic (and arguably, ultimately normative) terms.[41] The fact that this aspiration to universality can never be successfully concluded, however—because any particularity by definition never ceases to carry the birthmark reminding it of its lowly origins—means that the process of universalization conceived in these terms will always remain a universalization relative to other, similarly constructed and oriented projects. Such "particular universalities" will thus always need to be on their guard against potential challenges from similarly constituted rivals, as they also attempt to make claims to represent exhaustively a completed totality that remains constitutively impossible.

From unity, to subject, to total hegemonic struggle over the universal: Laclau and Mouffe's great achievement was to have provided an articulated and consequential formalization of previously vaguely suggested rather than coherently argued understandings of hegemony as predominance, informal sovereignty, ideological influence, or generalized power. Their formalized notion has subsequently become the foundation for the operationalization of hegemony in a wide variety of research projects over the last 30 years, both theoretical and—rarely for political philosophy today—empirical.[42]

Despite what has sometimes been assumed or asserted, Laclau and Mouffe consciously did not seek to present their own theorization as a faithful inheritance of Gramsci's thought. On the contrary, one of the central arguments of *Hegemony and Socialist Strategy* was that hegemony in the *Prison Notebooks*, despite Gramsci's innovations with respect to the prior use of the term in the debates of the Bolsheviks, nevertheless remained tainted by its affiliation with a residual "economism" and the specter of class "reductionism."[43] Their claim was instead that their own theory constituted a coherent development of an "implicit logic" in the history of the "concept" of hegemony, a history that certainly passed through Gramsci's *Prison Notebooks*, but which Laclau and Mouffe proposed to take far beyond them. The success of this initiative can be measured by the fact that their version of hegemony has effectively entered into the vocabulary of contemporary radical thought as the most influential understanding of hegemony, presumed to exhaust—in all senses of the word—the political potential of hegemonic politics in its entirety.

Both historical distance and subsequent scholarship allow us to a take up a more critical perspective on this claim today, one which recognizes the overdetermining influence of the context in which Laclau and Mouffe developed their understanding of hegemony and the limitations of the presuppositions on which it was based. From a distance of over 40 years, we can now see that *Hegemony and Socialist Strategy* was clearly marked by the debates of the Marxist left throughout the 1970s and early 1980s to a much greater extent than it was by engagement with the text of Gramsci's work itself. It is notable, for instance, that Laclau and Mouffe's textual references to the *Prison Notebooks* are surprisingly rare and do not in fact include notes that directly discuss the definition of hegemony (or passive revolution, which they do not mention even indirectly). They instead engage much more extensively with the secondary literature and debates over Gramsci's legacy that were then underway.[44]

Even in their more textually grounded, individually authored works on Gramsci from the late 1970s, this predominance of the theoretico-political conjuncture over a closer reading of the *Prison Notebooks* is still discernable.[45] Indeed, it is in these earlier texts that the influence of the contemporaneous debates that took passive revolutionary processes to be paradigmatic of hegemony in general on Laclau and Mouffe's general conceptualization of hegemony is explicitly highlighted, even more so than in *Hegemony and Socialist Strategy* itself.

At the legendary seminar of Latin American Gramsci scholars and activists held in Morelia in 1980, for instance, Laclau presented a paper entitled "Theses on the Hegemonic Form of Politics." He argued that "the historical form of articulation of the set of positionalities of a society is precisely what constitutes its hegemonic principle. And this hegemonic principle presupposes power and domination. Hegemony is not, therefore, a relationship of alliance between preconstituted social agents, but the very principle of constitution of those social agents."[46]

The historical examples of such a "hegemonic principle" that Laclau immediately provides, however, are revealing of the extent to which his argument relies on an implicit equation of "hegemony" and "passive revolution." For these examples—Disraeli in England, Bismarck in

Germany—were embodiments of the types of dynamics that Gramsci came to see as characteristic of the passive revolutionary processes instigated by the western European bourgeoises in the long nineteenth century and not those of hegemony in a more expansive and strategic sense. "Disraeli's social policy in England," Laclau argues, "was hegemonic insofar as he managed to disarticulate certain social demands of the masses from the radical popular discourse in which they had until then been made and to re-articulate them in an alternative conservative discourse."[47]

It is this process of "disarticulation and re-articulation of positionalities" that Laclau sees as central to what he calls the "hegemonic form of politics," even in its variation between rightist and leftist variants (or between "transformism" and "popular rupture").[48] Both disarticulation and rearticulation are conceived in terms of a paradigm of representation, that is, in terms of the capacity of particular political actors to present themselves as the legitimate bearers in the political field of a diversity of interests that must by definition remain "merely social," even after their "hegemonization." In effect, the specific political features that Gramsci studied in terms of passive revolutionary processes—the exclusion of popular initiatives from the political field, the subalternization of "civil society" to "political society," the "formal perfection" of a certain conception of Jacobinism in the "representative" parliamentary regimes of the nineteenth century—are here formalized and presented as a "logic" of hegemony in general.

The interpretative tradition that had seen the primary significance of Gramsci's use of hegemony in its delineation of a general theory of the structure of power in political modernity here finds one of its most coherent conclusions: a theory of politics as an endless struggle to impose order on the chaos of the social not by a "God, Caesar, or tribune," but by the contingently constructed and ephemeral political subjects that have assumed those empty places in political modernity.[49]

The "Hypothesis" of Hegemony

Understandings of hegemony in terms of passive revolutionary dynamics have resulted in compelling stories of the consolidation of bourgeois political modernity—stories that have proved to be particularly compelling and even consolatory for generational structures of feeling shaped by the traumas of leftist defeat and retreat in the late twentieth century, whether they be the involution of the New Left in the "North" or disillusionment in the promises of decolonization in the "South." Large-scale historical narratives and sophisticated theories such as those proposed in different ways by Laclau and Mouffe, Hall, Guha, and Chatterjee, among many others, can certainly be elaborated by valorizing particular passages and famous notes in the *Prison Notebooks* as the basis for creative readings and extensions of Gramsci's thought. And "hegemony" understood in this sense undoubtedly continues to provide significant currents of contemporary leftist politics with a powerful analytical theory of the mechanics of the securing of political order.

Conceptual elaboration, theoretical systematization, or historical narration, however, are not the only ways in which Gramsci's uses of hegemony can be understood; arguably, they are also not the most significant ways, either historically or in terms of the contemporary use that can be made of them. Indeed, viewed from the perspective of our own different "historical present," the primary significance of hegemony may not be that it outlines a distinctive concept, theory, or history of the contradictions of political modernity. Rather, it could instead be that it provides a strategic perspective from which to elaborate practices of self-emancipatory politics that correspond to the diversity of interests and perspectives in the intersectional sociopolitical movements of today.

This is not primarily a question of proposing yet another definition of hegemony, in a divination of a conceptual core that Gramsci supposedly "intended" but unfortunately did not consistently express. It is instead to focus on what Gramsci was "doing" with hegemony at different times in the *Prison Notebooks*, in the Wittgensteinian sense emphasized by one dimension of Quentin Skinner's conception of methodology in the history of political thought.[50] For Gramsci was neither a philosopher, political theorist, nor historian in any conventional sense, however interesting some of his reflections may be for those contemporary disciplinary identifications. He was instead a political organizer and strategist, and his many other concerns were consistently shaped by these overriding political concerns. To understand the varied uses of hegemony in the *Prison Notebooks* as such a strategic perspective is therefore to grasp it less as a concept and more as a "hypothesis" in an evolving "thought experiment"; not as a systematic theory but as a "failure" of this thought experiment; and rather than as a historical narrative, as a "visual angle" from which to intervene into the past, present, and future of the politics of subaltern self-emancipation.

In the first instance, one of the often unstated interpretive claims that characterized the debate on hegemony since the 1950s was that the many varied analytic and descriptive uses of hegemony throughout Gramsci's work are ultimately derived from—or should be related to— a unitary and univocal concept. This presupposition was intensified and driven to at least one of its potential conclusions in the debate on passive revolution in the 1970s and its afterlives. The claim has become harder to sustain as the relative "novelty" of hegemony has faded, and hopes that it might represent a singular panacea to the blockages of revolutionary politics has given way to more nuanced historical contextualization of its many contested forms. Already in the debates of the 1970s, Valentino Gerratana had emphasized that Gramsci's *Prison Notebooks* do not propose a single understanding of hegemony but instead study the very different forms of hegemonic politics in different historical periods, and the diverse nature of hegemony in relation to the different conditions of opposed class projects. More recent works have also emphasized the multiplicity of hegemonies, as a field of conflicting interpretations, in both Gramsci's writings and more generally in the broader Marxist tradition.[51]

Such readings attentive to the rhythm of the development of Gramsci's usage of hegemony throughout the *Prison Notebooks* suggest that rather than understanding it as a more or less unitary concept, however (in)coherent or (in)complete, it might be more useful to regard it as a provisional hypothesis in Gramsci's evolving carceral thought experiment. A hypothesis here indicates not a stage of uncertainty prior to the affirmation of the solidity of the concept but an active intervention that attempts to reorder the possibilities of knowledge in a given situation by imagining it differently. The given situation is thought, that is, in terms of the potential for transformation that resides even in its most seemingly self-assured constitution.

In the *Prison Notebooks*, Gramsci deploys this hypothesis in a novel type of thought experiment, one that is distinct from other approaches in the history of modern political thought. The thought experiments of the social contract tradition, for instance, either imagine a mythical past as foundation for the present (as in the state of nature for Hobbes or Rousseau), or posit a purely "hypothetical" model that aims to legitimate a particular political conception (as in Rawls's "original position"). Gramsci's thought experiment, on the other hand, openly takes (to use Rawls's words) a particular "actual historical state of affairs"—that is, the experiences in the Russian revolutionary experience summarized in the formula of hegemony—as the basis for imagining the history of political modernity in general in radically new ways. Gramsci experiments with the range of meanings and historical resonances of this term in order to determine the extent of its translatability. The goal of this experimentation consists not in the definition of the "real meaning" of hegemony but in novel insights that could be produced by means of the term's deployment as an analytical and strategic perspective in entirely different contexts.[52]

Strikingly, for a figure frequently characterized as the paradigmatic "western" Marxist, Gramsci's thought experiment assessed political modernity in occidental Europe in terms of its "lack" of the political principle and practice of hegemony that had been most coherently developed in the so-called East. The significance of the intensity of Gramsci's engagement with the practical and theoretical uses of hegemony in the nascent Soviet state during his sojourn in Moscow in 1922–1923 cannot be overstated. Hegemony as he encountered it there was not a single fixed concept. It was neither a metaphor for command or sovereignty, nor simply a politics of alliances, nor merely the "concessions" of the New Economic Policy, nor even the widespread forms of cultural revolution encouraged by socialist construction. It signified instead an entire ensemble of economic, political, and cultural practices of mobilization and activation of the popular masses in a "revolutionizing of the revolution." Hegemony was, in other words, a contested condensation of the meanings and values at the center of debates over the history, present, and future of the revolutionary movement.

This multiplicity of references provided Gramsci with a concrete historical example, and the basis for his similarly pluralistic thought experiment. In the first instance, this experiment involved the translation of hegemony from the multiple ways in which it had been elaborated in the struggle of Russian Social Democracy against a crumbling absolutist state (and even more importantly in Gramsci's case, its creative "retooling" in the early years of socialist construction) into the very different context of the Western European bourgeois state, characterized by the theoretical if not practical dominance of the notion of popular sovereignty since the French Revolution. In Gramsci's precarceral activism, this thought experiment consisted in the attempt to think through the ways in which "Eastern" forms of political organization and struggle might be successfully "translated"—or "stretched," in Fanon's sense—in order to confront the very different tasks of a revolutionary movement in the "West" challenged by the rise of Fascism.[53]

In the *Prison Notebooks*, this thought experiment may appear to shift from immediately practical concerns to theoretical and historical reflections, particularly when individual passages are read in isolation from Gramsci's overall project. This evolution, however, always remains subordinated to the political objectives that motivated Gramsci's though experiment in the first place. Thus, for instance, in a significant line of research in the *Prison Notebooks*, hegemony becomes a key term in a distinctive history of the formation of the modern state, in nineteenth-century Italy, Western Europe more generally (particularly France), and eventually the modern capitalist state internationally, in its variety and unity. Many later readers have been inspired by the novelty of this narrative and have attempted to extend its general approach to revisit the history of societies partially or wholly absent from Gramsci's own narrative. Similarly, the seemingly conflicting "definitions" of hegemony that are scattered through various notes in the *Prison Notebooks* (hegemony as a combination of "force and consent," as distinct from "dominance," as equivalent to "democracy"), or apparently incompatible reflections on hegemony's "location" (in civil society or political society, or in their interstices), have led readers to suppose that one of the other of these formulations, or their combination, might be taken to signify "what Gramsci really meant" by hegemony. Once discovered, such a true meaning could then be redeployed for the analysis of wholly different situations, if not of politics in general itself.

In each of these cases, however, Gramsci was not applying a fixed definition of hegemony but experimenting with the range of meanings condensed in the word as hypotheses in order to clarify the political stakes of the specific arguments or controversies with which he was engaging at any particular moment. To understand the use of hegemony in the *Prison Notebooks* as such a thought experiment enables a shift in perspective in terms of the ways in which Gramsci's thought has often been inherited in contemporary debates. The proposal to reconstruct the history of modern state formation in Western Europe by hypothesizing the "presence" of hegemony in a context in which, historically, it was "absent" as a "political language" can be understood as preliminary considerations subordinate to Gramsci's real focus: namely, the challenges confronting contemporary autonomous subaltern political organization. It is precisely these themes that conclude the famous note on the Risorgimento from Gramsci's first notebook, which undoubtedly became the most influential note for hegemony's later reception.[54] In the same way, notes that have been read as genial but frustratingly incomplete elaborations of a metatheory of political modernity's "organic composition of power" (to use Guha's stimulating formulation) can instead be understood as concrete interventions into particular political and theoretical debates. It is not hegemony that is defined as a political institution in these notes. It is instead the memory of hegemony's wide-ranging function in the revolutionary experience that is posited as a hypothesis in order to deconstruct the self-referential definitions of so many institutions of bourgeois political modernity.[55]

In a precise sense, "politics" here provided a lens with which to read "history" and only thereby to construct "theory." The *Prison Notebooks* do not aim at a type of Rankean "recovery" of the past but to understand how that past continues unceasingly to flow into the now; and rather than aspiring to a normative standard of hegemony, Gramsci instead sought to develop it as a "mobile strategic perspective"—a perspective from which to experiment in imagining different futures.

The Failure of Hegemony

Recognition of Gramsci's usage of hegemony in the *Prison Notebooks* as a hypothesis in a strategic thought experiment enables us to resituate the discussion of the relation between hegemony and passive revolution in terms not of their commensurability within a general theory of modern political power, but instead in terms of their radical historical discontinuity. Rather than a consistent elaboration or formalist consummation of hegemony, as the late 1970s debate and its contemporary iterations assume, passive revolution in the development of the *Prison Notebooks* instead comes to represent something akin to a "failure of hegemony." This failure, however, is not simply a mimetic one, as if passive revolution were only a derivative imitation of hegemony devoid of its vital force, or in the terms that Guha used to describe the colonial state, a "spurious hegemony."[56] The failure of hegemony represented by passive revolution is instead hegemony's immanent deformation, in a dual sense: a deformation that is both substantive and conceptual.

Substantively, the development of Gramsci's historical analyses of what he had initially thought of as "bourgeois hegemony" throughout the long nineteenth century leads him to place an increasing emphasis on its passive revolutionary tendencies. Passive revolution is the name that Gramsci comes to give to the bourgeois project as he emphasizes the constitutively un-universalizable nature of its founding principles (above all, the sanctity of private property) and its practical denial of the emancipatory ideals that it rhetorically proclaimed. Key moments in Gramsci's realization of these dimensions include his early rereading of the bourgeois class limits encountered in the French revolutionary process (particularly in 1793, with the bourgeoisie's betrayal of the mobilized popular classes), his reflections of the renewal of these limits in 1848 (with the bourgeoisie's turn to an uneasy alliance with the aristocracy and the old order against a nascent militant workers' movement), and his studies of the epoch opened by the savage repression of the Paris Commune.

In all cases, these limits were not simply internal to the bourgeois hegemonic project but actively provoked and produced by its direct antithesis, namely, the autonomous militancy of rebellious subaltern social classes. When the hegemonic project of the subaltern classes is blocked, deformed, or repressed, passive revolution is what the ruling classes implement in order to maintain and extend their dominance. For this line of research, passive revolution comes to represent the negation of hegemony's emphasis on popular empowerment, expansive democratization, and historical progress.

Passive revolution in this sense arises when hegemony fails; it is the result of the failure of the bourgeois class project to be genuinely hegemonic, and to instead promote hegemony's distorted counterfeit image. The primal scene of this involution was represented for Gramsci by the "formal perfection" of Jacobinism (of an "inverted" type) in the consolidation of the parliamentary regime throughout the nineteenth century.[57] Gramsci depicts this formal perfection as in one sense a perversion of the most vibrant dimensions of early Jacobinism, whose impulses were instead inherited by the radical wing of the nineteenth-century proletarian movement (a type of "Metajacobinism," in Tosel's efficacious formulation).[58] Yet in another sense it was also a formalist repetition of the originary contradictions of Jacobin politics and its inherent class limits, which marked it out even in its most radical phases as yet another party of order. Were these failures of hegemony "merely" a betrayal of the original promises of hegemonic politics, when hegemony had ceased to be properly hegemonic? On the contrary, passive revolution is the name that Gramsci developed to indicate that this failed bourgeois hegemony had never really been hegemonic in an integral sense at all.[59]

Passive revolution also represents the failure of hegemony in another sense, however. It is also a *conceptual* failure, the product of the incapacity of hegemony to do the work of the concept that Gramsci's thought experiment had asked it to do. The relatively belated elaboration of the notion of passive revolution is the product of Gramsci's dawning realization that his initial thought experiment of translating hegemony from popular politics in the East to elite politics in the West was compromised by their fundamental incompatibility. In the distinctive formulation provided by the Bolshevik debates and usages that gave Gramsci's thought experiment its initial impetus, and which remained for him paradigmatic, hegemonic politics requires a dynamic sense of historical progress as its necessary complement and ultimate conclusion. Hegemony in that revolutionary context, that is, signified a political intervention that aimed to encourage the popular classes to travel toward an unknown but promising future, rather than slumping back into the certainties and disappointments of the past.

As Gramsci came to understand, however, the sequence that he had attempted to characterize in the early phases of the *Prison Notebooks* (particularly in early 1930) as a historical instantiation of bourgeois hegemony (the experience of the Italian Risorgimento, read through the lens of the Jacobin tradition), denied precisely that possibility.[60] In other words, the application of hegemony to bourgeois politics does not work; it is unable to comprehend the historical experiences of the development of the bourgeois class project because that project, in its dual reliance on relations of exploitation and subalternization, structurally denies the presuppositions and goals of hegemonic politics.

It is from Gramsci's realization of this conceptual blockage and its significance that the formulation of passive revolution emerged, as an alternative characterization of the nature of bourgeois political modernity. Tentatively formulated in November 1930, Gramsci at first projects passive revolution backward, inscribing it in the margins of his earlier notes on bourgeois hegemonic practice in a way that fundamentally transformed their meaning (and set the terms for their later reception). He then develops it in a series of notes on different topics written between early 1932 and mid-1933. While remaining a significant theme of reflection until the end of Gramsci's carceral writings, passive revolution nevertheless undergoes a process of "molecular dissolution" in the final phases of the *Prison Notebooks*. Under the aegis of Machiavelli, Gramsci's attention returns more strongly to "vigorous antithesis" of popular militancy contesting passive revolutionary processes, and to the nature of subaltern self-emancipatory politics.[61]

As a concept, passive revolution is the result of the "failed translation" of hegemony from the East to the West; in Fanon's terms, passive revolution emerged from stretching hegemony so far that it "snapped." Rather than a form of hegemony, or a variation of its fundamental logic, it is instead better understood as a "simulacrum" of hegemony, in a classical sense: a deceptive appearance that conceals a qualitative difference between the two political practices and projects. Hegemonic politics involves the overcoming of relations of subalternity and the emergence of practices of self-emancipation and self-direction. Passive revolution, on the other hand, involves the consolidation of subalternization and its extension as a principle of social organization. In other words, it deepens the very experience that hegemonic politics aims to end.

To posit passive revolution as the paradigmatic model of hegemony in general, or to conflate hegemony and passive revolution in a way that valorizes the latter's fundamental features and elevates them to the level of a general theory of modern politics, is thus not merely a conceptual confusion. It is also complicit with the simulacrum of passive revolution itself, whose deceptive shifting shapes appear to satisfy the cravings that give rise to hegemonic politics while leaving them famished in reality. It is precisely this that occurred in the 1970s debates focused on passive revolution, and which has been continued in various ways by its latter-day inheritors.

The failure of hegemony, however, need not mean its demise. As in the case of Gramsci's precarceral use of hegemony as an organizational practice or his later mediations on hegemony as a strategic perspective, it can also mean its liberation from an ultimately historiosophical narrative and its restoration to the arsenal of a concrete political theory that aims to intervene in the present.

Hegemony's "Visual Angle"

Just as hegemony in the *Prison Notebooks* is neither a precise concept nor a totalizing theory, so is its historical status very different from what has often been supposed by the interpretative traditions based on their thematic publication. Rather than a secularizing narrative of the emergence of bourgeois political modernity or even the discovery of its distinctive "logic," hegemony for Gramsci instead functions as a "visual angle," to use one of Labriola's most fascinating formulations, with which to focus on the self-emancipatory politics of the subaltern classes and social groups.[62]

In its main lines, Laclau and Mouffe's narrative of the emergence of hegemony from the late-nineteenth-century crisis of Marxism continued a general perspective in the (post) New Left of the 1970s and early 1980s regarding both the historical status of Marxism in general (thought to be defined by an originary, "orthodox" hard core of economic determinism in need of purification) and Gramsci's understanding of hegemony in particular (sometimes still today thought to represent his own heretical innovation or even nascent departure from such vulgar origins). Laclau and Mouffe's fused these presuppositions into the argument that the emergence of hegemony in the late Second International, as a "crisis concept," could be regarded as a first "crack" in the fortress of Marxism's economic determinism, and thus as a type of "antechamber" to an exit into what their critics, much more than Laclau and Mouffe themselves, later defined as "post-Marxism."[63]

Impressive in its historical range and persuasive in its teleological coherence, Laclau and Mouffe's almost Nietzschean tale of the birth of hegemony out of the spirit of economism nevertheless neglected rival accounts of this history—including above all one particularly significant narrative offered by Gramsci himself. In that famous long note from his first notebook that begins from the experience of the Italian Risorgimento, Gramsci had offered a very different genealogy of hegemony, one which has profound implications for understanding the nature of hegemony as a method of political work.[64] Rather than a response to a "crisis of Marxism" in the late nineteenth century, as Laclau and Mouffe suggested, Gramsci instead located the origins of hegemonic politics much further back in the mid-nineteenth century, at the moment of the primal crisis of (German) radical democracy.

For Gramsci, the original formulation of hegemony within Marxism was to be found in "the 'Jacobin' slogan" of the "Revolution in Permanence" essayed by Marx and Engels in the wake of 1848, most famously in their 1850 March "Address of the Central Committee to the Communist League."[65] Rather than originating in a politics of alliances, Gramsci saw the beginnings of hegemony in the Marxist tradition in this moment of the assertion of an autonomous politics of the proletarian political movement; "autonomous," that is, from those bourgeois and petit bourgeois elements that had betrayed the most radical demands of what had seemed to Marx and Engels in the

Vormärz to be a revolutionary cross-class alliance assembled under the banner of "The Democracy." It was in effect a self-critique of the position famously embodied in the *Communist Manifesto*'s ambiguous programmatic conclusions.

In the conclusion to the note that contains the first significance usages of hegemony in the *Prison Notebooks*, Gramsci argued that the central perspective of Marx and Engels's contested slogan was later "employed it in its historical, concrete, living form adapted to the time and place" by the Bolsheviks, in their translation of the revolution in permanence into a new political vocabulary: "as something that sprang from all the pores of the society which had to be transformed, as the alliance of two classes with the hegemony of the urban class."[66] It was this visual angle that allowed Gramsci to understand the origins of hegemony in the Marxist tradition not as a response to the dilution of a supposedly prior "purity" of a revolutionary subject, or as a later supplement to a hard core of a Marxist politics already constituted around an economic fundamental class, but instead as a primacy of self-emancipatory politics. Far from indicating a crisis of the presuppositions of the materialist conception of history, hegemony figures in Gramsci's reading as the necessary conclusion to be drawn from the political presuppositions of the Marxist tradition, which he proposed to inherit in the form of a "philosophy of praxis."

This perspective continues the understanding of hegemony operative in Gramsci's precarceral activism, as a strategic orientation toward the organizational independence of the working class movement. He understood hegemony in this period not primarily as a concept or theory but as a method of anti-Fascist struggle. This was the case both in an immediate sense—as the mobilization of broad layers of the popular classes against the still insecure new regime—and also, even more fundamentally, as a long-term perspective for the foundation of a "new order."

The Italian proletariat could only become genuinely hegemonic or a leading force among the popular classes, Gramsci argued, if it elaborated a program that could concretely address and resolve the problems of uneven- and underdevelopment that had been exploited by the Fascists in their rise to power. This focus on the central role of the proletariat in the struggle against Fascism in texts such as the

Lyon Theses or *On Some Aspects of the Southern Question* was not due to it being a "fundamental class" in a narrowly economistic sense. Rather, it was because it alone, among all the pulverized subaltern classes and social groups in Italy, had a history of militancy and still possessed, however precariously, organizational resources that could represent a credible political alternative to the Fascist infection of Italian society.

It is the strategic orientation that provides the impetus for all of Gramsci's carceral writings, even if its centrality has often been overlooked in favor of a focus on hegemony as a normative concept, totalizing theory of political modernity, or compelling historical narrative. Yet the emphasis on the link between a "metajacobin" revolution in permanence and hegemony is one of the most consistent leitmotifs of the *Prison Notebook* and remains the implicit architecture and immanent measure of Gramsci's entire carceral project.[67] His varied returns to the range of meanings condensed in the term hegemony, in notes written in changing contexts over a period of more than 5 years, were all different ways of revisiting the fundamental hypothesis of his thought experiment: the historical experience of hegemony as the basis for imagining a politics that would be autonomous from the fundamental logic of the modern state and its processes of subalternization. It is an emphasis that reaches its high point in the formulation of the mythical figure of the modern Prince as a "categorical imperative," assessing each and every political action on the basis of its capacity to increase the self-emancipatory powers of the subaltern classes.[68]

Previous seasons of interpretation have often read this strategic understanding of hegemony through the lens of the dimension of Gramsci's thought experiment that culminates in the notion of passive revolution as a characterization of the non-hegemonic nature of bourgeois hegemony. They were readings often elaborated at the end of a cycle of struggles, utilizing Gramsci in order to identify a viable explanation for that cycle's exhaustion. A reading of the *Prison Notebooks* today, on the other hand, undertaken in a period of reviving struggles and with an openness to future innovations, gives us the opportunity to undertake our own "thought experiment": namely, to think how the distinctive visual angle of hegemony conceived as a strategic approach can help to clarify challenges of subaltern self-emancipation in contemporary movements. The result of such an experiment might be a rediscovery of the original critical force of hegemonic politics as a concrete critique of the contradictions of the existing political order, and as a distinctive method of political work.

Hegemony as a method of political work

Recovery of the real complex historical development of hegemonic politics as a strategic perspective in the Marxist tradition and in the *Prison Notebooks* provides the basis for an alternative thematization of hegemony as a strategic "method of political work," or as simultaneously the goal, nature, method, and form of self-emancipatory politics. Instead of beginning from the assumption of dispersion as a condition to be overcome for effective political action, this strategically focused understanding of hegemony valorizes dynamic and enduring differentiation as an enabling feature of self-emancipatory politics. Rather than concluding in a theory of political unity, a hegemonic method of politics actively seeks to mobilize differences as resources for a struggle on multiple fronts, in ongoing relations of reciprocal translations. And in place of a focus on (partial, contingent, or strategic) universalization, hegemony understood in this sense openly champions particularity and partisanship as the expression of dynamic tendencies in historical development.

In short, this understanding of hegemony is not an inheritor of the Hobbesian–Rousseauvian paradigm of unity that has dominated political modernity, and it cannot be reduced to a mechanism or logic of sovereignty or state formation. It is instead a strategic method for the production of a politics of a completely different type: a politics of self-emancipation.

This strategic method can be thematized in terms of the four central perspectives of the previously delineated "aitiology of emancipatory politics": the goal of constructing a new order, the nature of self-emancipatory politics as the production of historical progress, the method of leadership conceived as fragility and experimentation, and the organizational form of a pedagogical laboratory.

New order

From the time of his apprenticeship in revolutionary politics in the workers' movement in Turin during and after WWI, Gramsci was committed to a vision of the goal of emancipatory politics as the construction of *la città futura* (future city), or *L'Ordine nuovo* (new order)—the titles of some his most memorable early publishing initiatives. This appetite for the new was only further stimulated by his sojourn in Moscow in 1922–1923, in a visceral form clearly recounted in his later correspondence reflecting on his time in what was then the capital of world revolution.[69] The Sorelian "spirit of scission" with the old world that marked Gramsci's early activism remained a dominating motif even in his carceral writings, products of a defeat that were nevertheless unable to destroy what Gramsci himself called, half-ironically, an incorrigible "optimism of the will."

Gramsci was of course far from alone in his urge to "make it new"; many others of his generation were caught up in the desires of political and artistic revolts, from the European-wide upsurge on the left during and after WWI to the Italian Fascist "revolution" on the right that followed in their wake; from the "high" artistic European modernisms to the first significant stirrings of mass revolutionary national liberation movements in the colonized world. What is distinctive about Gramsci's conception of this new order, however, is his understanding of the temporality of the New. He views it neither as the irruption in the present of the totally unprecedented (a theory of miraculous event), nor as the simple negation of the past by the present (a theory of teleological superannuation); the theological figures explored by some of his near contemporaries, such as Lukács, Benjamin, Schmitt, and Bloch. The new order is instead thought by Gramsci as an active mode of dis- and relocation internal to the existing situation in which the new is "pre-figured" in a literal sense in struggles against the old.

This conception of prefiguration is not a theory of the actualization of a latent potential in which a partial social element, marginal or excluded from the existing political order, "expands" and progressively displaces its antagonist. The new order of hegemonic politics, that is, is not a process in which the compromised Old is replaced by a pristine New. This is because, according to the theory of the integral state that Gramsci develops in the *Prison Notebooks*, there is no element—either social or political—that is not already a function of, and functional to, the existing state order. To imagine the construction of a new order as the becoming universal of a previously "mere" particularity would thus constitute nothing more than a formalist ruse by means of which the old order continues to subsist within the new one—precisely the condition that Gramsci had diagnosed in his critique of the fatalism that had deformed the prior Italian socialist tradition, and which he later extended in his carceral writings into an analysis of the relation between passive revolution and processes of subalternization.

The new order of hegemonic politics instead aims to construct the relations of force and institutional forms capable of representing a radical and viable alternative to the existing state of affairs from within it. As this construction, however, is forced to occur within the determining coordinates of the existing political order of the bourgeois integral state, it is a construction that can only occur simultaneously as a deconstruction of the reigning relations that are dedicated to blocking its emergence. "Prefiguration" therefore is here just as much "refiguration," a sublation of the old oriented to the future that it actively constructs. The present order here gives way to a process of reordering without end. Hegemony in a strategic sense is the name of this mode of prefigurative struggle; the goal of a new order occurs within this struggle itself, as a new practice of ordering, and not at some end point of a liberated society lying beyond it.

From these insights derives Gramsci's conception of a new order of formerly subaltern social classes and groups as a potentially autonomous new order. The political autonomy of the subaltern social classes is not given from the outset but must be actively constructed and made to endure in those modes of struggle against the existing order that are never entirely freely chosen, but always to a greater or lesser degree constrained by the existing order itself. For this reason, Gramsci insists the construction of a new order can only be thought of concretely as the conjunction of moral and intellectual reform (conceived as subtraction from the principles governing the existing political order) with a concrete economic program (understood in an expansive, political-economic sense, as the conscious self-regulation of society's reproduction). The new order just is this ongoing process of autonomization without end. It is precisely this dynamic that is condensed in Gramsci's vibrant metaphor of the modern Prince as a "concrete utopia"—not a messianic moment deferred to the horizon but an expansive practice within the present, as a politics that simultaneously prefigures and enacts.[70]

The notion of the new order as a new practice of ordering already underway reflected, in Gramsci's time, the still undiminished revolutionary enthusiasms that emerged in the midst of the crisis of classical imperialism in the first world war and its aftermath. It could appear as a realistic political strategy because it theorized political relations of force that were already operative, attempting to provide them with theoretical coherence, consistency, and direction. In other words, it was a "timely" conception and intervention. Even when the simulacra of Fascist counterrevolution latter appeared to drain the modernizing impulse of its progressive force, the active sense of constructing the New, as relation and institution, remained the utopian dream that nourished repeated attempts to renew self-emancipatory politics throughout the long, dark night of the twentieth century.

To envisage the goal of emancipatory politics today as the construction of a new order, as a new practice of ordering, on the other hand, can seem like nothing if not "unrealistic" and "untimely." For well over 30 years, so the story goes, emancipatory politics has labored in a minoritarian key, focused on immediate resistance to this or that injustice—civil, ethnic, gendered economic, or ecological—without any totalizing strategic vision. It is precisely as a response to this self-fulfilling prophecy that the critical force of reinstating the construction of a new order as the goal of self-emancipatory politics lies: to remind our present fallen from itself that its "outside" is already "within" it.

The multiplicity of movements over the last 30 years have not been isolated instances of reactive and particularistic protest, or rehearsals for some "real revolution" to come. In their generational learning processes, complicated inheritances, and creative extensions, they have represented moments in the emergence of a new critical imaginary of the Left, broader in its concerns and sometimes even more radical in its demands than the oppositional cultures that preceded it. The clearest example of this is the centrality assumed in contemporary radical discourses and activity by themes of social reproduction initially highlighted by socialist feminists, in stark discontinuity with the patriarchal structures and forms of older political cultures. Leftist practice today impatiently posits an immediate relation between means and ends, seeing the intersection of demands against injustice as constitutive of their nature as demands. To recognize the ensemble of these movements as experimentations in new practices of ordering in the here and now is thus also to project them beyond the present, in their prefigurative capacity of beginning the construction of our possible futures in the midst of the struggles of the present.

Historical progress

The new order that self-emancipatory politics aims to bring into being is characterized unashamedly in the *Prison Notebooks* as an instance of "historical progress."[71] It is true that few concepts today have fallen out of fashion quite so decisively as that of progress, however it is defined—and for good reasons. It is not only the association of notions of progress with generations of reformisms—the type of naïve faith in a historical destiny that Benjamin condemned so forcefully in German social democracy—that seems to compromise this notion.[72] Nor is it only the observation, theorized by recent currents of critical theory on the basis of an older critique of Enlightenment rationality, that notions of (linear or normative) progress have been and remain complicit with histories of colonialism, eurocentrism, and domination.[73] It is also the fact that a banalized conception of progress, cynically masked as "modernization," figures among the weapons of the dominant politics of order of our time. Progress and modernization have been regularly invoked as battle slogans in neoliberalism's drive over the last 30 years to roll back the reforms secured by popular struggles in the postwar period, just as today they are routinely called on to justify automation and AI in capital's restructuring of labor relations, in so many cliched repetitions of the ignominious slanders hurled against the honorable Captain Ludd. Given so many betrayals and deformations, it is thus unsurprising that many engaged in emancipatory politics today may feel that the word "progress" can leave only a bad taste in one's mouth.

For Gramsci and his generation of internationalist revolutionaries at the high tide of popular struggles in the early twentieth century, the problem of historical progress was posed in very different terms. For those figures, historical progress was not understood in terms of the teleological guarantees of an abstract philosophy of history but as the very stakes of their struggles contesting the immanent limits of bourgeois political modernity. Rather than simply given by the flow of a homogenous time, progress for this perspective was something that had to be produced through the resolution of the actually existing contradictions of political modernity: contradictions between the egalitarian rhetoric of the bourgeois revolution and its substantial continuity with the hierarchies of the feudal order, between the declaration of political liberty and the reality of enduring relations of disenfranchisement.

Historical progress was thus here fundamentally understood not as a linear accumulation directed toward a predetermined goal but in the comparative perspective of a learning process and of problemsolving. To understand hegemonic politics as the production of historical progress is thus to conceive it as a type of immanent critique. It begins from existing contradictions in order to valorize the critical acts and practices capable of resolving them in an enabling fashion. In the late nineteenth and early twentieth centuries, this critique was focused on the claims of classical liberalism and its belated adoption of democratic legitimation. If popular sovereignty was affirmed in theory but not in practice, hegemonic politics aimed to build the expansive institutions in which meaningful popular participation in political deliberation and determination could occur; if slavery was abolished on the basis of an inalienable claim to personal liberty, hegemonic politics aimed to extend that claim to the regulation of the "normal" labor relations still entrapped within the servitude of private property of the means of production of social wealth. In each of these instances, hegemonic politics aimed to force bourgeois society to progress beyond itself, in an immanent sublation of its own constitutive limits.[74]

This conception of historical progress is not a normative one, at least not in the sense in which normativity is commonly understood today. Normativity in contemporary political philosophy most often is invoked in the aestheticized sense of the realization of a "model," or a formalization of the "ought" as moral prescription. Rather than recommending "how things ought to be," a conception of historical progress is better understood in terms of the Machiavellian tradition of the "concrete fantasy" in which Gramsci's thought was formed.

For Machiavelli, the realistic reformulation of a supposedly moral imperative involved recognizing that the desire for transformation overcoded in moral (and ultimately legalistic) appeals was not in itself an abstract utopia but an already operative element in any given situation, one that needed to be valorized and developed on its own concrete terms, without reference to any supposedly justifying instance. So too for Gramsci, progress was not an ideal toward which to aim, but, in Viconian terms, a concrete "making" whose efficacy was to be verified in comparative terms. Rather than a determining ideal at the end of a process, this conception of historical progress is thus better comprehended as a categorical perspective from which to begin, from which consequences can be drawn, and on the basis of which responsibilities are assumed.

In the political culture of international Communism in the early twentieth century, the conception that the popular classes could engage in purposive, independent, political action was a "heresy" of what Gramsci sardonically characterized as the "religion of liberty," or of nineteenth-century liberalism's betrayed promises.[75] Even when negated by Fascist counterrevolution and Stalinist corruption, this notion of the transformation of the unfinished emancipatory tasks of the "bourgeois revolution" into practices of self-emancipation remained an orienting perspective that defined a continuity of the revolutionary tradition at the moment of its deepest defeats.

Today, to argue that the nature of emancipatory politics consists in the production of historical progress is equally heretical. It represents an explicit refusal of the ruling order's declaration of the impossibility of any alternatives to its daily production of historical regress. Attempts to propose solutions to the concrete problems that prevent an improvement in the life conditions of the subaltern classes and social groups thus do not need to rely on any philosophy of history or normative guarantee. It is the acts of resistance of contemporary movements themselves—against the atomization by legal mandate of institutions of collective popular deliberation such as trade unions, against the divisions promoted by mobilizations around ideologies of racism and sexism, against the originary accumulation undertaken by the renewed commodification in the private and public spheres alike, against the threat of extinction posed by state-sanctioned environmental destruction—that demonstrate the possibility that the future could be different from the present: indeed, unashamedly "better" than the present if the dynamics condensed in those acts were to be generalized as a new beginning for society at large. To advocate historical progress today is thus not to fall into any easy ideology of a fatalistic "progressivism." It is rather to understand contemporary oppositional movements as the actually existing alternatives to the current order.

Leadership

While the post-New-Left explosion of references to hegemony have most frequently understood it in terms of the paradigms of domination or sovereign power, the Bolshevik tradition that directly inspired Gramsci's understanding of hegemony's strategic significance instead most often conceived it as synonymous with social, cultural, and political leadership (in Gramsci's Italian translation, *direzione*).[76] Even when this affiliation has been noted, the overwhelming influence of the notion of hegemony as a system of power has still tended to understand leadership in this context in terms of a conventional conception of supremacy, command, and authority; in short, the notion that leadership is a concentration of power in a hierarchical relationship that consigns "mere" followers to a lesser and derivative condition. Such an understanding of leadership is ultimately compatible with a Weberian notion of charismatic power as self-foundational, if not a Schmittian conception of the groundless decision at the foundation of modern sovereignty.

Leadership in the Bolshevik debates both before and after the October Revolution, however, focused not in the first instance on the achievement of power as a capacity to order (whatever the impression to the contrary created by the hierarchical military metaphors so often used by this generation of revolutionaries, Gramsci prominently among them). Rather, it was primarily a strategic response to the necessarily temporally disjointed process of mobilization of the subaltern classes and social groups. The notion of a struggle for hegemony in Lenin's writings, for instance, does not signify a bid for a (political or governmental) power that could be however provisionally or definitively attained (a process that Lenin discusses with the very different vocabulary of dual power, insurrection, and seizure of the *vlast*). Hegemony for Lenin instead consists in the active process of mobilizing the "followers" of a political program. It is a mobilization that, in a Machiavellian sense, creates those who will receive and act on its message in the very act of calling them forth.

For this perspective, the "hegemony of the proletariat" among the popular classes did not signify the dominance of the industrial working class over, for instance, the peasantry. Rather, it means the "prestige" (to use the term from Italian historical linguistics with which Gramsci sometimes comprehends this process) of the proletariat's political program among the peasantry and other subaltern classes.[77] Hegemony in this sense "occurs" when the wider popular classes re-cognize—in an etymological sense—the political program of a leading class as a rethinking of their own interests and the forms of their potential satisfaction. It was precisely this more expansive sense of leadership that characterized the postrevolutionary developments of hegemonic politics in the early 1920s in Soviet Russia, and which makes at least this dimension of hegemony irreducible to a merely mechanical conception of an "alliance" between fundamental and "non-fundamental" classes.[78]

In Gramsci's precarceral and carceral writings, this relational understanding of hegemony is accentuated and elevated to the level of a conscious political method. Precisely insofar as hegemonic leadership is a capacity to mobilize and activate followers, it is not a self-referential source of power but depends on those following it to maintain its hegemonic status. Rather than the sovereign command that grounds its own decision, this is an image of the risk of the proposal that seeks assent; the fragility of the tentative foray that hopes for reinforcement; and above all, the productive difference between leaders and those they hope to inspire to follow them. This type of hegemonic leadership does not command, and nor does it merely seek to persuade. It aims actively to empower.

Herein lies Gramsci's reformulation of what he characterizes, following Machiavelli and in polemic with the elitist theorists of his day, as the "primordial fact of politics." "There really are the governed and governors, leaders and the led," he freely admits; but that recognition is only the beginning of the real problem.[79] The question then becomes how this given condition is to be comprehended not as an obstacle to self-emancipatory politics but as a productive resource for its development. Everything depends, Gramsci insists, on whether this distinction is regarded as permanent and inevitable, or as the expression of the possibility of historical movement. The relationship between leaders and followers is thereby reformulated not as given, and not as a qualitative difference of type. Rather, it is much more similar to the constitutive temporal difference between an avant-garde and those it seeks to inspire to travel along the path it has highlighted as a viable mode of development. Between the moment of proposal and its operationalization, or between political formulation and its "sedimentation" in social movements, there exists a productive tension that drives emancipatory politics forward in an exploratory mode.

This conception of leadership is thus not the static relation of hierarchical command but the exposed and fragile relationality of the experimental hypothesis. As a hypothesis, its veracity can never be presupposed but is always at risk in the experimental process of discovery, which may in fact negate its continuity, utility, and validity. Hegemony, then, instead of the self-assurance proper to sovereign power, actively works to remind itself of the possibility of its own failure, in those moments when leadership no longer works, when the followers refuse to continue to travel along the path indicated by their leaders and instead propose an alternative project, in effect, themselves assuming a hegemonic role. To engage in hegemonic politics is to accept the possibility of just such a "successful failure" at every moment: the failure to produce the productive tension between the political initiative and its social base, but also the failure that results precisely from the fine-tuning of this tension and its reversal of polarities. Hegemonic politics in this sense aims to put itself out of business by enabling those who were led yesterday to become their own leaders today.

The understanding of hegemonic leadership as risk, as fragility, and as dynamic differentiation represents a distinct understanding of the nature of the empowerment represented by and in emancipatory movements. Above all, it signals the autonomous nature of hegemonic politics from the "normal" forms of political power comprehended within the paradigm of modern sovereignty. The Bolshevik and later Gramscian development of this perspective was remarkable for the extent to which it refused the descent into decisionistic and ultimately nihilistic conceptions of political authority that marked the early twentieth century, and which continue unabated today. Harnessing the dynamic dialectical differentiation between leaders and followers as an enabling resource of mobilization signified a new understanding of the nature of leadership, not as a mechanism of domination but as a learning process and as an ethico-political relation of self-emancipation.

To imagine leadership in these terms today is to rediscover the essentially strategic dimensions of hegemony as a method of political work. In a time when the mere mention of leadership is still regarded by some with suspicion—or on the other hand, is all too easily asserted by others in entirely fetishized and ultimately sovereign forms—this understanding of hegemony reminds us that leadership is both "normal" and inevitable. An intervention in the life of a political movement—a proposal for this or that priority, for the short- or long-term value of this or that action—is always an instance of leadership, however brief or modest. What is decisive is not the temporal endurance or nominal authorship of any such intervention but its openness to experimentation and the risks that are always implicit in its nature as a proposal. It is precisely such risks that the plurality of contemporary movements encounter as they intersect with each other in the rhythms of the recurrent mobilizations that define our times.

Pedagogical laboratory
If the strategic perspective of hegemony aims toward the development of a new process of ordering, and not merely the rearrangement of an existing order; if the nature of hegemonic politics consists in the production of historical progress, as the concrete and immanent critique of the current state of affairs; and if leadership as intervention is a method for undertaking such a dynamic and partisan project, hegemonic politics nevertheless still confronts a potentially disabling paradox. By taking its distance from the reigning sovereign forms of politics, does hegemony not run the risk of simply falling behind them? Might hegemony, that is, not come to represent anything more than an ephemeral moment prior to the affirmation of sovereignty, destined to be replaced by its antagonist precisely insofar as it seeks to

make its own dynamic endure? Is hegemonic politics, that is, incapable of any form of durable institutionalization, without losing the distinctive features that make it what it is?

This was the paradox that Gramsci confronted in his carceral solitude. It was a solitude that was not merely the physical separation of confinement but an ideological "aloneness" from the sectarian isolation into which so many of his fellow leaders of the international Communist movement fell in the early 1930s. The *Prison Notebooks* are in large part an extended attempt to find the strategic perspectives and forms that would be able to make of hegemonic politics a realistic and viable alternative to the sectarianism of the grotesque "revolutionary purity" of the counterrevolutionary Stalinist "Third Period." Present from the outset of his carceral researches, as their guiding horizon, Gramsci intensified this dimension of his project in 1932 with the formulation of the Machiavellian notion of the "modern Prince" and its articulation with his long-standing call for the Italian anti-Fascist movement to understand its potential as a form of constituent struggle.[80] The result was a distinctive conception of political organization not as an administrative "apparatus" of order, condensing "machine" of force, or "monopoly" of command, but as a "pedagogical laboratory" of self-emancipatory politics.[81]

The notion of "laboratory" here refers not to the figure most commonly associated with word today, that is, the organized infrastructure of experimental technique. As the site of the modern natural scientific process in contemporary capitalism, the laboratory is called on to provide a stable institutional basis for the observation of regularities and tendencies and the formulation of predictions that can master or offset contingency. It has also, however, increasingly become an institution of control, isolation, and technocratic regulation, most often under the direct or indirect control of capitalist ownership interests and therefore in the service of neoliberalism's new round of originary accumulation at "immaterial," biopolitical, and ecological levels.

If political organization is thought in these terms, it would reproduce all the dynamics of subalternity, imposed passivity, and of separation between intellectuals and the *semplici* that Gramsci's entire project was designed to overcome. In other words, a conception of political organization as this type of laboratory would provide an almost empirical description of the distanced calculation and "experimentation" that political elites already conduct on those they claim to "re-present"; that is, to make absent from the political processes of deliberation and decision, in order to stand in their place.[82] Political organization thought as this type of laboratory would represent little more than a repetition of Fordist disciplinary social policies' extension of Taylorist productive techniques from the factory to society as a whole.

There are, however, other conceptualizations of the laboratory that suggest a more expansive perspective and seem closer to the type of productive relation that Gramsci envisaged as the heart of his party "of a new type," as an "organization of struggle." In the golden age of the Florentine Renaissance, for instance, the famous laboratories of the Uffizi were not merely sites of experimentation or production (though they were that as well). They were also places of combination and communication between different dimensions of artistic and cultural practice, zones of dissemination, cross-fertilization, and contamination. This mode of experimentation was not one of speculative reflection but of active participation and transformation. It aimed not at the production of unity but consisted in the multiplication of diverse practices and the exchange and interchange enabled by their proximity in common relations of world building.[83]

Gramsci's project of the modern Prince as concrete mythological expression of hegemonic politics is best thought in these terms, as a productive and transformative laboratory. It is a pedagogical laboratory in the sense that its dynamic of combination and communication aims to create the conditions for a learning process of the already existing potentials for self-emancipation among the subaltern classes and social groups. This is a Socratic pedagogical mode, guidance rather than instruction in the process of critical reflection on already existing but dimly comprehended capacities. For Gramsci, the modern Prince and its institutional concretization in the dynamic of the constituent assembly of anti-Fascist forces provided forms in which the subaltern classes could discover collaboratively their own capacities for self-governance. Its function was to make enduring and productive the differences, tensions, and conflicts that are constitutive of hegemonic politics as an intervention in the historical process. As an expansive process of moral and intellectual reform, it was situated simultaneously in the midst of, outside, and beyond the relations of subalternization inherent to the modern bourgeois integral state: a space in which the subaltern social groups could reforge themselves into autonomous political forces.

The reformulation of political organization as a pedagogical laboratory of self-emancipation was for Gramsci linked to the needs of the anti-Fascist struggle in the 1930s, as a viable form in which the subaltern classes could rediscover their potential for social and political autonomy. It was an attempt to provide an institutional vehicle for the "unprecedented concentration of hegemony" that he saw as the concrete and actual form of revolutionary praxis in unpropitious conditions.[84] Neglected in Gramsci's own time, its spirit soon deformed in the Italian Communist Party's capitulation to the postwar constitutional process and resulting republican order, the modern Prince has long remained a tantalizing but still abstract utopian figure.

To think of self-emancipatory politics today as a type of pedagogical laboratory is to rediscover a language to describe the dynamic of learning and cross-fertilization that is already occurring in so many of the contemporary intersectional sociopolitical movements, as anti-racist protests, feminist struggles, and ecological movements each in their own way confront the consequences and causes of state-inflicted or endorsed violence. The pedagogical laboratory of hegemonic politics in this sense represents an attempt to develop the dynamic institutional forms in which the subaltern classes and social groups, precisely in their diversity and divisions, can collectively unlearn the habits of subalternity, discovering new forms of conviviality, mutuality, and collective self-determination. The organization of hegemonic politics, by providing an institutional context in which the fragility and risk of learning processes can be valorized, represents a concrete way for subaltern social groups and classes to rehearse the conditions of their own self-emancipation.

Hegemony as Self-Emancipation

The wide diffusion of hegemony understood as a concept of power since the 1950s, first in Italy and increasingly in the many international translations of Gramsci's thought, gave rise to many significant theoretical and practical initiatives. It defined a new paradigm for discussing the nature of modern political and state power, even if that paradigm has increasingly been neutralized and reintegrated into the mainstream of what today passes for "political science" and even "critical theory." The contemporary usage of hegemony as a leftist euphemism for sovereignty is evidence of the domestication that has accompanied such a successful and widespread reception.

Were this the only way in which hegemonic politics can be understood, it would be difficult not to concur with those contemporary critics who have condemned the "hegemony of hegemony" as a block on critical energies. The multiple dimensions of reflections on hegemony, however, are much richer than the dominant ways in which the word is understood today, as we are only beginning to understand. Gramsci, as the most influential figure in the popularization of hegemony over the last 50 years, is central to this process of reevaluation. To re-situate the reading of his work, and to explore the polyvalent meanings of hegemony within it, is thus to open up a new perspective on hegemony not as a description of the functioning of power in the current order but as a strategy for the new ordering of self-emancipation.

When conceived as an articulated theory of the structure of self-emancipatory politics, synthesizing a new process of ordering, historical progress, pedagogical leadership, and a new practice of political organization, hegemony can no longer be limited to, or reintegrated within, the main currents of modern political thought. Rather, it represents an opening to an unprecedented future in which emancipation is not given but actively constructed in the daily practices and strivings of subaltern classes and social groups to become artificers of their own destiny. Hegemony represents in this sense not a state to be achieved, definitively or provisionally, but a new way of doing politics: potentially, a politics capable of going beyond the sovereignist limit of modern politics itself.

4

Formal Cause

The Question of Organization

Organizational debates were central to the development of the alternative globalization, social fora, and antiwar movements that straddled the turn of the century. Like the practices of what was sometimes called a "movement of movements" itself, these debates undoubtedly sometimes fell into overly dichotomized and abstract oppositions between movements and parties, anti-power and counter-power, micro- and macropolitics, as faint echoes of the classic couplet of spontaneity and organization. Nevertheless, debates between figures such as Naomi Klein, Michael Hardt and Antonio Negri, John Holloway, and Daniel Bensaïd had the redeeming merit of "re-actualizing" some of the classic organizational debates on the relationship between social movements and political forms, on the nature of state power and its consequences for oppositional politics, and on the most effective means of durable political organizing.[1]

Viewed in retrospect, we can now see how this season of discussion constituted something like a "pivot" between the cultures of emancipatory politics in the twentieth and twenty-first centuries. Whatever the limitations of the positions that were essayed, and however far their concrete results fell short of the hopes they had aroused, they helped to establish the theoretical framework in which more recent organizational debates and forms of experimentation have occurred.

Yet these debates from the early years of the new century are also significant in a longer-term perspective. For the very fact of posing the question of organization precisely as an *open* question has long been symptomatic of a decisive stage of revitalization of emancipatory politics. For "politics as usual," the answer to the question of organization is always already given in existing political regimes. Political order qua order constitutively reduces and traduces the question of organization

Radical Politics. Peter D. Thomas, Oxford University Press. © Oxford University Press 2023.
DOI: 10.1093/oso/9780197528075.003.0005

into one of the shabby simulacra promoted by the main currents of modern and contemporary political thought: from a technocratic assertion of the question of justification, to a liberal displacement of the question of justice-as-reward, to the social democratic concession of the question of subaltern redistribution. In all cases, "what (merely) exists" is accepted as the basis for proposing more or less exhaustive "emendations" of its (supposedly merely contingent) insufficiencies.

The posing of the question of organization as an open question, on the other hand, signifies the movement from the limitations of any merely immanent critique of the existing order to the active self-constitution of an alternative practice of ordering. It means to think the future not as a passive state-to-come, but as a dynamic process of construction within the contradictions of the present. It is in this sense that the organizational debates of the early years of the century remain significant today—not simply as a transition between older and newer cultures of emancipatory politics but as a moment of rupture that began to delineate a new way of thinking and doing radical politics. Viewed in this light, the movement of movements still constitutes today something like our contemporary "primal scene," to be continuously revisited, de- and reconstructed, disavowed and remembered.

A New *Vormärz*?

Despite the vibrant debates and the culture of mobilization in which they occurred in the early years of the twenty-first century, the onset of the global financial crisis of 2007 nevertheless seemed to some commentators to coincide with an "interregnum" for radical politics. Both Slavoj Žižek and Alain Badiou, for instance, argued in different ways that the end of the first decade of the twenty-first century represented a "zero point" for a new beginning of radical politics. This perspective was most succinctly encapsulated in the notion that the most intense structural crisis of the ruling order since the 1960s could be characterized as a "pre-political" conjuncture.[2] Forms of social discontent and inchoate rebellion multiplied; but a properly "political" response—"political" here defined in an almost apophatic way, as what existing movements were *not*—was argued to be lacking.

While ostensibly oriented to a future, properly political moment, this argument in reality drew on models from the past, above all those that were (retrospectively) developed in order to account for some of the most signification moments of political transformation in the nineteenth century. Žižek and Badiou's argument regarding the pre-political nature of the conjuncture was not limited to the late 2000s, as if there had been a merely temporary lull in political energies. More radically, both suggested that the entire post-Cold War period, from the 1990s onward, could be usefully thought in terms of affinities with the famed German *Vormärz* of the mid-1840s. Just as that earlier conjuncture had been a chaotic period of competing forms of "critical criticism" that were later sublated (in the full Hegelian sense, as su-perannuation and transformative preservation) by the "fully political" moment of the uprising of 1848, so the social and political movements of this new period were characterized as an absence of the "real" politics that was supposed to succeed them.

It was a suggestive comparison that undoubtedly captured some-thing of the chaotic energies and enthusiasms that the two very dif-ferent periods seemed to share. Just as what Heine characterized as "our German misery" had witnessed a multiplication of critical perspectives and proposals—from Feuerbach's militant atheism to Bauer's austere universalism, from the radical democracy of the young Marx to the first stirrings of autonomous working-class politics—so the initial movements at the end of the twentieth century had explored a wide variety of mobilizing terrains: the intersection of indigenous and ecological struggles, articulated with critiques of the global finan-cial architecture, flowing into a revival of the critique of imperialism in militant antiwar movements. Despite their many differences and the centuries that separate them, these conjunctures can indeed both be characterized as examples of "primitive political accumulation": not full-blown alternatives to the existing order but forms of resistance and experimentation in which a new culture of dissent and opposition was haltingly being developed.

Žižek and Badiou's invocation of the *Vormärz*, however, was less concerned to valorize the forms of experimentations of the movement of movements than it was to establish a periodizing narrative.[3] In a classic instance of what Louis Althusser had cautioned were the risks of history written in the *futur antérieur*, this periodization sought to define the present as but a prelude to what was hoped would follow it.[4] Just as the mid-nineteenth-century *Vormärz* after all only became recognizable as such after the fact, *nach dem März*, so our millennial misery was thought in terms of its expected superannuation. The debates of the alternative globalization and antiwar movements of only a few years earlier were thereby represented not simply as surpassed by changes in the conjuncture, such as inevitably occurs in any extended political sequence. Rather, they were represented as having been a "false start," confined to the "pre-political" or the "merely social" in a way that did not fundamentally challenge the coordinates of the existing state of affairs. Only the arrival of something entirely different could endow them, retrospectively, with their true historical meaning.

From the Idea of Communism to the Idea of Socialism

It was against this periodized background that the debate on "the Idea of Communism" was staged. The initial impetus for this discussion was Alain Badiou's analysis of the electoral victory of Sarkozy in France in 2007, but it soon overflowed its local and polemical formulation to engage a wide range of prominent theorists from many leftist traditions on an international scale.[5] Unexpectedly and audaciously, it became possible to discuss once again communism as a positive political program and not simply a failed historical experiment. It is true that the terms of these debates sometimes seemed more in tune with the concerns of the academic seminar than the tasks of the trade union branch meeting or movement assembly. Similarly, the rush to defend the "Idea" of Communism without an extended reckoning of accounts with the causes and effects of the realities associated with communism throughout the twentieth century, or the significant theoretical traditions that had previously dedicated themselves to this task, undoubtedly displayed both historical and political limitations.[6] These limitations, however, do not negate the singular political and theoretical achievement of this season of discussions: the valorization of communism as a name not of and from the past but as a potential future.

Nevertheless, there was undoubtedly something "untimely" about this debate, which seemed so different in tone and temper from the organizational debates that had directly preceded it. Badiou argued, for example, that we should resist the notion that the affirmation of communism should be accompanied by a renewed consideration of the role of the political party. Rather than an ineludible moment in that idea's realization, he instead understood the political party to be a historically superseded instantiation of "communist invariants," which were now searching for different and new modes of historical existence.[7] In its sense of historical exhaustion, this perspective seems as distant from the anarchistic urgency of the alter-globalization movement straddling the turn of the millennium as it does from the chaotic forms of organizational experimentation that have emerged in the intersectional sociopolitical movements of more recent years.

Yet there is something even more "untimely" about this discussion of an "idea" of communism when we consider it in relation to the concrete political history of the last two decades. For this has not been a period characterized by a turn toward communism, at least if communism is understood in its classical Marxian sense. For Marx, communism signified in a particular sense a society of conscious inequality. It directly opposes the formal equality (of individual actors in the marketplace, of juridical subjects) that lies at the foundation of the capitalist mode of production. Communism in this sense would be an organization of society in which all give unequally according to their specific abilities and qualities, and receive according to the qualitatively distinct criterion of their inevitably unequal needs and desires.

This conception of communism, in other words, is not a zero-sum game because it presupposes relations of incommensurable qualities. Understood in this way, it makes no sense to talk of communism as a "fair" distribution of resources, rights, or recognition, or as an equality of either opportunities or outcomes, because it is not a species of egalitarianism.[8] It is instead an acceptance and indeed a valorization of qualitative inequality as the basis of a new type of mutuality. Given the dominance of the very different quantitative inequalities produced and exacerbated by neoliberalism over the last 30 years, however, it is not surprising that this dimension of Marx's critique of the capitalist mode of production has rarely constituted the focus of recent debates.[9]

It has instead been the paradoxical revival of the historically much more difficult problem of "socialism" that has defined our historical present. This revival seems well underway on a global scale, whether as an ideological position in those countries (particularly in what is now increasingly characterized as the "North") where neoliberalism's "idea of capitalism" remains dominant, or as concrete policy proposal in societies (frequently in the so-called South, in both regional and global senses) in which movements, parties, and sometimes even "governments of the left" have grappled with the contradictions of post-neoliberal, neo-developmentalist, or simply "old-accumulationist" paradigms. Socialism here is intended in the sense in which it was most often understood throughout the nineteenth and particularly the twentieth centuries: that is, as a society in which a still substantially bourgeois-capitalist law of value at the socioeconomic level is regulated by political intervention at the level of the state. It is this contradictory compromise formation, and not a maximal program of communism, that has been the immediate challenge of the international left in the early twenty-first century—or rather, as the examples of Brazil, Bolivia, and Greece make clear, our obstacle.[10]

Recent revivals of social democratic practice and theory, understood in the broadest sense, provide ample evidence of the "inactuality" of the Idea of Communism. Various forms of "socialism" have gained a much wider audience in popular political movements in an understandable if naive desire for some type of immediate defense against the anarchy that has been "loosed upon the world." Strengthening the social welfare state against the lures of right-wing populism, state-led economic interventionism, and investment to counter the worst excesses of a market unbridled for too long, even expropriated bourgeois state power wielded against pandemics and climate change: almost anything now seems better than the continuing rightward drift of mainstream politics and the sad theoretical reflections that tried to justify its genesis in the epoch of the ideology of a third way—including and especially nostalgia for a supposed golden age of postwar social democracy.[11]

The most "successful" social and political movements of the early twenty-first century—if success is measured by the dubious criterion of the assumption of governmental power—have been characterized by just such a "preemptory" realism. Politics as the art of the possible was the focus in the first decade of the century of the *Partido dos Trabalhadores* in Brazil and (arguably even more significantly, given its constitutional transformations) the *Movimiento al Socialismo* in Bolivia. It also provided a watchword for more recent projects such as those of *SYRIZA* in Greece, the Corbynite revitalization of the British Labour Party, or the campaigns around Sanders's runs for the US Presidency. Even when these movements have advocated a longer-term strategic goal of fundamental sociopolitical transformation—and it is not insignificant that many of them do—their immediate tactical concerns have nonetheless been the type of reforms traditionally associated with the social democratic tradition.

This unexpected revival in the practice of socialism has been echoed at a distance by revivals of its Idea. Much contemporary critical theory, for instance, particularly but not only in the global North, has been engaged in an effective reformulation of social democratic theory as a counterweight to the dominance of an often nebulously defined "neoliberalism."[12] These currents constitute an Idea of Socialism to the extent that they accept, explicitly or implicitly, the coordinates of the current situation as both the starting point and structuring dynamic of their projects. Whether conceived in terms of an identitarian recognition as a cure to the pathologies of social injustice, or its supposed opposite in an economistic emphasis on the restorative powers of redistribution, a yearning after the forms of justification of an (imagined) sociopolitical order, or a more ambitious philosophy of steady but inexorable historical development, the presuppositions are remarkably similar: the assertion of a virtuous primacy of politics over the social, or the desirability of the statal regulation of the inherent anarchies of the (inevitability of the) market. Compared to the practical and theoretical diffusion of such forms of socialism, the assertation of a mere "Idea" of communism risks becoming a reminder only of its effective inactuality.

The Communist Hypothesis

The debate on communism can begin to seem less untimely, however, when it is thought not in terms of the assertion of a mere "Idea" but instead as an exploratory hypothesis. Badiou's formulation in *The Meaning of Sarkozy* had in fact originally emphasized the more concrete notion of a communist "hypothesis" as a proposition in need of demonstration and historical actualization, rather than the mere austere (and frequently caricatured) "pseudo-platonic" sense of an "Idea."[13] This perspective was also emphasized by Daniel Bensaïd's preference for the notion of communism as a "strategic hypothesis."[14] Such experimental metaphors are better positioned to capture the key political stakes of the discussion as something more than an instance of the speculative leftism to which it has sometimes been reduced.[15]

Conceived as a hypothesis rather than idea, the "inactuality" of communism can be understood in a more positive sense. Unlike the certainty sometimes associated with an idea or concept, standing over and sometimes against the reality they claim to comprehend, a hypothesis is constitutively provisional and open to revision in the experimental process that it both enables and in which it is implicated. A hypothesis in this sense doesn't aim to describe an actually existing condition; nor does it aim to establish a normative standard by means of which the existent can be measured as lacking. Rather, similar to the interventionist conception of hypothesization I have argued is operative in Gramsci's *Prison Notebooks*, it attempts to act a guide for exploration, opening up new perspectives that remain to be verified, refuted, or modified in the concrete process of discovery of what reality both is and can become. A hypothesis, that is, always represents an attempt to think otherwise.[16]

By considering communism as a hypothesis rather than an idea, it also becomes possible to rethink the relation of the debate on communism to the theoretical discussions in movements of a decade earlier in less antagonistic and periodizing terms. For although the connections have not always been immediately apparent, the debate on communism in fact inherited significant dimensions of the discussions in the cycle of movements at the beginning of the millennium. Both theoretical conjunctures were defined, for instance, by attempts to break the deadlock of a present imagined without emancipatory alternatives; both proposed novel and often heretical mobilizing slogans that aimed directly against the clichés that had become all too "common sense."

These continuities are perhaps most viscerally discernable in the "enthusiasm" (in a Kantian sense) that greeted both sets of debates. Just as the declaration that "another world is possible" was understood as a "sign of moral progress"—finally, a clear and militant refusal of the end of history consensus of the 1990s—so the debate on communism seemed to signal a direct affront to the "post-communist" presuppositions of the new century. Here, there was a continuity in terms of the ways in which both debates energized those engaged in emancipatory political movements. Theoretical debates were experienced as points of condensation, intensification, and amplification of the perspectives that activists and militants had already been exploring in practical terms.

To note these continuities at the level of the political "base" of these theoretical debates' "superstructures" is thus also to argue that the periodizing gestures that accompanied the initial formulations of the debate on communism do not adequately capture its own political significance, considered in the context of the long cycle of movements from the 1990s onward. Indeed, in many respects, such periodization moved directly against the matrix of the energy and engagement that made the debate on communism such a signal moment or "event." Resituating this debate as a displacement into a theoretical register of central themes of the previous sequences of struggles in the late 1990s and early 2000s enables us to recognize that the debate on communism did not, unsurprisingly, emerge from nowhere, as a purely subtractive event irreducible to the coordinates of the existing situation. Rather, the energies that determined its reception and reverberation—and therefore ultimately defined what was at stake in it politically—both preceded and exceeded it. Viewed in this alternative light, the debate on communism can instead be understood as a resumption of "unfinished business."

Refusing a periodizing logic, finally, also enables us to understand the extent to which the new movements that fortuitously emerged immediately in the wake of the debate on communism—student movements across North America and Europe from 2009 onward, the global wave of Occupy in 2011, the Arab revolutions and growing anti-austerity movements in Europe (particularly in Spain and Greece) from 2012 onward—did not represent a return or "rebirth of history," but its revenge. The uprisings in the Middle East and North Africa in the early years of the twenty-first-century's second decade, for instance, did not come from nowhere. Their preconditions had been steadily prepared by the entire history of European colonial and imperialist interventions in the region and by traditions of subaltern struggle and organization against them.[17]

Rather than miraculous irruptions, moments such as these should instead be understood in more profane terms: as expressions of the accumulation, displacement, and transformation of tendencies of previous cycles of mass struggles. Albeit in often obscure and predominantly minoritarian forms, they had been surreptitiously burrowing away, like Marx's old mole, under the surface of what we can now see was only an apparent and decidedly temporary pacification of the "interregnum" of the early years of the century.

The spontaneous rediscovery by Occupy and the movements that followed in its wake of the *aporiai* that had plagued the alternative globalization and antiwar movements—tensions between spontaneity and organization, between the immediacy of revolt and the mediation of organized resistance—provides a clear illustration of the substantial continuity of unresolved problems across the different conjunctures of the ebbs and floods of the social and political movements of the last 20 years. They are challenges that remain just as evident today in the post-crisis, intersectional sociopolitical movements, with their search for the historical memories and organizational practices that could valorize intersectional analyses of the multiple forms of oppression, exploitation, and subalternization in contemporary societies.[18]

The debate on communism can thus finally also be understood, like the debates in the movement of movements, as a "pivot" of transmission. It was one of the means by which the concerns of movements in the early years of the century were formalized and transmitted to more recent cycles of movements. The ultimate political significance of this discussion may thus consist not in any of its own terms of self-comprehension but in how it contributed to clarifying the strengths and limits of the debates that came before and after it.

In particular, the formalizing dimensions of this discussion, read against the grain, might provide a productive point of reference for attempts to comprehend the arc of organic development of contemporary emancipatory politics. Viewed in this way, it might also enable us to comprehend some of the most significant "structures of feeling," in Raymond Williams's sense, that informed the posing of the question of organization in these different conjunctures, from the alternative globalization movement to recent mobilizations on a myriad of fronts.

Between Past and Present

Debates in the movement of movements at the turn of the twenty-first century posed the question of organization in at least three distinct registers:

- First, as active remembrance, or as institutions in which traditions of struggle could be bequeathed, inherited, and re-actualized. This approach posed the problem of the forms of "translation" of the past into the present; that is, not simply the "transmission" of the past in the present but its renewal as a "tradition" in the fullest sense of the term, in an act of transformative inheritance.
- Second, as prefiguration, or as the production of outlines of the future within the struggles of the present. Existing organizational practices were valorized as the potential beginning of alternative forms of more general social organization. This approach represented an attempt to think the possibility of orienting the present toward the future, in a "localization" of utopia.
- Third, as political form, or as the type of political organization that would be able to express and strengthen the demands and goals of the movements. Alternative answers to this question ranged from supposedly "horizontalist" networks to an ostensibly "verticalist" and "traditional" party-form. Despite the substantial differences between them, these positions shared the common project of moving beyond the expectation of what may come, toward its purposive construction.

Transformative inheritance, utopian prefiguration, and political form: these were some of the central themes and energies that flowed in subterranean channels from the alternative globalization and antiwar movements into the debate on communism, and which continue to define the terms and conditions of emancipatory politics today. To map these continuities and transformations is to produce an account of the changing yet consistent structures of feeling that have shaped emancipatory politics over the last 20 years.

Transformative inheritance

The alternative globalization movement had posed the question of organization as one of active inheritance of previous traditions of struggle. Figures from the past were remobilized as "forerunners" of the contemporary movements: Zapata's insurgent peasants in the Mexican revolution, for instance, were evoked to characterize contemporary indigenous struggles for autonomy; the Wobblies in the wake of WWI were called on to provide a model for a new militant labor movement; key figures in revolutionary anti-colonialist movements after WWII were summoned up as inspiration for struggles against neocolonialism.

At their most creative, these debates aimed at the transformative rethinking of those traditions in relation to new demands. It was a question, that is, of the "translation" of the past into the present, in the fullest sense of the term: not repetition of or derivation from an origin but communication and transformation in different contexts. The context of the practical mobilizations in which these debates occurred tended to reinforce these active dimensions.

These debates were nevertheless not always immune, however, from what Walter Benjamin famously called the conformist overwhelming of the present by the past, or in other words, the reverential relation to tradition that is characteristic of dogmatism and sectarianism. Attempts to characterize those movements' exploration of new models of participation and decision-making as a mere restaging of old debates between a supposedly "classical" Marxism and Anarchism, for instance, reduced them to simple re-proposals of known figures and forms.

The debate on communism only a decade later initially seemed to have been inspired by a very different historical sense. Rather than emphasizing potential continuities with the past, it appeared at first sight to privilege the notion of rupture, of the emergence of novelties irreducible to the coordinates of any preexisting situation. "Communism" was in this sense an old name re-signified in order to designate an incompatibility with the reigning order in its totality, that is, including the forms in which oppositional forces had previously sought to oppose it.

Yet from another perspective the debate on communism was fundamentally animated by an attempt to inherit the past in a transformative mode similar to the ultimately "historicist" structures of feeling that informed debates in the movements at the turn of the century. Indeed, the very nomination of "Communism" as the stake of the debate was premised on the notion of a potential "re-activation" of a presently repressed but not definitively vanquished tradition. Both Badiou and Žižek formulated this in terms of a subterranean continuity of the "Idea of Communism," the former in terms of "eternity" and the latter in terms of "persistence."[19] Badiou even framed his argument in strongly visceral terms, suggesting that we might be approaching a new phase of "incorporation" of the Communist Idea.[20]

The implicit theory of history here—as a dialectic between repression and reemergence, between forgetting and remembrance—corresponds to what I have previously characterized as contemporary radical thought's "reconstructive-transcendental style." This attempt to determine the conditions of possibility for future political engagement by reconstructing them on the basis of a (more or less implicit) comparison to previous political formations undoubtedly represents a stimulating thought experiment, in its conception of history as an archive of "models" of political action. But precisely in this emphasis on an "excavation" of the past, it is not as distant from the reactivating dimensions of debates in the movements at the turn of the century as Badiou himself sometimes seemed to think.

Despite Badiou's own post-Althusserian orientation, and in particular his acceptance of the early Althusser's critique of (teleological or metaphysical) "historicism," this perspective nevertheless continues to rely on and imply a certain type of historicism—in effect, a highly stylized or even "aestheticized" historicism.[21] Badiou's invocation of communism as something akin to a Habermasian norm (communism as a meta-historical condition of history substituting for Habermas's meta-social condition of sociability), however, made it more difficult to understand the transformative dimensions of this actualization, that is, the way in which the present could not simply "receive" the past but needed actively to refigure it. Just as in the debates of a decade earlier, the attempt to inherit a tradition pressed up against the weight of all those dead generations.

Movements in the wake of the 2007–2008 financial crisis confronted similar temporal challenges. Benjaminian constellations between past and present abound, as we continue today to search for points of reference and orientation. It is notable, however, that the mobilizations in the wake of the 2007–2008 financial crisis and over the last 15 years have placed a greater emphasis on the construction of consciously "selective traditions" as a mode of reinforcing contemporary experimentation. One of the most dominant modes of radical theorizing over the last decade, for instance—the rediscovery of neglected traditions of Marxist theory emphasizing the integral and not supplementary nature of gender, race, and sexuality—has most often understood the past not as passively given in the singular but as actively constructed by a plurality by contemporary, antagonistic, orientations. Inheriting such potential "future pasts" has therefore functioned as a translation in a profound sense, that is, an interpretation that retroacts back on its object, transforming it in the process.

Utopian prefiguration

One of the enduring achievements of the "moment of Seattle" in 1999 was to have restored utopian prefiguration to its rightful centrality in any form of genuinely emancipatory political practice. The militant assertation of the possibility of "another world" posed the problem of how the present could be experienced not simply in terms of lack of the past but in terms of its potential to become a different future. Prefigurement functioned as a way of actively constructing such a future, already in the struggles of the present. The appeal of horizontalism, for example, as an ethico-political experimentation in new forms of mutuality and collective self-determination, was based in this constructive orientation.

The debate on communism exhibited a similar understanding of the potential of imagined futures to refigure the present. The assertation of the idea of communism functioned in this sense not only as a memory of the past but also as a type of "catapult into the future." For Badiou, "subjectivation" by the idea of communism in the present is the initial form of communist restructuring of society in general in the future.[22] Daniel Bensaïd's notion of the *puissances du communisme*, in a very different way, similarly emphasizes the presence of "traces" of communism in the present with the capacity to grow into genuine communist powers in the future.[23]

The challenge that such positions confronted was that of resisting the reduction of communism to a normative standard to which the present was expected to adjust. This dimension was highlighted by Žižek's response to the charge that a focus on an "Idea" of communism risked falling into the indeterminateness of a Kantian "regulative idea."[24] For Kant, a regulative idea constitutively lacks an empirical referent. It is deployed in a heuristic sense merely in order to regulate enquiry, but explicitly does not figure as a *telos* that such an enquiry could attain. As Kant writes, it directs "the understanding towards a certain goal upon which the routes marked out by all its rules converge, as upon their point of intersection."[25] The inactuality of communism would seem to configure it precisely as such a regulative idea.

However, as Žižek rightly observed, if communism is understood as such a regulative idea—that is, not as a presently deferred goal toward which program and organization strive, or as a hypothesis open to revision in the course of research, but as constitutively unattainable heuristic guide—we would be left with the revival of "an 'ethical socialism' taking equality as its apriori norm-axiom."[26] In an inversion of Bernstein's famous maxim, the goal would be everything; the movement, much less, if not simply a continuous reassertion of the goal itself.

The future here would be conceptualized merely as a "horizon of expectation," to use Koselleck's phrase, or as the present's "inoperativity" (in Agamben's sense)—that is, not as an active construction but as potentiality defined by the impossibility of its actualization.[27] The Communist Idea, that is, would fall back into precisely those abstract utopian dimensions that its proponents claimed had

constituted the chief theoretical weakness of the preceding movement of movements.

How to orient the present to the future without falling into the
abstraction of normativity remains a challenge for contemporary
movements, but their focus has fallen much more strongly on the prefigurative dimension of utopian thought. The International Women's
Strike, with its conjugation of traditions of feminist organization and
trade union mobilizations, for instance, has found its strengths precisely in a fusion of means and ends; ending the normal functioning
of social reproduction is not the goal of this movement, but the immediate practice in which its claims are made concrete and the movement
itself expands.[28]

The relationship between the tactics that are pursued today and
the longer-term strategic perspective that sustains them is thus not
conceived as one of sequential and potentially contradictory stages but
as one of coherence in an immediate and concrete sense. Prefiguration
here ultimately becomes direct figuration: the transformation of what
had previously only been a potential future into a different present in
antagonism with the existing state of affairs.

Political form

One of the central preoccupations of emancipatory politics at the end
of the 1990s was the debate regarding the political forms that could
deepen and extend the movements that were already underway. Did
the struggles against neoliberal globalization require a new conceptualization of the relation between the social and the political, given
that they involved a range of interests and actors stemming from
very different cultural and social contexts? The sheer range of sometimes contradictory perspectives—from ecological crises to indigenous liberation to anti-corporatization and anti-commodification
movements—could only with difficulty be homogenized into existing
practices of politics as expressive representation. Or could the dynamics of those disparate movements be made effective by rethinking
them within a political form derived from previous cycles of struggles,
such as the mass party of the post-fordist era? What was involved in

these debates was a non-formalist conception of political form, that is, a focus on political form not as a static "model" but as the expression of evolving historical tendencies.

The opposition between "horizontalism" and "verticalism," as different ways of conceiving both organizational form and practice, was one of the key sites in which these debates were played out. At stake was not the legitimacy of the notion of political organization as such, as was sometimes assumed by critics quick to reduce the debate to a mere rerun of the clash between Marx and Bakunin that led to the dissolution of the First International. Rather, the debate was about the particular type of political organization that could be durable and effective in the post-Cold War world. As Daniel Bensaïd noted in his response to John Holloway's *Change the World Without Taking Power*, the frequently invoked opposition between "network" and "party" occluded the more substantial issue that lay beyond the mere names: that is, the actual organizational practice that gives meaning to any political form, regardless of what it is called, and sometimes in direct contradiction to the tradition from which it emerges.[29]

The way in which political form was later discussed in the debate on communism demonstrated some continuities with these themes, yet in other respects it was radically different. On the one hand, the focus on political form as a mode of constructing the future in the present was strongly present in the emphasis on communism as a process of subjectivation. Communist subjectivities that are minoritarian today were seen as prefiguring the realization of the Idea of Communism on a larger scale in the future. The construction of subjects to the "truth" of communism (in Badiou's specific ethico-political sense) was thus viewed as an evental site of the realization of the Idea of Communism, in a type of "neoplatonic war of position." Blocked on the terrain of history, communism had retreated to the stronghold of the Idea, awaiting the moment of its renewed "emanation" or even "incorporation" in "courageous" communist subjects, conceived as preludes in a mimetic chain to the moments of a communist program and organization "of a new type," according to a tripartite schema of "grades" of political reality.[30] Subjectivation was here conceived as the intimation of a political form-to-come.

On the other hand, the debate on communism sometimes seemed to lack, when not deliberately to ignore, the extensive engagement with "classical" organizational debates that had characterized discussions in the earlier, alternative globalization movement. Indeed, in its initial formulations, there was even a deliberate resistance to thinking organization as a concrete problem at all. In continuity with "post-Maoist" positions that he had first essayed in the 1980s, for instance, Badiou insisted that what the current conjuncture required was not organizational elaboration in the form of a political party but the more fundamental work of "affirmation" of the Idea of Communism. Only on this basis could organizational practices "of a new type" emerge that would be worthy of the Idea that constituted their ever present, formal condition of possibility.

It was thus notable how quickly the question of organization reasserted itself. Already at the first conference on the Idea of Communism in London in 2009, Alberto Toscano had emphasized that "communism as the name for a form of political *organization*" should be understood as the necessary complement of, rather than alternative to, a philosophical comprehension of the tasks of a communist politics.[31] Subsequent interventions strengthened this tendency. From Peter Hallward's ongoing exploration of the unifying dimensions of a "political will," to Jodi Dean's post-Occupy calls for the centrality of the disciplined agency of the political party, to Bruno Bosteels's engagements with interactions between movements and party in contemporary Bolivia, the most significant theoretical projects to emerge from the debate on communism have all demonstrated important continuities with the themes that animated the organizational discussions at the beginning of the century.[32]

These developments intersected with both short- and longer-term tendencies in the organizational discussion of contemporary emancipatory politics. On the one hand, the felicitous arrival of the moment of Occupy soon after the beginning of the debate on communism provided a concrete problem on which to test out the practical consequences of communism not simply as an idea but as a hypothesis. Jodi Dean, for instance, argued that communist politics called not simply for organization but the specific organizational form of the political party. Far from the caricature of homogenous or "totalitarian" unity, Dean argued that the party—and the Leninist party in particular—should be understood as constituting a "vehicle for maintaining a specific gap of desire, the collective desire for collectivity."[33] In a related vein, Jan Rehmann argued that the nascent counter-hegemonic dimensions of Occupy made it possible to repose the question of the renewal of the mass political party. He emphasized that such a renewal would involve experimentation in new forms of the political party, including notions such as those of a "mosaic left" or a "connective party."[34]

On the other hand, the exploration of communism as an organizational hypothesis intersected with an extended moment of reflection on the practical experience of leftist regrouping internationally over the last 30 years. These include the reconfiguration of the Latin American Left during the so-called pink tide (particularly the experience of the Bolivarian revolution in Venezuela and the *Partido dos Trabalhadores* in Brazil), to the various alliances and fronts formed to engage in parliamentary competition in Europe for shorter or longer periods (with formations such as *Die Linke* in Germany, *Izquierda Unida* and *Podemos* in Spain, *Bloco de Esquerda* in Portugal, *SYRIZA* in Greece, the *Front de Gauche* and *La France Insoumise* in France, among many others). The debate on communism provided a lens through which these developments could be analyzed; but equally, it was itself transformed by the encounter, pushed to reformulate itself in more explicitly organizational terms.

The most recent cycle of struggles—that is, all those struggles in the wake of Occupy and the Arab Spring that have confronted the post-neoliberal consensus and its populist, racist, and nationalist morbid symptoms over the last decade—have been grappling with precisely the same organizational challenges. At times the potentials of more traditional, "stable" political forms have been explored, such as the attempts to "occupy" the US Democratic and British Labour parties in the campaigns of Sanders and Corbyn.[35] In other moments, innovative proposals for mobile and networked infrastructures to support the endurance of social movements have been developed, as in the uneven but steady international of reverberation of the Black Lives Matter movement before its explosion in 2020 as a defining instance of popular response to an unfolding global pandemic.[36]

The intuition shared by these varied experiences is the recognition that the political party, after a long season of minoritarian neglect, has returned as a central problem for the organization of contemporary emancipatory politics. But what type of party is feasible under contemporary conditions? And how should such a party relate to the existing and emerging intersectional, sociopolitical movements of today?

In the Mirror of Party-Forms

Rather than the assertion of the "party-form," in the singular and the abstract, the initial point of orientation for reposing the question of organization today must consist in the actual organizational experiments that have emerged in recent political struggles.[37] The most striking thing about them has been their sheer range and variety, from more or less structured alliances and united fronts to networks and convergences of various types. I propose to view these experiments through the lenses of three exemplary moments or "models" of political organization drawn from the experiences of emancipatory politics in the long twentieth century.

These three moments can be considered significant today not only as historical achievements, or highpoints in the history of the struggles of subaltern social groups within and against the bourgeois integral state. They are also exemplary in a stronger sense, providing us with ways to think how the complex and contradictory pasts of emancipatory politics might be transformed into our potential futures. These three figures are the following:

- First, there is the notion of the "compositional party" derived from the experience of early Italian *operaismo* [workerism] in the late 1950s and early 1960s, reproposed in Hardt and Negri's recent works. This figure thinks the political party as a coalitional process of communication and coordination between proliferating movements and demands grounded in diverse experiences of capitalist exploitation and oppression. Attractive in its ostensible

openness to innovation, it runs the risk of descending into a
type of political "informalism" in which a charismatic instance
deforms the compositional process.

- Second, there is the conceptualization of the party as a unifying
  and totalizing "political subject," theorized most coherently in
  the early work of Lukács in the 1920s. This approach poses the
  question of the political party as an instance of unity of disparate
  interests by means of their reduction to a common denominator.
  It ultimately results in a political formalism, or even a formalism
  of (a thoroughly traditional conception of) politics.
- Third, there is the understanding of the political party as a
  harnessing of political modernity's constitutive conflictuality in
  an expansive and constituent process, expressed most forcefully
  in Gramsci's call for the formation of a "modern Prince." This
  conception attempts to a chart a course between the "occasional
  decisionism" that ultimately results from an informalist resolution of the compositional process and the austere formalism of
  theories of the political subject.

Each of these models or "exemplars," in different ways, capture important dimensions of the experiences of unity, diversity, and conflict
in contemporary movements. Each can in this sense be regarded as a
"mirror" that reflects past experiences, experiments, and hopes into
the present. Deciding which, if any, of these models can help us to see
ourselves anew today constitutes the central organizational and strategic challenge of emancipatory politics.

The Compositional Party

The fundamental problem confronted by the organizational
experiments of emancipatory political movements over the last
30 years has been the challenge of finding an effective way of coordi-
nating the diversity of interests, demands, and perspectives that have
risen up against it. Given the weakening or even dissolution of many
of the traditional mass organizations of the radical left (particularly
at the political level) at the end of the Cold War, there is no center to

hold: things have already fallen apart. The proliferating sites of resistance have thus frequently needed to find ways of acting together,
however provisionally, in order to achieve immediate or longer-term
shared goals.

The way in which this process has occurred has varied, depending on
the issues, contexts, and objectives involved. Among social movements
focused on specific issues—antiwar movements or local ecological
campaigns, for instance—tentative forms of regrouping have frequently occurred in mobile networked forms, more or less enduring
depending on the case. At the strictly political level, it has been notable
that the inherent nature of the political party as an alliance or coalition
of different tendencies has usually not been subordinated to the claims
of ideological purity characteristic of many traditions of the radical left
but instead explicitly acknowledged as the form in which viable mass
organizations can be built today. Indeed, many of the most significant
forays of the radical left into electoral politics in recent years have expressly occurred in the form of more or less durable coalitions of otherwise conflicting tendencies, from the *Partido dos Trabalhadores* in
Brazil in the late 1990s, to *Rifondazione comunista* in Italy at the time of
the alternative globalization movement, *Die Linke* in Germany in the
mid-2000s, and *SYRIZA* in Greece and *Podemos* in Spain in the post-
crisis conjuncture. What I am referring to as the figure of the "compositional party" can be understood as an illuminating metaphor for
comprehending the theoretical significance of this process.

An attempt to renew the political party as a "compositional party"
can be found in the experience of Italian *operaismo* in the late 1950s
and early 1960s. At first sight, this claim may seem paradoxical, particularly given the widespread perception (particularly in the anglophone
world) that this tradition of "heretical Marxism" was defined by a rejection of purportedly "classical" Marxist organizational positions.[38]
It is the type of half-truth of which spurious legends are often made,
based on a particular (and contentious) interpretation of a limited moment of *Autonomia* in the second half of the 1970s. Italian workerism
in its full historical context and development, however, and particularly what has become known as early workerism [*primo operaismo*],
was not opposed to the political party as such. On the contrary, as
Mario Tronti has provocatively suggested, whatever else the workerist

tradition became in the Italian "Long 68," it was also at its origins in the late 1950s an attempt to rethink the political party as an organization of struggle rather than the administrative apparatuses that both the Italian Communist and Socialist Parties had become in the post-constituent phase of the so-called first Italian Republic.[39]

The specificity of the Italian context is here decisive to grasp the innovation that the workerists introduced into the Marxist tradition. For the post-war Italian Communist Party within which many, though not all, of the workerists struggled (often "within and against," to use Tronti's often repeated and almost Augustinian formulation) was not the type of minoritarian "cry in the wilderness" that has long characterized leftist and far-leftist traditions in the anglophone world (an experience that has undoubtedly overdetermined the latter's perception of the former). Nor was the PCI simply a mass party, such as emerged in other countries in Europe and beyond where communists had played prominent roles in the anti-Fascist and anti-Nazi resistance in the war years, such as was the case in France. Rather, the Italian Communist Party was qualitatively distinguished from those experiences by its overwhelming size and social reach, but also, and perhaps even more significantly, by the extent of its involvement in the state formation process of the post-Fascist Italian Republic.

In a very real sense, the PCI was "within and against" the state that it had helped to found. This involved not merely Togliatti's various declarations of a "party of a new type" aiming at a "progressive democracy" (following the mythical "Svolta di Salerno" in 1944), or an "Italian Road to Socialism" (particularly in the wake of 1956). It also included active participation in the constitutional process at the foundation of the Italian republic in the late 1940s. The post-Fascist Italian republic was to be, both Christian Democrats and Communists concurred, a republic in which "sovereignty belongs to the people." But this sovereignty, Italy's founding fathers immediately added, could be exercised only "in the forms and within the limits of the Constitution."[40] It amounted to an immediate disempowerment of those popular initiatives that questioned the very limits of the existing legality and legitimacy formalized in the constitution—precisely the limits that the PCI had originally been founded to contest.

The Italian Communists thereby earned themselves unprecedented room for maneuvering within the existing political institutions, in comparison to communist forces in other Western European states. If they were rapidly excluded from national government already in 1947, they could nevertheless consolidate their hold on significant regional power bases, which in turn reinforced their legitimacy as an essential, albeit subaltern, element in the material constitution of the republic. As soon became apparent, however, this Faustian pact came at a high price. It was not that the PCI's engagement with the "commanding heights" of state power led to its neglect of the life of the Italian popular classes, as if it had forgotten Machiavelli's lesson that one must be "a man of the people [in order] to know the character of a prince."[41] A mass base of 2 million members at its peak ensured that the PCI remained more deeply integrated with popular social and cultural life to a greater degree than any other Western European Communist Party.

Rather, the PCI was compromised by the very nature of the relationship between party and people that the process of statalization presupposed and reinforced. Rather than an active expression of the subaltern classes striving for autonomy, the PCI instead became yet another agent of the processes of subalternization of the social by the political that characterizes the bourgeois integral state's most intimate and essential logic. "Marooned" in the political, the PCI, unwittingly or not, became one of the key supports for a democratic republic "founded upon labor," in a revealingly ambiguous formulation that simultaneously valorized and subjugated the working class movement, as the republic's subaltern raw material.[42]

In this context, *operaismo* represented a return to Marx's "hidden abode of production," to the labor relations and realities that constitute the popular "base" on which the modern State arises as a subalternizing "superstructure." Given the explicitly political nature of those labor relations in the fledgling Italian republic, however, such a turn to labor was never the type of "negation of politics" that many post-New Left critiques have frequently associated with the "economism" claimed to characterize "orthodox Marxism." The focus on the contestation of labor relations was instead necessarily a political intervention, which sought to generate the matrix for a politics of another type, based on workerism's distinctive assessment of the dialectical interaction between the political constitution of the socioeconomic and the social constitution of the political in processes of class composition.

This focus was already present in the pioneering works of Raniero Panzieri and Romano Alquati, and constituted the "red thread" uniting the disparate projects published in the early volumes of *Quaderni rossi*. It was here that the key methods of the workerist theoretico-political program—particularly those of "co-research" (*conricerca*) and "workers' enquiry" (*inchiesta operaia*)—were most coherently elaborated.[43] For Panzieri, it was necessary to study the contemporary levels and forms of "technical composition" of the working classes in transformed relations of production in the postwar period in order to be able to determine the possible forms of their "political composition" in institutions and formations of political struggle—above all, in that of the political party. This necessitated a strategic perspective rooted in the realities and experiences of class struggle, conceived not as a "content" subordinated to the party's "form" but as the material and final cause of the party itself.[44]

Composition was here conceived as an active and relational process, more akin to the dynamism of "structuration" than the fixity of "structure." It issued in a perspective of the primacy of sociopolitical content over political form. The party had meaning only insofar as it enabled this content to express and compose itself into strategic interventions into each and every given relation of forces. Indeed, the "class party" simply was this process of composing the socioeconomic into the "genre" of the bourgeois political, in order all the better to demolish it.

This early project, however, soon pressed up against the political limits that defined it. Divisions among workerists emerged already in the 1960s and intensified in the 1970s into an opposition between perspectives emphasizing the conjuncturally determined tactical necessity of an "autonomy of the political," and an opposed current insisting on the transformation of the conditions and subjects of social movements.[45] This was not, however, a division between a "political" and a "social" inheritance of early workerist themes. Rather, it was primarily a dispute over the *type* of political party that would be adequate for the growth of anti-systemic politics during the changing conditions of the 1970s.

On the one hand, some—Tronti and Cacciari most prominently—argued that the workers' political formation (now understood to be already given in the PCI, rather than to be reconstructed in a new synthesis) needed to exert control over an increasingly bureaucratized state apparatus and rationalized course of capitalist development. It was a task that the bourgeoisie was held to be no longer capable of fulfilling, but which also could not be expected of the workers themselves in the period of declining industrial militancy of the early 1970s.

The autonomy of the political in this context signified an exertion of political force on behalf of, rather than by, the working class, in a consciously historiosophical perspective. In so doing, however, this current ended up proposing a model of political organization that, in practice, was difficult to distinguish from precisely the conception and form of "sovereignist" politics with which the early workerist experiment had attempted to break. From its autonomy, the political soon passed to its Nietzschean "twilight" (*tramonto*), before exhausting itself in a Weberian "destiny"—finally bathetically realized in support for neoliberal labor market reforms.[46]

On the other hand, the experience of *Potere operaio* in the late 1960s and early 1970s, involving Negri and others, continued the attempt to think and practice the possibility of a party "of a new type."[47] The notion of *Autonomia* as an "area" of political engagement to the left of the established parties of the left represented an attempt to keep open the question of the relation between the then emerging new social movements and their potential political expressions, even as the *compromesso storico* (historical compromise) then underway in the PCI closed down the space for any direct political intervention into the existing political formations of the Italian Left. In this sense, the Italian experience replicated the failed generational transmission between older communist and New Left political cultures that occurred unevenly internationally.

Notably, this attempt was formulated in terms of the search for the new political subjects and subjectivities and the organizational forms that would most adequately valorize their potentially revolutionary nature. Subsequent state repression and the dissolution of *Autonomia* as an organized current did not negate the fundamental impulse behind the project of rethinking political organization and its subjects outside the bounds of the sovereign state apparatus. It is a perspective that continued to define, for instance, Negri's theoretical production throughout the 1980s and 1990s, in its consistent emphasis on the self-organizing potentials of a revolutionary constituent power.

Hardt and Negri's collaborative works over the last 20 years represent a sustained attempt to update and internationalize this research project. Appearing in the context of the debates in the alternative globalization and antiwar movements, *Empire* and later *Multitude* were most often regarded as the most prominent expressions of a "horizontalist" focus on the spontaneous capacities of networked forms of political activism, and not infrequently thought to be antithetical to the problem of the political party. Undoubted rhetorical and often organicist excesses aside, however, both books posit the question of organization as their ultimate horizon. This is nowhere more evident than in their attempt to determine the potential of the multitude to assume the decision-making capacities of a properly political actor.[48]

Negri's contribution to a conference on Lenin held at the height of the alternative globalization movement in 2001 had already set out the key terms in which the question of organization was pursued in *Empire* and *Multitude*. How could the multitude, as cipher for the general intellect, achieve organizational consistency, Negri asked?

> In order to make the event real, what is required is a demiurge, or rather an external vanguard that can transform this flesh into a body, the body of the general intellect. Or perhaps, as other authors have suggested, might the becoming body of the general intellect not be determined by the word that the general intellect itself articulates, in such a way that the general intellect becomes the demiurge of its own body?[49]

The opposition was thus marked out as one between what was presented as a classically "Leninist" (in truth, Kautskian) notion of "consciousness" being brought in "from the outside," and the multitude as a sort of Baron Munchausen lifting itself up by its own bootstraps.[50] The hope here, as in *Empire* and *Multitude*, was that the multitude might achieve "self-governance" of itself.[51] But it was a hope haunted by the possibility that, should the multitude fail to live up to this expectation, an "external vanguard" or "demiurge" might arrive "from outside," imposing on the amorphous multitude the "body" that it been unable to achieve on its own.

It has above all been in the later books of their expanding series that Hardt and Negri have attempted to confront this antinomy in terms of what can be understood as a "compositional party." *Commonwealth*, for instance, issued a call for the "becoming prince" of the multitude, in a process described as that of "governing the revolution."[52] One of the significant advances of *Commonwealth* is that it immanently breaks with the spontaneist and arguably even economistic tendencies of *Empire* and *Multitude*, in which the multitude was argued already to have arrived. In *Commonwealth*, explicitly political organization figures not as a supplement to an already ontologically fulfilled political subject, as sometimes seemed to be the case in the previous books. Rather, political organization is here configured as the necessary solution to the multitude's constitutive lack. The multitude is not given, but must be actively made, through a strategy of developing the "revolutionary parallelism" of a manifold of identities into "insurrectional intersections."[53]

"Making the multitude," however, "is not a process of fusion or unification . . . but rather sets in motion a proliferation of singularities that are composed by the lasting encounters in the common."[54] The organization of such lasting encounters is presented as a cathartic process of purification of the "juridical corruptions" that have hitherto prevented the multitude from becoming itself. The aim of this process is to enable the multitude to make the transition from a subaltern technical composition within the "Republic of Property" to self-determining political composition within "the common."[55]

Political organization thus figures for Hardt and Negri in *Commonwealth*, unlike was arguably the case in the earlier books, no longer as something external or additional to a multitude that is already given. Rather, organization is now posited as a potential of the multitude-to-come, a potential to throw off the constraints imposed on it by the terrains of the public and the private alike. It is from this process of liberation, and not as an already given "plane of immanence" (as Hardt and Negri sometimes still seem to suggest, in continuation with the Deleuzian vocabulary developed in *Empire* and *Multitude*), that "the common" emerges, as an artificial construction.[56]

This focus on the multitude's organizational potential and on political construction is continued in *Assembly*. In arguments that directly respond to the blockages encountered by emancipatory political movements over the last decade, Hardt and Negri here focus on possibilities for the emergence of durable decision-making capacities that avoid the descent into any autonomy of the political. It is in the practice of assemblying, or of democratic convergences and encounters, that they identify the political form in which the multitude can act as a force of innovation at the political level in a way that mirrors the innovations that its cooperative production has already to have produced at the level of the socioeconomic. What is decisive is to endow these transformative coalitions of singularities with a material consistency in nonrepresentative and non-sovereign institutions structured by forms of delegacy and revocation.[57] In this way, the long-term strategy elaborated by the multitude would be able to exert an organizational discipline over the tactics implemented by temporary leaderships in any given conjuncture. In effect, Hardt and Negri here propose a theory of "meta-organization," or a theory of the "organization of organization" as an articulation of distinct terrains of struggle.[58]

Perhaps paradoxically, or at least for those readings of Negri that continue to depict him as an arch-anti-constitutionalist, these books readily acknowledge that institutionality remains an ineluctable moment in the formation of any emancipatory political project. Unlike the immediacy championed in *Empire* and *Multitude*, Hardt and Negri now acknowledge that the nature of the multitude as "multiple-singularities," as ensemble of irreducible differences, means that any formation of it into a collective singular could not occur in an organic or expressivist fashion but would necessitate a strategic decision to valorize one dimension of singularity over others. In the words of an older vocabulary, the contradictory socialization within the various levels of the working classes, in the unity and distinction of their experiences of exploitation and subjection, means that their composition at both technical and political levels always occurs unevenly, temporally, and spatially—and it is from this unevenness that the need for organization at all arises.

In other words, *Commonwealth* and *Assembly* ultimately propose, in the very act of explicitly repudiating certain historical formulations of the party-form, a theory of the necessity of the political party—at least if that term is understood as a dynamic process of political composition rather than mere apparatus of command. Hardt and Negri's periodization of party-forms in the twentieth century, and critique of their limitations, in fact elevates the compositional method as a key criterion for determining the type of organization that would be adequate to the current phase of the capitalist mode of production's expansion—and even more crucially, to the multitude's emerging "political entrepreneurship."[59]

Yet if *Commonwealth* and *Assembly* can be understood as making a significant contribution to the renewed discussion of the political party, it is notable that their proposals remain haunted by the image of an external organizational form. This is highlighted by Hardt and Negri's uncertainty in *Commonwealth* regarding the formal nature and agent of this party composition, and in particular, the terms in which they attempt to think organization as the result of an effectively organic transition between technical composition (in the social relations of production) and political composition (at an institutional level).[60] Rather than thinking the specificity of political composition as a strategic intervention that dialectically and retrospectively reorders the technical composition, the "weak" historicism of their approach in this book risks reducing organization to a moment that subordinates the contradictory dimensions of technical composition to a mere "pre-history" of the "truth" that political composition reveals, in a caricatured Hegelian fashion.

Assembly explicitly repudiates any merely linear transition between technical and political composition, for reasons consistent with Negri's long-held claim for the fall of the law of value and the consequently unmediated political command exercised by capital.[61] Under conditions of biopolitical production, technical composition itself (in relations of production and reproduction) is regarded as having already become political composition, in the composition of the multitude as productive organizer both of itself and of society. The notion of a transition between the two different levels that was so central to earlier formulations of class composition is thereby jettisoned, but only by accentuating and making immediate the underlying organicism that it expressed. Rather than changing technical composition determining the need for new forms of political composition, it is now an already achieved political composition that drives innovations at the technical level. The problem of organization is thereby reposed as one of gradations of authenticity within political composition itself.

This is nowhere more evident than the way in which Hardt and Negri remain firmly wedded to a dichotomized external opposition between spontaneity and organization, movement and political form, tactics and strategy. One of the central innovative proposals of *Assembly* regards the future development of so-called leaderless contemporary movements. The multitude, they argue, should be viewed as responsible for the longer-term strategy of contemporary movements, while "leaders"—that is, those operative in more or less formalized contexts of existing political organizations—can be ceded responsibility (within undefined limits) for immediate tactics.[62] The multitude in its plurality is thus posited as the artificer of the strategic framework within which the tactical maneuvers of (conventionally understood) political leaders can occur. What remains entirely unclarified in this conception, however, are the conditions under which the political composition of the multitude as a political actor occurs, or of the mediating instances between tactics and strategy, between spontaneity and organization, or between "apparent" (merely tactical) and "real" (strategic) leaders.

The solution offered in *Assembly* to the Kautskian aporia of the externality of consciousness only displaces and finally reproduces it at another level. In this case, however, it is no longer a question of existing political organizations arriving to tutor nascent spontaneity. On the contrary, it is the "spontaneity" of the multitude that arrives as a disciplinary instance from "outside" existing political formations in order to organize them in a longer-term strategic perspective. The polarities may be reversed, but the form remains the same. In other words, the multitude's organizational status is that of a vanguard. Unlike theories of a vanguard that see it as merely a temporally advanced instance of a more general tendency, and therefore as expression of a movement, however, this is a vanguard that arrives like a Pauline "thief in the night." Unauthorized if not by itself, self-foundational in a strongly charismatic sense, the multitude finally appears as a properly political actor—"the demiurge of its own body"—by functioning as type of decision that decides on itself.[63]

The fundamental problem up against which this conception runs is the problem of "political informalism." Existing political forms—the apparently spontaneous and the seemingly organized—are accepted as given and related externally. It can thus be only an excess of subjective force that decides on the result of their encounter, an excess that can be above and beyond each of those forms only by leaving them structurally in place. Having refused a mediating instance between spontaneity and organization, Hardt and Negri thus ultimately conceive the political composition of the multitude in "katechontic" terms, that is, as a charismatic moment of innovation that continually restrains the temptation of a descent into ossified organizational form. Their informal solution to the compositional problem thus remains arbitrary, if not in the last instance dependent on a vaguely conceived "will to organization" in the abstract.[64]

Hardt and Negri are not alone in adopting such a provisional resolution to an enduring problem. For it is precisely the same indeterminate informalism that characterizes so many initiatives in contemporary emancipatory politics, whether they think of themselves in horizontalist or verticalist terms. Organization is thought as the assertion of a subjective force that disrupts the order of a given situation and its technical and political forms, and not in terms of a dialectical synthesis that aims at overcoming their mutually reinforcing limitations. Advocacy of the "democratic" strength of social movements as a discipline on the political parties that aim to represent them (as was the case in the initial phases of Podemos in Spain, for instance), or counselling that the blockages encountered by recent social movements demonstrate the need for their subordination to enlightened political guidance (as occurred in the wake of Occupy), are in this sense two sides of the same abstract coin. Moving beyond such a schematism is one of our central political tasks today.

The Party as "Political Subject"

If what I have characterized as the problem of a compositional approach's potential informalism constitutes an obstacle to rethinking the question of organization in contemporary emancipatory politics, might a focus instead on reconceiving the form of organization itself provide a more promising orientation? Rather, that is, than attempting to think organization as the external combination of the social and the political, is it possible instead to conceive it in terms of their internal relation, or as a form that is the expression of their immanent fusion? At stake here would be the valorization of an organizational form that would not be partial but total, and that could prefigure in the particular organizational practices of the present struggles of emancipatory politics the principles that should animate a future emancipated society in general.

The Lukács of the final phases of the theoretico-political journey charted in *History and Class Consciousness* provides one powerful model of such a valorization of an innovative political form. The concluding essay of that astounding collection of interventions, "Towards a Methodology of the Problem of Organization," was written in late 1922, in the midst of the broader debate in the international communist movement on the United Front, and before the imposition of the limited party-form associated with the Comintern-directed process of "Bolshevization" (a monstrosity, in the classical sense of the term, that continues to deform communist political practice even today). Lukács argues that "organization is the form of mediation between theory and practice."[65] It is a mediation that operates not in a merely linear fashion, in a teleological sense (the word-become-flesh, or a movement from Idea to Program to Organization). Rather, this mediation reacts back on that which it instantiates. As Lukács argues, "only an analysis oriented towards organization can make possible a genuine criticism of theory from the point of view of practice."[66]

The question of organization for Lukács involved a dialectical integration of spontaneous action of the class and conscious regulation by the party.[67] Sometimes, he argued, this process could even involve a temporary "detachment" of the party from the broad mass of the class. For Lukács, however, this temporary detachment did not lead to the affirmation of any "autonomy of the political." It was instead an argument regarding the specificity of the political moment embodied in the party, and its irreducibility to the socioeconomic conditions that structured the class as a class. It was thus ultimately an advocacy of the "primacy of politics" as decisive instance of transformation. As Lukács immediately emphasized, this notion of provisional separation does not imply what he characterized (not entirely fairly) as a Blanquist strategy of substitutionism. Rather, such a "distance taken" is determined by the uneven nature of the social formation, which Lukács conceives in subjectivist terms as so many different layers and levels of an uneven but potentially unitary consciousness.

Yet rather than positing a fixed limit between fundamentally unbridgeable levels, the detachment of party and class is only momentary. It is representative of the processes of distinction that are necessary for a class to be constituted fully as a class, that is, not only at the socioeconomic level (in itself) but also in political terms (for itself). The temporary separation of party and class is thus thought to be "itself a function of the stratification of consciousness within the class, but at the same time the party exists in order to hasten the process by which these distinctions are smoothed out—at the highest level of consciousness attainable."[68]

In this model, the party relates to the class as a laboratory in which the future of the class is essayed, an "*autonomous form* of proletarian class consciousness" that prefigures, in a particularist form, the disciplined communist "freedom" that it is the task of the revolution to make universally attainable.[69] For Lukács in the early 1920s, the class is reforged into a properly political subject under the pressure of this intensity of the party's conscious discipline.[70] But this reforging is only possible insofar as the class in itself is defined negatively, in terms of its lack, that is, on the basis of its expected but as yet unrealized unity at the political level. Rather than a nominalist description of the real existing multiplicity of struggles at the socioeconomic level, "class" here is instead thought as the potentiality of what can become actual only at the level of the political. The class, that is, is understood as a latent tendency toward unity, a unification that occurs in the encounter of this tendency with the political form that retrospectively validates it.[71]

One of the most common critiques of supposedly "Leninist" conceptions of organization such as that advocated by Lukács is that it implies an elitism of a party that remains "above" and "outside" the movement, in a hierarchical relationship. It is of course a critique with a long lineage throughout the nineteenth and twentieth centuries,

intensified into a quasi-shibboleth in the wake of New Leftist disillusionment with promises of a revival of heretical Marxist currents in
the 1970s and 1980s. The limits of Lukács's organizational proposal,
however, does not reside in its ostensible "vanguardism," or at least not
in the sense in which that term is often understood today. As Terry
Eagleton has judiciously noted, a vanguard need not be understood
as an external or permanent elite, but sometimes might simply be
what it is in a literal sense: an advanced guard, a temporally distinct
element within a broader movement, to which it must remain inte-
grally linked in order to be defined as a vanguard at all.[72] In this sense,
vanguardism—or rather, the fact that some move in certain directions
earlier than the others who later may follow along the same path—is
an unavoidable dimension of any political process, indeed, of sociality
itself.

The limits of the organizational figure proposed in the conclusion
of *History and Class Consciousness* consist, instead, in its reliance
on a figure that can be legitimately regarded as Lukács's own inven-
tion: namely, the curious figure of a self-constituting "political subject." Today, following the exhaustion of the theoretical anti-humanist
moment of the 1960s, the concept of the subject has returned with a
vengeance in broader philosophical discussions (albeit often in terms
very different from those of the subject-as-essence valorized by previous philosophies of consciousness), and particularly in the fields of
political theory and philosophy (as practiced in both academic and
militant contexts). A "renovated" concept of the subject as (contingent) construction is regularly deployed by theorists from a wide variety of otherwise antagonistic political traditions, to such an extent
that it seems obvious that politics is of course something that is "done"
by subjects—of a particular type.

Yet considered in a literal sense, the notion of a distinctly *political*
subject represents either a contradiction in terms or a self-defeating
tautology. Viewed from one perspective, the notion of the political
subject affirms with its qualification precisely that which the substantive denies. For according to the anthropological presuppositions that
define much of modern bourgeois philosophy, the subject (understood
in terms of the interiority of a consciousness) is precisely that which
is preeminently pre-political. Political process can only begin on the

basis of the subject's prior constitution, whether in the ethical (as for Kant) or the aesthetic (as for Croce). The subject is in this sense, etymologically, "that which lies beneath" politics; its autonomy ends precisely there where politics begins.

For a very different perspective, however, the political subject is simply a tautology, repeating itself needlessly. For the tradition of modern thought descending at least from Hegel (if not already from Hobbes) to Althusser, the subject itself is always already political. For Hegel, the subject is a function and expression of the ethical life (*Sittlichkeit*) of the state; for Althusser, it is an effect of the interpellative powers of the state and its apparatuses. But insofar as the very notion of the subject is inherently political, and insofar as all subjects in their generic function are politically constructed, it makes no sense to attempt to identify a specific type of subject that would be more political than any other.[73]

No less anomalous is the notion of the political subject when considered in terms of the history of Marxism. Despite its widespread contemporary usage, one searches in vain for either the word or the concept itself of the "political subject" in the so-called classical Marxist tradition prior to Lukács's intervention. In a literal sense, the notion of a "political subject" is not to be found in the political texts of Marx and Engels. They instead most often use a vocabulary in which notions of political actors, interests, and above all "relations of force" are central. Indeed, it is notable that, after discussions of the subject in his philosophical critiques in the 1840s, Marx rarely uses the concept in his later political texts; when the word does appear in the successive drafts of the critique of political economy, culminating in *Capital*, it is used in relation not to the proletariat, as a "political subject" of revolutionary praxis, but in relation to capital itself, as an "automatic" and "dominant" subject whose expansion is driven by its mode of positing all relations as merely its relation to itself.[74]

Similarly, Lenin does not theorize the party as a "political subject," whether collective or singular, but rather as the site of the construction and intensification of knowledge; such a "learning process" is embodied for Lenin in the concrete form of the agitational slogan, an "objective correlative" capable not of comprehending or reproducing its time in thought, in Hegelian fashion, but of intensifying the contradictions of socioeconomic relations via their articulation with and expression of determinant interests.[75] Nor is the notion of a "political subject" prominent in the works of Korsch and Gramsci, supposedly Lukács's "co-founders" of the tradition of Western Marxism in the 1920s and 1930s.[76]

It was thus not "Western Marxism" in its totality that embarked on a search for a missing "revolutionary subject," as is today sometimes supposed.[77] Rather, this concept represents the young Lukács's own distinctive addition to Marxist vocabulary, or rather, its translation into the concepts of what is arguably more neo-Kantian than post-Hegelian philosophical thought.[78] Unlike the organicism of a compositional approach (in either its variants of a linear transition between technical and political composition or their charismatic conflation), this theory thinks organization as the immanent fusion of the socioeconomic and the political. But this immanence is possible only by according primacy to political form as the measure both of itself and the social content that it seeks to organize. Precisely insofar as Lukács's response to the question of organization ultimately falls back into the assertion of privileged moment that can give to social movements the "comprehension" that they lack on their own, rather than the immanent development of the organizational relations that are already operative within them, his approach starkly presents us with an image of one of the most significant limits that confronts attempts to rethink the political party today as a political subject.

Yet the limits of this constructed political subject are clearly not those that were identified by significant currents of European critical theory in the mid-twentieth century as the limits of the subject that was affirmed as central to the modern Western philosophical tradition since at least the seventeenth century: namely, its "essentialism" and concomitant philosophical anthropology. One of the enduring achievements of the theoretical anti-humanist offensive of the early 1960s was the critique of the ultimately theological dimensions of those theories of the subject, from Descartes to Kant and beyond, that posited it as the bearer of consciousness, an interiority opposed to an exteriority, author of actions that were conceived as the externalization of an interior intention.

This critique emphasized the extent to which the notion of sub-ject as agent (an active, grammatical notion) was not contradicted by but presupposed the only seemingly opposed notion of the subject as "subjected" (a passive, politico-juridical notion). It argued, that is, that to be a subject implies a previous moment of subjection to an authority that "author(ize)s" it as a subject in its constitutive ambiguity, with its Faustian powers. Far from being self-evident or explanatory of actions, the concept of the subject thereby became precisely that which needed to be explained, a result rather than an origin.

It was on the basis of this analysis of the subject as the product of processes of subject(iva)tion that their later occurred a revival of discourses of the subject, particularly prominent throughout the 1980s and 1990s but continuing as a significant pole of attraction today. Rather than the rehabilitation of essentialist conceptions of human agency and freedom for which critics of post-structuralism had fre-quently called, it was instead an extension and deepening of at least some of the dimensions of the initial theoretical, anti-humanist cri-tique of them.

If the subject seemed to have returned, it was nevertheless in a very different incarnation. Rather than given, the subject was now in-stead conceived as effectively a contingent "action of the structure," in Jacques-Alain Miller's influential formulation.[79] Artificial rather than essential in its nature, this subject was thus configured as a complex point of confluence of contradictory tendencies in temporal motion: as a construction, and as a "gap" in the existing structure, the subject was simultaneously determined by the past from which it constitutively subtracted itself, as well as being the herald of a different future, or even the "origin" of a new structure.

It is precisely in these non-essentialist terms that the "post-post-structuralist subject" is most often invoked today. It is also in these terms that its variant of the political subject has been projected back onto the history of emancipatory politics in political modernity. For this narrative, our present is distinguished from high points in revo-lutionary struggles over the last two centuries—from 1789 to 1848 to the Paris Commune, from October 1917 to May 1968—by its lack of the type of constructed political subjects that are thought to have de-fined these conjunctures: "the Third Estate," "the people," "the working class," "the proletariat," "revolutionary youth," and so forth. In accordance with what I have previously argued is contemporary radical thought's "reconstructive-transcendental style," "recovering" a comparable political subject in the present—or more precisely, overcoming its lack—is often regarded as a, if not *the*, fundamental task of contemporary radical politics.

In different ways, many of the most prominent experiments in contemporary radical thought reproduce, unwittingly or not, the fundamental coordinates of Lukács's paradigm. In this sense, despite the profound distances separating his epoch from ours, Lukács can legitimately be regarded as one of the theorists of the current politico-philosophical conjuncture, defining in advance positions that we are rediscovering again today.[80] Badiou's entire political thought, for instance, is structured around thinking the consequences of the notion of the subject for the consistency and endurance of a political intervention. We are subjects to (a) truth insofar as we explore the always retroactive significance of an event. It is the intensity of this exploration that determines both the possibility of fidelity to its universal dimensions (and therefore the emergence of a subject from it), as well as that of its betrayal in forms of abandonment or simulation. In a related vein, though with a stronger Lacanian inflection, Jodi Dean has argued that the subject is not an action of the structure of existing capitalist social relations but a potential gap in them. In excess of any attempt to enclose "collective political subjectivity into the singular figure of the individual," the notion of the (political) subject thus becomes a central way to understand the formation of the conflicted collective body that is the political party.[81]

Above all, however, it is arguably in the later theorizations of Laclau and Mouffe that we encounter the most elaborated and stylized attempts to think the consequences of the constructedness of the political subject. In texts following in the wake of *Hegemony and Socialist Strategy*, Laclau increasingly emphasized that the fundamental and simultaneously impossible task of (radical) politics consists in the formation of a collectivity that would be capable of embodying political order. For Laclau, only insofar as equivalential chains condense into the "nodal point" of a hegemonic subject, a particularity standing in for an impossible universality, does politics occur at all. Politics simply is this clash of—contingent, provisional—hegemonic subjects. And politics conceived in this sense is necessarily "populist" insofar as these hegemonically constructed subjects must compete to represent the "empty signifier" of "the people" that lies at the foundation of the modern democratic order.[82]

Building directly on the interpretation of the notion of "collective wills" explored in *Hegemony and Socialist Strategy*, Mouffe for her part has argued for the centrality for politics of the formation of shared intentionalities. In a type of pacified Schmittianism, democratic politics for Mouffe consists in the "sublimation" of antagonistic oppositions into an agonistic pluralism of competing identifications and the demarcation and negotiation of their frontiers. In whatever way they are regulated by what are ultimately juridical limits (the rule of law embodied in deliberative institutions as check on the descent into hostilities), however, Mouffe's conception of the nature of a "collective will" clearly marks it out as ultimately a representative claim, a claim once again to represent, however fleetingly, the "will of the people."[83] In their different ways, Laclau and Mouffe thus arrive at a thematization of the logical conclusion of each and any theory of the political subject as a unified collective body: the night in which all political subjects are communitarians.

There were at least some tendencies in the earlier season of theoretical anti-humanism, however, that had outlined a critique of the subject in a very different perspective. It is from this vantage point that the political limits of the theory of the political subject can be most clearly discerned. For the "young" Louis Althusser, the fundamental problem with the philosophical theory of the subjected consisted not in its presupposition of an anthropological essence or interior consciousness. Unlike many of his contemporaries (and arguably his own later development), that is, Althusser's initial critique of the subject did not amount merely to a "destitution" of "the subject as *arche* (cause, principle, origin)," or as "constitutive," in order to reconstruct it as "effect," or as "constituted subjectivity."[84] More radically, at least some of the early Althusser's formulations point toward a more thorough-going critique of the entire philosophical grammar of subject–object thought that has dominated modern Western philosophy since at least Kant.[85]

Althusser's fundamental argument consisted in the claim that the concept of the subject (and its mirror in the concept of the "object") was unable to think the primacy of relationality over the related terms.[86] The concept of the subject itself, and not merely its essentialist variants, thereby stood condemned due to its "formalism," that is, due to its privileging of the genericity of a given form over any singular content. The subject represented in this sense is a concept of the priority of order, whether or not that order is thought in an enduring or ephemeral sense. To use terms employed by the later Althusser, it is a representative of the "party of the state" in the philosophical field.[87]

Herein lies the fundamental limits of a theory of the political subject, even as constructed, contingent, and provisional: it is the form of the political subject, as locus of purposiveness and efficacy in the political field, that dominates over the social contents that it aims to unify and to order. It is only by means of assuming this form, however fleetingly, that any movement, protest, or struggle can "count" as political at all; without its subject(ivat)ion, it remains a subaltern expression of the merely social. In contemporary theories of the political subject, just as in Lukács's response to the question of organization in the early 1920s, the social struggles that such a formalist instance should organize are characterized not in terms of their own immanent dynamic but in terms of what they are supposed to lack. Organization thus once more arrives "from outside"—in this case, outside the actual current realities of the struggles themselves.

Contemporary movements of emancipatory politics have been haunted by the legacies of this paradigm over the longer term and in a more immediately urgent sense. On the one hand, over the last 30 years, variants of the political subject have frequently been invoked as panacea for our current woes. If only the regularly occurring outbreaks of protest and rebellion could have unified their disparate demands and interests, it is suggested, they would have been able more effectively to reach their immediate goals—against wars, ecological degradation, racism, austerity, and so forth. At the same time, the tale continues, they would also have been able to pose a more genuine alternative to neoliberalism's continuing dominance because they would have achieved the type of more enduring organizational consistency that is claimed to have characterized previous cultures of oppositional politics. As seductive as this narrative may be, particularly in cyclical periods of defeat and regress, such a hope of rescue arriving from some beyond ultimately reinforces the minoritarian disempowerment that it aims to overcome.

On the other hand, the current conjuncture is increasingly marked by the valorization of just such a formalist political subject, in references across the political spectrum to the centrality of "the people." Whether in the menacing "populism" of the right denounced by liberal good opinion as "undemocratic," or in the scrambling tailism of a left that seeks to win this "populist moment" for its own cause, the presupposition is the same: the possibility of the (re)emergence of "the people as a 'good' political subject."[88] Yet despite claims made by its defenders and detractors, "populism" in its broadest sense (i.e., understood as the unmediated reference to the people as the foundation of political legitimacy) is not a negation of modern democracy or popular sovereignty but their most coherent elaboration. From at least Rousseau's reformulation of the Hobbesian tradition of political order onward, modern political order has been "populist" precisely in its affirmation of a substantive absenting of popular political initiatives and their simultaneous, formalist re-presentation as a "People" unified by and under the tutelage of political elites (even and especially those claiming to be "of the people").[89] It can thus not be a question of "capturing" this populist moment as a way to chart a course beyond it; because populism itself is already internal to the homogenizing, absenting/re-presentative logic of the bourgeois political order.

To think beyond such a homogenizing formalism is a fundamental challenge for the growth of genuinely self-emancipatory politics today. Rather than waiting for the endlessly and constitutively deferred arrival of a juvenescent political subject, what contemporary movements instead need is a theory of organization that can reinforce the expansive dynamics of their current struggles, precisely in their struggles within and against the reigning order's attempted populist capture of their innovations.

The Expansive Party-Form

Is it possible to think the dynamic dimensions of political organization not in terms of a Janus-faced (in)formalism ultimately brought "from outside" but as a process that "condenses" the associational relations already operative in existing social and political movements, intensifying them into forms of self-organization and self-governance? Is it possible, that is, to think political organization not in terms of the affirmation of any particular party-form, or a content that miraculously exceeds it, but precisely as an expansive process? Instead of supposing an exterior opposition between spontaneity and organization, this approach would involve thinking the dialectical relation that always exists between the two in the broader organizational relations of force from which spontaneity emerges, just as in the spontaneous initiatives that regularly transform any organizational form itself.

Such a project would emphasize the compositional processes without finishing in the informalism of subjective force, while valorizing an immanent totalizing process that refuses the fusion of origin and telos in a predetermined, privileged political form. Taken in its dual aspects, it would amount to a search for the material constitution of the political party as a pedagogical laboratory for new practices of ethico-political socialization and self-emancipation.

An approach to the question of organization of this type can be found in Gramsci's reflections in the *Prison Notebooks* from the early 1930s regarding the complex process of formation of a "Modern Prince," conceived as an immanent condensation of political relations. It has often seemed to commentators that Gramsci is also, like Lukács only a decade earlier, a theorist of a unitary party-form, conceived as a political subject. In one of the most famous citations of the *Prison Notebooks*, for instance, Gramsci famously argued that

> The modern Prince, the myth-Prince, cannot be a real person, a concrete individual. It can be only an organism, a social element in which the becoming concrete of a collective will, partially recognized and affirmed in action, has already begun. This organism is already given by historical development; it is the political party, the modern form in which the partial, collective wills that tend to become universal and total are gathered together.[90]

In even stronger terms, he also characterized the modern Prince as a process of unilateral totalization. He argued that

The modern Prince, as it develops, revolutionizes the whole system of intellectual and moral relations, in that its development means precisely that any given act is seen as useful or harmful, as virtuous or as wicked, only in so far as it has as its point of reference the modern Prince itself, and helps to strengthen or to oppose it.[91]

Read on their own and out of context, it is not surprising that citations such as these have led some commentators to see in Gramsci's thought a universalizing synthesis of the dynamism of the compositional party with the formalism of a theory of the political subject. The figure of the modern Prince could then be understood as an updating of Machiavelli's "new Prince," a twentieth-century addition to a sixteenth-century gallery of "innovators." It has even been suggested that Gramsci's conception of political organization has important affinities with Weber's theorization of charismatic domination, Mosca's elitism, or Schmitt's self-referential decisionism.[92]

Such readings derived from the way in which Gramsci's carceral writings were first published in the late 1940s and early 1950s, initially in Italian and later in translation. For Gramsci's original editors, Felice Platone and Palmiro Togliatti, the modern Prince, like so many other novel terms in the *Prison Notebooks*, was to be understood as a "codeword," a mythological euphemism for the Italian Communist Party employed in order to evade the prying eyes of a Fascist prison censor. It was in this sense that the notion of the modern Prince became most widely known throughout the 1960s and 1970s as a type of shorthand for the political party in general, a usage that remains influential today even when the term is invoked in discussions otherwise distant from Gramscian themes.[93]

We now know, however, that the modern Prince signified something more than a tantalizing rhetorical figure at the historical moment of its original formulation, and that its significance cannot be limited to any known version of the political party (a topic that Gramsci was not at all afraid to discuss extensively under its own name). No mere metaphor, the complex development of the notion of a modern Prince in the *Prison Notebooks* points to a distinctive and positive content, to the attempt to name a new practice of political organization, and a new way of conceiving the nature of the political party.

The figure of the modern Prince is not present at the beginning of Gramsci's reflections in prison in the late 1920s and early 1930s. Rather, his early notebooks are dominated by the exploration of the distinctive processes of subalternization that constitute the historical dynamism of the bourgeois "integral state." It is a line of research that is consolidated in the tentative elaboration of the notion of passive revolution, conceived in terms of a substantive and conceptual "failure" of hegemony.[94] This failure gives rise to Gramsci's dawning realization of the exhaustion of his early project. In a Machiavellian sense, it had been a "landscape" drawn from the perspective of the "high mountains" of the Prince rather than from the "plains" of the people.[95] It was necessary to invert the perspective.

The figure of the modern Prince irrupts onto the pages of the *Prison Notebooks* between January and May in 1932, explicitly nominated in just a handful of notes among the thousands that Gramsci writes in over half a decade. Engaging intensively with other anti-fascists readings of the Florentine Secretary, one of Gramsci's primary concerns in these notes is to outline the political consequences for the subaltern classes of a novel reading of *The Prince*. Machiavelli, Gramsci argues, was more radical than even his most "democratic" readers had previously supposed. While that tradition focused on Machiavelli's "revelation" of political knowledge to a hitherto ignorant people, Gramsci instead argues that the true lesson of *The Prince*, and thus the starting point for any modern Prince, consists in a distinctive type of popular realism founded on the "merging" of political power and the political knowledge that seeks to regulate it.[96]

This merging, however, is not a case of the "becoming-Prince" of the people, or of the transition of hitherto atomized subalterns to the consistency of a "People" that has expropriated the Prince's knowledge and his role as organizing instance. This type of "popular" sovereignty—whether understood as the unity of a Rousseauvian General Will, a heterogeneous post-national People, or the singular multiplicity of an intersectional multitude—is for Gramsci not a cure for subalternization but its formalist foundation. It does nothing but change the name but not the place of authority. The modern Prince is instead a merging of political knowledge and power, of organization and association, a merging that deconstructs their distinction. In this process, the subalterns are empowered with a knowledge not of the Prince but of themselves; above all, of the capacity of their own associational forms and practices for self-organization, self-governance, and self-emancipation.

Although it appears only for a brief season, the figure of the modern Prince sketched out "from the plains below" in early 1932 effectively functions as a refoundation and reorientation of the theoretico-political project of the remaining *Prison Notebooks* composed between 1932 and 1935. The institutions of abject subalternity induced by the bourgeois hegemonic project that Gramsci had analyzed in the earlier notebooks under the rubric of passive revolution are re-dimensioned in this transition to the later notebooks into forms of potential self-emancipation of the subaltern social groups. The modern Prince in this sense becomes an absent cause of the later phases of the *Prison Notebooks*, the dramatic discourse that redefines them as a "living book" in which Machiavelli's radical merging of political knowledge and political power is re-actualized.[97]

This perspective has a decisive impact on Gramsci's understanding of the question of political organization in the anti-Fascist struggle in the 1930s. Fascism had reduced the Italian subaltern classes to a status similar to that which Machiavelli had diagnosed in his own time: "More enslaved than the Hebrews, more oppressed than the Persians, more widely scattered than the Athenians; leaderless, lawless, crushed, despoiled, torn, overrun."[98] Only a thorough-going constituent process, and not the arrival of any singular redeemer, could liberate the Italians from the barbaric Fascist yoke. What could be the forms and modalities of such a constituent process of political struggle?

In the early 1930s in Italy, Gramsci argued that such a project needed to involve a renewal of the neglected politics of the United Front from the early 1920s. His repeated calls in this period for a *Costituente* of anti-fascist forces was not simply a re-proposal of the Republican Assembly of 1924–1926, or a suggestion of the possibility of a post-fascist "pre-parliamentary convergence" of political elites, such as later occurred in the pre-constitutional phase of the post-war Italian Republic. Rather, Gramsci was arguing for an expansive Constituent Assembly as a deeper process of coordination of the anti-fascist forces already within and against the Fascist regime, in a durable and substantive, rather than merely tactical or ephemeral, way.

Central to Gramsci's political proposal was the translation of the "living book" of the modern Prince into modern organizational form, a translation that he conceived in the terms of what he had earlier characterized as a type of "living philology."[99] The formation of the "collective organism" of the political party, Gramsci argues, should involve a process of "active and conscious co-participation," "compassionality" [con-passionalità], and the "experience of immediate particulars."[100] When these conditions are realized, he argues, the political party becomes not merely an institution or apparatus, but an ongoing practice of the "living philology" of popular political "relations of force" capable of intervening on the terrain of mass politics. It is this dimension that makes the modern Prince, as an organizational form, something much more than a euphemism for an already known type of political party. On the contrary, as the historically concrete realization of the practice of a living philology, the modern Prince as an organizational form is represented as a process of experimentation in the construction of an unprecedented future.

In their own historical moment, Gramsci's *Prison Notebooks* and the notion of a modern Prince were like a message in a bottle, set adrift against the current of their times. It is a message that arrives to us today as an untimely but yet uncannily contemporary meditation. There are at least four decisive elements of this dense Machiavellian metaphor that are directly relevant to thinking the question of organization in relation to contemporary movements of self-emancipatory politics.

Constituentism beyond Constitutionalization: The modern Prince signifies no pre-existing form of organization. Just like Machiavelli's invocation of a not-yet existing Prince, Gramsci calls for a new form and practice of political organization. The modern Prince is not a "concrete individual," and still less a political subject. Rather, it is a dynamic process, which aims at nothing less than a totalizing expansion across the entire social formation, as a new organization of social and political relations. The modern Prince thus ultimately represents the simultaneous point of departure and summation of the process of the "unprecedented concentration of hegemony" that Gramsci had indicated as the goal of an offensive war of position against the logic of the passive revolution.[101] For this reason, the modern Prince also cannot be limited to its articulation as a new party-form, as decisive as this institutional dimension is to its historical becoming and efficacy. Rather, the modern Prince's distinctive nature consists in the fact that this institutional level represents only the tip of the iceberg of a broader process of collective political activation of the popular classes, in all of the instances of deliberation and decision-making throughout the society. It is precisely for this reason that the modern Prince, even when thought as a party-form, is not an instance of political formalism, for it is a form that constitutively and continuously exceeds its own limits in the practices that it enables. It thus cannot be conceived in terms of "constitutional law, of a traditional type" but only in the non-statal terms of an expansive constituent power.[102]

Categorical Imperative of Self-Governance: The modern Prince, un-like at least some other readings of its Machiavellian ancestor, does not emerge from a "void" in order to impose its unity in a process of transcendental ordering, either in an act of self-validating charisma or miraculous decision.[103] Rather, it is a historical process of the emer-gence of increasingly articulated forms of self-governance throughout the society. It aims to gather up the partial "collective wills" already in motion, but not in order to fuse them into an identity or submit them to a sovereign instance; the modern Prince is not a Hobbesian figure, a type of communist Leviathan. It thus does not signify an or-ganizational form that can be reduced to one of the common figures of modern state theory. For the tradition that runs from Hobbes, via Rousseau, Hegel, Weber, and Rawls, the state is that type of social or-ganization in which unity and stability dominate over difference and conflict, which can then only appear as "un-" or "pre-" political, as the social chaos that (state) politics must organize. Gramsci's proposal for a new party-form develops as an alternative to both the formal and the material constitutions of the existing bourgeois integral state. This party-form does not function as a discrete "political" instance of organ-ization besieged on all sides by the anarchy of the associative "social"; on the contrary, the modern Prince is conceived as a relation of self-governance that invests the social from within. For this reason, Gramsci argues that the modern Prince is to be understood as a "categorical imperative," the "organizer [of a popular-national collective will] and simultaneously active and effective expression" of the same.[104]

Tumult of Collective Conscience: The modern Prince, conceived in this expansive "civilizational" sense, includes within itself processes of disaggregation and conflictuality as constitutive moments. As both political party formation and broader dynamic of self-emancipatory practice, the modern Prince functions not simply as an organization of a political struggle external to itself but institutionalizes political struggle as the very form of its historical existence; a fully and properly political organization that valorizes the conflictuality inherent to political modernity as one of its immanent expansive dynamics. Gramsci thus does not think unity in terms of identity and homogeneity, but rather in terms of constitutive difference as the precondition of processes of differentiated unification that necessarily always remain incomplete. There can be no unification of the identical, which by definition is always already present to itself. Real unification—that is, unification as an active process rather than achieved state—in fact presupposes and requires irreducible differentiation, in an expansive dialectic without definitive synthesis: an "orchestra" that never ceases rehearsing.[105] It is only on the basis of the differences and conflicts that constitute the modern Prince that it can continue to grow, with the productive harnessing of conflict as motor of totalizing expansion, rather than its expulsion or exclusion by the delimitation of distinct subjects ranged one against the other, in a vision of politics that effectively reduces the party-form to a vehicle of militarized parliamentarianism. "The vital question," Gramsci argues, "is not one of passive and indirect but active and direct consent, and hence that of the participation of single individuals, even though this gives an impression of disaggregation and tumult."[106]

Recomposition and Prefiguration: The modern Prince's institutional articulation as party-form functions as an active organizational synthesis of all the levels and instances of the struggles of subaltern social groups. The modern Prince was a proposal for the political recomposition of the decimated Italian subaltern classes within and by means of an expansive party-form, which integrates the strengths of both the "compositional" and "laboratory" party models. On the one hand, Gramsci's modern Prince represents a proposal for a mass party capable of effecting the political recomposition of all subaltern social groups and classes, actively expressing and thereby transforming their myriad interests and forms. In this sense, it can be interpreted as including important dimensions of a "compositional" party. On the other hand, the modern Prince is also conceived as a laboratory for processes of negotiation and dialogue between these differences, recognizing that dynamic leadership is both a necessary consequence of and potential solution to the unevenness and contradictoriness of the historically existing relations of subalternization. This party-form thus represents no "political formalist outside" in relation to the "social" instances its aims to organize, but instead their valorization and mobilization within an ongoing process of "constitutent assemblying." Both process and prefiguration, the modern Prince should thus be understood as a constitutively open-ended new practice of political organization: the "Revolution in Permanence" invoked by Marx after 1848 as the foundation for an autonomous and enduring working-class politics, and continually recalled by Gramsci as the original formulation of hegemonic politics. The modern Prince thus, to echo Marx's reflections on the organizational significance of the Paris Commune, represents an expansive party-form discovered—provisionally rather than finally—in which to work out the self-emancipation of the subaltern social groups and classes.

From the alternative globalization movement, to the debate on the communist hypothesis, to the intersectional sociopolitical movements of today, the last 30 years have been marked by a proliferation of new organizational models and radical experiments. It has been an attempt to find the organizational forms that could correspond to the novelty and particular challenges confronted by contemporary movements, to develop coherently the organizational practices already animating these movements in their particularity into general instances of a new culture of self-emancipatory politics. But it has also been a struggle to reimagine the movements of today in relation to often neglected traditions, at least some of which no longer seem as distant from today as yesterday once claimed.

The cycles of advance and retreat that have marked radical politics in the twenty-first century show no signs of abating, and the challenges for emancipatory political movements in the next decades will, if anything, be even more dauntingly multiple and contradictory than anything we have yet seen. But the concrete utopia of the figure of the modern Prince at least provides us with a visual angle for viewing the goal, nature, method, and form of this ongoing process of collective experimentation: self-emancipation as the simultaneous horizon and reality of our efforts to bring about an end to the current state of affairs.

Conclusion

Contemporary Self-Emancipation

Radical politics in the early twenty-first century has witnessed a series of cycles of struggles, with demands, tactics, and energies from one particular moment spilling over in others. This cross-fertilization of perspectives and orientations has been intensified and accelerated in the intersectional sociopolitical movements of the last decade. Viewed from a certain visual angle, the convergence in a short time period of movements against gendered and sexualized violence, racialization, climate change, repression of trade union organization, or state-led exacerbation of a global pandemic, form something like a collage of denunciations, not of any particular wrong but of the contemporary faces of Injustice as such.

Yet have these movements, either recently or over the longer term, advanced the cause of emancipation any further than the initial stages of protest against the proclaimed post-Cold War "New World Order" in the 1990s? Resistance may abound even today, just as it always does, but does it amount to anything more than an ultimately subaltern reaction? The end of supposedly "progressive" governmental programs in Latin America; the blockages on leftist interventions in parliamentary politics in Europe and North America; neoliberalism's continuing dominance as technocratic governmental logic even in the midst of its seemingly interminable crisis; the rise of far-right, xenophobic, and authoritarian movements and governments on a global scale, with a menacing intensity compared by some to interwar Fascism—the defeat can seem to be general. Is it possible that these defining features of the beginning of the third decade of the century are not merely temporary cyclical refluxes but instead indicative of longer-term trends? Has anything really changed since the deep defeats that marked the 1990s, if not changes for the worse?

Radical Politics. Peter D. Thomas, Oxford University Press. © Oxford University Press 2023.
DOI: 10.1093/oso/9780197528075.003.0006

I have argued throughout this book that the movements over the last 30 years, whatever blockages and setbacks they have all encountered, should be viewed in their totality as a learning process in the challenges of a genuinely emancipatory politics for today. These movements have begun to articulate a new vocabulary of radical political action, based on an intergenerational structure of feeling and modes of response to the diverse processes of subalternization that continue to structure the capitalist mode of production and reproduction on a global scale. The questions that these movements have posed to themselves, in the unity of their differences, can be regarded as a potential aitiology of contemporary emancipation—less explanations than explorations of what radical politics might be able to become.

Gramsci has constituted a privileged dialogue partner for these explorations, not primarily because his work can be read today as a prefiguration of our own concerns, as if his *Prison Notebooks* might be able to say to us directly, "*de te fabula narratur.*"[1] Rather, it is due to the potential for the issues raised by our contemporary intersectional sociopolitical movements to translate his thought in productive and unexpected ways, and thereby to cast new light on—to provide a new "visual angle" from which to view—the very nature of those contemporary issues themselves.

The challenges for an aitiology of contemporary self-emancipatory politics that have been thereby illuminated can be programmatically resumed as follows.

Goal (Final Cause)

Contra the cautionary tales that have re-emerged following the failures of projects of left governance or engagement in electoral politics in the last years, not to engage directly in the struggle over state power would be to retreat once again into the inevitable ephemerality of minoritarianism, whether in the name of a more authentic politics (cultural, ethical, industrial, philosophical . . .), or as a talisman against the risks of "dirty hands" or the lures of a nebulous "reformism." As a condensation and intensification of the manifold processes of subalternization that traverse society, the state remains the central antagonist of any genuinely radical politics today, and one that cannot simply be wished away.

Yet the state, understood in a limited institutional sense as the formal structures of bourgeois-capitalist political power, cannot be the goal of radical politics; rather, as an integral state or social relation of the generalized subalternization engendered within the capitalist mode of production, it is radical politics' terrain of struggle or field of operation. Such an integral state cannot be "seized" or even "smashed" with one decisive blow. Instead, its pervasive logic of the separation of association and organization must be deconstructed in the midst of the struggle against it, wherever and whenever it is encountered, from its purist presentation in parliamentary systems to its quotidian dissemination in the dull compulsion of marketplaces.

A situation of dual power is not something that awaits us in some "after" or "beyond"; it continuously re-emerges in each instance in which the logic of subalternization is contested. To be "more political"—that is, to engage directly with politics as it is currently constituted, institutionally and materially—is the primary means for generalizing these experiences on a mass basis. It is the demand for a politics capable of going beyond the sovereign system of the modern state in all its variations.

Nature (Material Cause)

Yet politics as it is currently constituted in its official forms is not an antidote to subalternization; in its usual reliance on a logic of the absenting of popular and subaltern demands and their re-presentation in the hierarchies of command condensed in the political and juridical fields, it is one of the most potent mechanisms for generalizing and normalizing the experience of subalternity across the entire social field. To engage in radical politics today is to do so in the full awareness not only of institutional or official politics' limits but also of the fact that politics as we know it, even and sometimes especially radical politics, remains an expression of the problems our movements aim to solve. Hierarchies of command, claims to predominance by restricted or restrictive groups, pacifying practices, or structural blockages on

energies and dispositions: none of these experiences are alien to oppositional political cultures, least of all to movements such as those of
today constituted at the intersections of diverse backgrounds, claims,
and goals.

Is there a type of politics that does not subalternize? That is, is
there a type of politics that does not reinforce the subordination of
association to organization on which political modernity rests? To be
simply "more political" within the confines of most current practices
of politics is not, in itself, enough. What is decisive is the type of politics in which emancipatory movements engage, both in relation to
existing political structures, and even more crucially, in terms of
their innovation of new political structures within those movements
themselves.

The fundamental challenge for radical movements today does not
consist in the politicization of supposedly merely social demands, or
their representation at the political level; our intersectional sociopolitical movements have already practically demonstrated the extent to
which political relations of force already traverse all social instances. It
is instead the form and the practice of politicization within movements
themselves that will determine their capacity to grow. The concrete critique of representation as a governing logic of political action through
experimentation in alternative practices of delegation is the first step
toward generating a de-subalternizing "politics of another type."

Method (Efficient Cause)

How such a politics of another type might be done is the most immediate question posed to radical emancipatory movements today. As
the logic of representation always sooner or later falls back into the
separation of organization from association, a key challenge is to develop a way of doing politics that instead valorizes the organizational
forms already at work in associative practices themselves. In this book,
I have argued that a strategically focused conception of hegemony
offers a particularly powerful model of a concrete method of political work that might be able to resist the re-imposition of the logic of
subalternization—but only if this widely diffused term is re-imagined

in terms very different from those in which it is most commonly used today.

We need to abandon the idea that leadership or hegemony is something that could ever be "won," either temporarily or definitively, or that its holder could emanate it down "from above." Hegemony is not a euphemism for authority or even power. It is instead the openness to innovation of an experimental risk. It is experimental in the sense that a hegemonic mode of politics involves making proposals in a given situation that aim to mobilize the widest possible involvement of subaltern social groups in activity to transform it; and it is a risk because such proposals must be made without any guarantee that they will even be heard, let alone be effective. In a hegemonic relation, everything depends on the "followers" realizing that what leads them is only the actualization of their own capacity for self-organization and self-governance.

It is in this precise sense that a strategically focused conception of hegemony provides a method for attempting to transform the demands for emancipation formulated in the languages of existing politics into concrete practices of self-emancipation. For it provides a method of engaging in politics as a learning process in overcoming politics' own limits as decisive instance of regulation of the conflicts that the process of generalized subalternization inevitably engenders. For the diversity of interests and experiences engaged in the intersectional sociopolitical movements of today, this type of hegemony as a method of political work represents not a goal of the preeminence of any one movement but a common path along which those movements can travel at their own speeds.

Form (Formal Cause)

Reports of the death of the political party as an essential dimension of the organization of emancipatory politics have been greatly exaggerated since at least the 1960s. Behind most of these claims lie myths about the nature of a supposedly "real" political party as a vehicle of static unity, rather than as a site of contentious and incomplete unification, as all historically significant mass political parties have been. Not even the palpable evidence of a veritable explosion in new political parties of the subaltern social classes and groups in numerous countries over the last decades have been enough to quell these rumors; the notion of some more desirable form of organization beyond the political party is sometimes still offered today as panacea for our supposed paralysis, even in the midst of novel organizational experiments on a global scale.

It is not the historical durability or conjunctural success of any particular political party formation that gives the lie to these perspectives; it is rather the consistency with which the political party has continuously been reproposed, either as goal or horizon, but always as an open question, historically and today. The question of organization can be posed realistically and concretely only if we leave such prejudices behind and acknowledge that, in the field of politics, conflict cannot be avoided or expelled but only valorized and made productive. This includes conflicts inside a political party itself. The problem that the political party has always designated—namely, how a diversity of interests and experiences could be empowered and coordinated in a shared struggle against their antagonists—remains as important today for radical politics as it has ever been. Indeed, in a period characterized by a diversity of movements and cycles of struggles, it has become even more central, as the reality of the intersections between them, whether those intersections call themselves or are known as a political party or not.

For the names are not ultimately as important as the actuality of the facts, and all reports based on these facts concur: ours is a period of proliferating and persistent translations between movements and protests of rebellion of the subaltern social classes and groups on multiple fronts. The real question of organization today regards how these intersecting movements can continue to grow alongside and within each other, in an expansive process of de-subalternization, as the self-organization of association. The creative forms of "constituent assemblying" occurring in these movements offer us a powerful reminder and concrete example of the categorical imperative that has always governed the very idea of radical politics: self-emancipation.

Notes

Introduction

1. G. W. F. Hegel, *Phenomenology of Spirit*, trans. A. V. Miller (Oxford: Oxford University Press, 1977), 6.

2. The notion of "Intersectional Sociopolitical Movements" is used in this book to designate those radical emancipatory movements (such as, e.g., Black Lives Matter, the International Women's Strike, Ni Una Menos, and the radical wing of the environmentalist movement, among many others) that have emerged in the wake of the global financial crisis of 2007–2008 as an intersection of demands and claims based on class, race, gender, and sexuality, among other lived experiences of injustice. "Intersectional" is thus understood here in more generic terms than those at work in the more strictly juridical conception at the base of Kimberlé Crenshaw's initial interventions, or the subjectivist focus that has been prominent in the subsequent development of intersectionality theory. The "Intersectional Sociopolitical Movements" of today can be further distinguished from the "New Social Movements" prominent in debates of the 1980s to the extent that the fundamental dynamic of these more recent movements has not been configured as an opposition between supposedly "class-based" interests (understood in economistic terms) and ostensibly "identity-centric" claims. Many recent movements have instead been characterized by an explicit acknowledgment, and deliberate operationalization, of the political construction of both the lived experience of class (conceived expansively) and various other identities in the context of concrete political projects.

3. Marx memorably formulated this as the "*categorical imperative to overthrow all relations* in which the human [*der Mensch*] is a debased, enslaved, forsaken, despicable being"; see Karl Marx, "A Contribution to the Critique of Hegel's Philosophy of Right. Introduction," in *Marx Engels Collected Works*, Volume 3 (London: Lawrence & Wishart, 1975–2005), 182.

4. In this book, the notions of popular or subaltern social groups and classes are used interchangeably, following their formulation in Antonio

Gramsci's *Prison Notebooks*. As I explore further in chapter 2, one of the analytic advantages of a vocabulary of subalternization is that it enables us to comprehend the relations of subordination, expropriation, and command that structure a society divided into classes, simultaneously both economically (in terms of disposal over capital or subjection to the commodification of labor power) and politically (in the separation of association from organization)—with each instance overdetermining the other historically and logically. Viewed in the expansive optic of subalternization, class should therefore be understood not in terms of a structural reduction to a common denominator (of whatever type) but as the zone of overlap in a Venn diagram in which sometimes radically diverse lived experiences encounter the temporary unity of their differences in the shared process of struggling against them.

5. Regarding the problematic "socialism for the twenty-first century" in general, see Michael Lebowtiz, *Build it Now: Socialism for the Twenty-first Century* (New York: Monthly Review Press, 2006). On the potentials and contradictions of the Bolivarian revolution in Venezuela, see George Ciccariello-Maher, *We Created Chávez: A People's History of the Venezuelan Revolution* (Durham: Duke University Press, 2013). A prescient early analysis of the limitations of left governance in Brazil can be found in Alvaro Bianchi and Ruy Braga, "Brazil: The Lula Government and Financial Globalization," *Social Forces* 83, no. 4 (2005): 1745–1762. Jeffery Webber provides a critical overview of developments in Bolivia in *From Rebellion to Reform in Bolivia: Class Struggle, Indigenous Liberation, and the Politics of Evo Morales* (Chicago: Haymarket, 2011).

6. Q3, §34, p. 311, June–July 1930. References to Gramsci's *Prison Notebooks* are given to the Italian critical edition: Antonio Gramsci, *Quaderni del carcere*, ed. Valentino Gerratana (Turin: Einaudi, 1975). I follow the internationally established standard of notebook number (Q), number of note (§), and page reference. The English critical edition of the *Prison Notebooks*, translated by the late Joe Buttigieg, currently includes notebooks 1–8. Dates of the composition of individual notes are given according to the chronology established by Gianni Francioni and the revisions contained in the appendix to Giuseppe Cospito, "*Verso l'edizione critica e integrale dei Quaderni del carcere*," *Studi storici* LII, no. 4 (2011): 896–904.

7. Drawing on a figure in Walter Benjamin, Wendy Brown proposed the notion of left melancholia in her homage to the thought of Stuart Hall in order to comprehend a type of traditionalism on the left that remained narcissistically attached to past verities. See Wendy Brown, "Resisting Left Melancholy," *Boundary* 2, no. 26: 3 (1999), 19–27. For a recent attempt

to think through the contradictions of left melancholia in a dialectical fashion, see Enzo Traverso, *Left-Wing Melancholia* (New York: Columbia University Press, 2017).

8. Hegel, *Phenomenology of Spirit*, 6–7.

9. Sigmund Freud, "The Aetiology of Hysteria" (1896), in *The Standard Edition of the Complete Psychological Works of Sigmund Freud*, vol. 3 (London: Hogarth Press, 1962).

10. Aristotle, *Metaphysics*, 1013a et seq.

11. A synthesis of some of the most significant findings of this season of philological and historical studies, largely but not only centered in the Italian discussion, is provided by the entries collected in *Dizionario gramsciano 1926-1937*, ed. Guido Liguori and Pasquale Voza (Rome: Carocci, 2009), building on the earlier pioneering collection *Le parole di Gramsci: per un lessico dei "Quaderni del carcere"*, ed. Fabio Frosini and Guido Liguori (Rome: Carocci, 2004). A summary of recent historical research can be found in Angelo D'Orsi's *Gramsci: una nuova biografia* (Milan: Feltrinelli, 2017). Curiously, despite the widespread reference to Gramsci's thought in the anglophone world, consultation of the recent Italian scholarship that has redefined our understanding of his thought remains the exception and not the rule.

12. See in particular Q11, §47, p. 1468, August–December 1932. As recent studies have emphasized, Gramsci's distinctive notion of "translatability" is central to the philosophical and political proposals of the *Prison Notebooks*. See Derek Boothman, *Traducibilità e processi traduttivi. Un caso: A. Gramsci linguista* (Perugia: Guerra Edizioni, 2004) and Peter Ives and Rocco Lacorte, eds., *Gramsci, Language and Translation* (Lanham, MD: Lexington Books, 2010).

13. On the temporal distinctiveness of Walter Benjamin's reflections of translation in relation to the mimetic tradition, see Andrew Benjamin, *Translation and the Nature of Philosophy. A New Theory of Words* (London: Routledge, 1989). I have previously explored some of these themes in relation to both Benjamin and Gramsci in Peter Thomas, ' "The Tasks of Translatability," ' *International Gramsci Journal* 3, no. 4 (2020): 5–30.

14. Ernesto Laclau and Chantal Mouffe, *Hegemony and Socialist Strategy: Towards a Radical Democratic Politics*, trans. Winston Moore and Paul Cammack (London: Verso, 1985).

15. Translations of both Kant's original intervention of 1796, "On a Newly Arisen Superior Tone in Philosophy" [*Von einem neuerdings erhobenen vornehmen Ton in der Philosophie*], and Derrida's later influential commentary on it, "On a Newly Arisen Apocalyptic Tone in Philosophy,"

can be found in *Raising the Tone of Philosophy: Late Essays by Immanuel Kant, Transformative Critique by Jacques Derrida*, ed. by Peter Fenves (Baltimore: Johns Hopkins University Press, 1998).

16. On the way in which Weber's class allegiances shaped his social theory, see Jan Rehmann, *Max Weber: Modernisierung als passive Revolution* (Hamburg/Berlin: Argument, 1998).

17. "Iron cage" was the translation adopted by Talcott Parsons, not unproblematically, to render Weber's use of *stahlhartes Gehäuse* in *The Protestant Ethic and the Spirit of Capitalism*. As Peter Baehr notes, while this translation choice can be contested and arguably reduces the complex resonance of Weber's original formulation, it has nevertheless become a significant figure in its own right. See Peter Baehr, "The 'Iron Cage' and the 'Shell as Hard as Steel': Parsons, Weber, and the *Stahlhartes Gehäuse* Metaphor in the Protestant Ethic and the Spirit of Capitalism," *History and Theory* 40, no. 2 (2001): 153–169.

18. *Sedimentation* and *reactivation* were the terms used by Laclau and Mouffe to characterize their approach to the history of Marxist theory. As they later noted, it was their critics who forcefully emphasized the post-Marxist dimensions of their work, though they were content both to adopt the characterization and arguably to deepen it in their later work. See Ernesto Laclau and Chantal Mouffe, *Hegemony and Socialist Strategy: Towards a Radical Democratic Politics*, 2nd ed. (London: Verso, 2001), viii–ix.

19. Sigmund Freud, "Mourning and Melancholia," in *The Standard Edition of the Complete Psychological Works of Sigmund Freud*, vol. 14 (London: Hogarth Press, 1957).

20. For instance, Joshua Clover's recent periodizing narrative—the Age of Riots giving way to the Age of Strikes before returning to Riot "prime"—draws on the type of philosophy of history that animated many dimensions of debates over "postmodernism" and "postfordism" in the 1980s and 1990s, while seeking to ground it in an Arrighian conception of transformations in the world system since the 1970s. See Joshua Clover, *Riot. Strike. Riot: The New Era of Uprisings* (London: Verso, 2016). For a critique of the limits of this conceptualization of our contemporaneity, see Alberto Toscano, "Limits to Periodization," *Viewpoint*, September 6, 2016.

21. Reinhart Koselleck, *Futures Past: On the Semantics of Historical Time*, trans. Keith Tribe (New York: Columbia University Press, 2004).

22. Antonio Negri, *The Savage Anomaly: The Power of Spinoza's Metaphysics and Politics*, trans. Michael Hardt (Minneapolis: University of Minnesota Press, 1991 [1981]), 229.

23. Alain Badiou, *The Century*, trans. Alberto Toscano (London: Polity Press, 2007 [2005]).

24. See Agamben's expanding *Homo Sacer* series and the return to the Greeks via the 1840s undertaken by Jacques Rancière between his *Proletarian Nights,* trans. John Drury (London: Verso, 2012 [1981]) and *On the Shores of Politics*, trans. Liz Herron (London: Verso, 1995 [1992]).

25. Among the journals founded over the last 30 years in which a re-imagining of what the signifier "Marxism" might mean today has taken place are (in the anglophone world) *Rethinking Marxism, Historical Materialism, Viewpoint, Jacobin,* and *Spectre,* among many others. In France, the slightly older project of *Actuel Marx* has been joined by new initiatives such as *Contre Temps* and *Période.* The international project of *Das historisch-kritische Wörterbuch des Marxismus (HKWM)*, based in Germany, represents both a continuity with older new leftist traditions and their renewal by a younger generation. Similarly, journals such as *Critica marxista* in Italy, and *Outubro revista* and *Crítica marxista* in Brazil, to mention only some of the bright points in an expanding international galaxy of new publications, represent original forms of exploration of the plurivocality of the international Marxist tradition.

26. Hegel, *Phenomenology of Spirit*, 492.

27. The notion of an "anxiety of influence," as the conscious and unconscious practices by means of which a tradition is constructed, is used here in the sense famously proposed by Harold Bloom in *The Anxiety of Influence: A Theory of Poetry* (New York: Oxford University Press, 1973).

28. Niccolò Machiavelli, "Letter to Francesco Vettori, December 10, 1513," in *Machiavelli and his Friends. Their Personal Correspondence,* trans. James Atkinson and David Sices (DeKalb: Northern Illinois University Press, 2004), 265.

29. Karl Marx, *The Eighteenth Brumaire of Louis Bonaparte, Marx Engels Collected Works,* vol. 11 (London: Lawrence & Wishart, 1975–2005), 104–6.

30. Marx, *Eighteenth Brumaire,* 104–6.

31. Norberto Bobbio, *Teoria generale della politica* (Turin: Einaudi, 1999), 70.

32. Fredric Jameson, "Marx and Montage," *New Left Review* 58 (July/August 2009).

33. Jameson, "Marx and Montage."

34. For an early formulation of this argument, see Massimiliano Tomba, *La "vera politica." Kant e Benjamin: la possibilità della giustizia* (Macerata: Quodlibet, 2006); and more recently, *Insurgent Universality: An Alternative Legacy of Modernity* (New York: Oxford University Press, 2019).

35. Notions of endurance, recollection, and de-foreclusion inform the approaches of some of the most significant recent studies of Gramsci, including Alberto Burgio's *Gramsci storico* (Bari: Laterza, 2002),; Fabio Frosini's *Gramsci e la filosofia* (Rome: Carocci, 2003),; Guido Liguori's *Sentieri gramsciani* (Rome: Carocci, 2006); Wolfgang Fritz Haug's *Philosophieren mit Gramsci und Brecht* (Hamburg/Berlin: Argument, 2006),; Alvaro Bianchi's, *O laboratório de Gramsci: Filosofia, História e Política* (São Paolo: Alameda, 2008); and Kate Crehan's Gramsci's *Common Sense: Inequality and its Narratives* (Durham: Duke University Press, 2016). I have previously explored Gramsci's thought in these terms in Peter D. Thomas, *The Gramscian Moment. Philosophy, Hegemony and Marxism* (Leiden: Brill, 2009).

Chapter 1

1. Daniel Bensaïd, "On the Return of the Politico-Strategic Question," *International Viewpoint* IV, no. 386, February 2007. https://internationalvi ewpoint.org/spip.php?article1199.

2. John Holloway, *Change the World without Taking Power* (London: Pluto, 2002); Jacques Rancière, *Disagreement: Politics and Philosophy*, trans. Julie Rose (Minneapolis: University of Minnesota Press, 1999); Alain Badiou, *Metapolitics*, trans. Jason Barker (London: Verso, 2005).

3. Michael Hardt, "The Withering of Civil Society," *Social Text*, no. 45 (Winter, 1995): 27–44; Michael Hardt and Antonio Negri, *Empire* (Cambridge: Harvard University Press, 2000), 212; Michael Hardt and Antonio Negri, *Assembly* (New York: Oxford University Press, 2017), 139.

4. For an example of the ways in which these translations have occurred, see the two quite different assessments of Álvaro García Linera's thought and practice offered by Bruno Bosteels sympathetic analysis in *The Actuality of Communism* (London: Verso, 2011), 225–268; and Jeffery Webber's sharp critique of García Linera's evolution in "Burdens of a State Manager," *Viewpoint*, February 25, 2015.

5. *Transformism* refers to the political culture of cooption, absorption, and not infrequently open corruption that characterized the post-*Risorgimento* Italian liberal state in the late nineteenth and early twentieth century. Gramsci saw it as fundamental not only to the development of the modern state in Italy but potentially to passive revolutionary processes in general. See Q8, §36, p. 962, February 1932.

6. In different ways, with their notions of neoliberalism's "hollowing out" or "depletion" of contemporary liberal democracy, Wendy Brown, Pierre Dardot, and Christian Laval fail to register the extent to which liberal representative democracy has always been—and continues to be today—constituted around a "center made absent," or the unruly practices of popular power that the modern state constitutively seeks to reduce to the merely social in need of political regulation. See Wendy Brown, *Undoing the Demos: Neoliberalism's Stealth Revolution* (New York: Zone, 2015); Pierre Dardot and Christian Laval, *The New Way of the World: On Neoliberal Society* (London: Verso 2013 [2009]).

7. Recent work has given us greater knowledge of the deeper historical roots of the open contradictions between neoliberal theory and practice vis-à-vis the state rightly noted by David Harvey. See David Harvey, *A Brief History of Neoliberalism* (Oxford: Oxford University Press, 2005), 70ff.; Quinn Slobodian, *Globalists: The End of Empire and the Birth of Neoliberalism* (Cambridge: Harvard University Press, 2018); Johanna Bockman, *Markets in the Name of Socialism: The Left-wing Origins of Neoliberalism* (Stanford: Stanford University Press, 2011).

8. On the strengths and limits of Polanyi's approach to such questions, see Gareth Dale, *Karl Polanyi: The Limits of the Market* (Cambridge: Polity, 2010).

9. On the contradictions of the state under neoliberalism, see Richard Seymour, *Against Austerity: How We Can Fix the Crisis They Made* (London: Pluto, 2014).

10. On the complex temporal dialectic between the oppositional and the alternative, see Raymond Williams, *Marxism and Literature* (Oxford: Oxford University Press, 1977), 113–114.

11. Mario Tronti, *Operai e capitale* (Rome: DeriveApprodi, 2006 [1966]); *Workers and Capital*, trans. David Broder (London: Verso 2019). Steve Wright's *Storming Heaven: Class Composition and Struggle in Italian Autonomist Marxism* (London: Pluto, 2002), remains an indispensable synthetic overview of the development of early workerism.

12. Different conceptions of the precise nature of Tronti's heresy can be found in Sara R. Farris, "Inimical Incursions: On Mario Tronti's Weberianism," *Historical Materialism* 19, no. 3 (2011): 29–62; and Étienne Balibar, "A Point of Heresy in Western Marxism: Althusser's and Tronti's Antithetic Readings of *Capital* in the Early 1960s," in *The Concept in Crisis: Reading Capital Today*, ed. Nick Nesbitt (Durham: Duke University Press, 2017), 93–112.

13. Tronti, *Operai e capitale*, "Poscritto di problemi," 269–315.

14. Mario Tronti, "Estremiso e riformismo," *Contropiano* 1 (1968): 41–58. In retrospect, this text can be seen as a decisive transition to Tronti's later "neo-reformism," particularly in its advocacy of a workers' political management of capitalist development.

15. Mario Tronti, *Sull'autonomia del politico* (Milan: Feltrinelli, 1977). In addition to the homonymous seminar from December 1972, this edition also includes "The Two Transitions" [*Le due transizioni*] from April 1976.

16. Tronti, *Sull'autonomia del politico*, 10.

17. *Sull'autonomia del politico*, 58. Tronti himself notes a certain irony in his use of the notion of "hegemony" in this context, precisely at the moment when he is proposing ideas that are effectively indistinguishable from Togliatti's championing of a hegemonic political strategy in the post-1956 conjuncture, against which much of Tronti's thought in the last 1950s and early 1960s had been defined. On the novelty of hegemony as a "political language" in 1950s Italy, see Francesca Chiarotto, "I primi dieci anni (1948–1958). Note sulla ricezione del Gramsci teorico politico: la fortuna dell'egemonia," in *Egemonie*, ed. Angelo D'Orsi (Naples: Edizione Dante & Descartes, 2008), 65–76.

18. Tronti, *Operai e capitale*, 87. I use "originary" here in the sense of Marx's characterization of "originary accumulation" (*ursprüngliche Akkumulation*—frequently and, in my view, misleadingly translated as "primitive accumulation")—not as a temporal stage preceding fully mature capitalist social relations but as their continually reproduced structural precondition. Tronti's valorization of workers' struggles over capitalist development exhibits the same logico-structural emphasis.

19. Tronti's conception of the potential "advance" of politics, as instance of command over the economic, is configured in terms reminiscent of Aristotle's definition of the capacity "to foresee with his mind"—to plan and program the future already in the present—as the foundation of the master's "natural" dominance over the slave. See Aristotle's *Politics*, Book I, 1252a.

20. Tronti's interest in the late 1960s and 1970s was directed in particular to the era of originary accumulation in England during the revolutionary events of the 1640s; see Mario Tronti, ed., *Il politico. Antologia di testi del pensiero politico. 1: Da Machiavelli a Cromwell* (Milan: Feltrinelli, 1979). Slightly later in the anglophone world, seemingly without any knowledge of Tronti's work, Robert Brenner and Ellen Meiksins Wood developed a comparable approach on the basis of similar materials, though they ended up drawing quite different political conclusions. See, among other exemplary works, Robert Brenner, "The Origins of Capitalist

Development: A Critique of Neo-Smithian Marxism," *New Left Review* I, no. 104 (July/August 1977): 25–92; Ellen Meiksins Wood, *The Pristine Culture of Capitalism* (London: Verso, 1992).

21. Foremost among these is Antonio Negri, who has repeatedly distinguished between a "good Tronti" of the early 1960s (to which Negri continues without hesitation to affiliate his own work) and the "bad Tronti" who broke away from his workerist origins. For Negri's most recent (and most devastating) rehearsal of this argument, see "*Sull'autonomia del politico di Tronti,*" Paris, 5 (April 2019), available at http://www.euronomade.info/?p=11933. Riccardo Bellofiore's diagnosis of the theoretical weaknesses of the early Tronti's conceptualization of labor power, however, provides some of the reasons for suggesting that Tronti's evolution may exhibit more continuities than Negri supposes. See Riccardo Bellofiore, " 'L'operaismo degli anni '60 e la critica dell'economia politica," *Unità proletaria*, no. 1–2 (1982). From a very different perspective, see also the argument for an underlying continuity in Tronti's evolution offered by Andrew Anastasi and Matteo Mandarini, "A Betrayal Retrieved: Mario Tronti's Critique of the Political," *Viewpoint*, February 25, 2020, https://viewpointmag.com/2020/02/25/a-betrayal-retrieved-mario-trontis-critique-of-the-political/.

22. For a sharp critique of the "residues" of historicism in Tronti's thought, see Massimiliano Tomba, "Tronti e le contraddizioni dell'operaismo," *Erre*, no. 22 (2007): 27–32. *Politics and Destiny* (*Politica e destino*) was the title of Tronti's final lecture at the University of Sienna in 2001. See Mario Tronti et al., *Politica e destino* (Milan/Bologna: Luca Sossella Editore, 2006).

23. Central here were the reflections of Carlos Nelson Coutinho, already at the end of the 1970s inspired by the approach of the Italian Communist Party leader Berlinguer, in the famous text "A democracia como valor universal," *Encontros com a Civilização Brasileira*, no. 9 (March 1979): 33–48.

24. Among the best studies of Poulantzas's thought remain those of Bob Jessop and Alex Demirović from the 1980s. See Bob Jessop, *Nicos Poulantzas: Marxist Theory and Political* Strategy (London: Palgrave Macmillan, 1985); Alex Demirović, *Nicos Poulantzas: eine kritische Auseinandersetzung* (Hamburg/Berlin: Argument, 1987).

25. Michel Foucault, *The History of Sexuality Volume I: An Introduction,* trans. Robert Hurley (New York: Vintage Books, 1978), 88–89. The theme is explored at greater length and in more nuanced forms in Foucault's lectures in the mid-to-late 1970s; for an analysis of their context, see Stuart Elden, *Foucault's Last Decade* (Cambridge: Polity, 2016).

26. Norberto Bobbio, "Esiste una dottrina marxista dello Stato?," *Mondoperaio* 28, no. 8–9 (August–September 1975): 24–31.

27. Notable exceptions include the authors of the texts collected in Stanley Aronowitz and Peter Bratsis, ed., *Paradigm Lost: State Theory Reconsidered* (Minneapolis: University of Minnesota Press, 2002).

28. Alongside re-editions of Poulantzas's major works, previously untranslated texts have been made available in English in *The Poulantzas Reader*, ed. James Martin (London: Verso, 2008). Among the many recent significant collections and special journal issues on the historical and contemporary significance of Poulantzas's thought, see Lars Bretthauer, Alexander Gallas, John Kannankulam, and Ingo Stützle, ed., *Poulantzas lesen: Zur Aktualität marxistischer Staatstheorie* (Hamburg: VSA, 2006); Jean-Numa Ducange and Razmig Keucheyan, ed., *La fin de l'État démocratique. Nicos Poulantzas, un marxisme pour le XXIᵉ siècle* (Paris: PUF, 2016).

29. Witness, for example, the diffuse presence of Poulantzian motifs in Chantal Mouffe's conversations with Íñigo Errejón in *Podemos: In the Name of the People* (London: Lawrence & Wishart, 2016), particularly p. 125: "We need a synergy between electoral competition and the wide range of struggles that take place in the social arena. It's clear that the democratic demands that exist in our societies cannot find an expression solely through the vertical party form, that they also need horizontal forms of expression. A new form of political organization that articulates the two modes—that's how I conceive 'left-wing populism.'"

30. Christine Buci-Glucksmann was the first to suggest such a close affinity, noting the presence of Gramscian themes in Poulantzas's work even from the time of *Political Power and Social Classes*; see Christine Buci-Glucksmann, "A propos de la théorie marxiste de l'Etat capitaliste: vers une conception nouvelle de la politique," *L'Homme et la Société* 11 (1969): 199–207.

31. Nicos Poulantzas, *Political Power and Social Classes* (London: NLB, 1978). For Althusser's early critique of Gramsci's historicism, see Louis Althusser, "Marxism Is not a Historicism," in *Reading Capital: The Complete Edition*, ed. Louis Althusser, Étienne Balibar, Roger Establet, Jacques Rancière, and Pierre Macherey (London: Verso, 2015 [1965]).

32. Poulantzas, *Political Power*, 39; see also 138–139, 194, 197, 201.

33. Poulantzas, 195.

34. Poulantzas, 226. The claim was later repeated almost verbatim by Perry Anderson ("The Antinomies of Antonio Gramsci," *New Left Review* I, no. 100 [Nov/Dec 1976]: 5–78), and by Althusser in his reflections on Gramsci from the late 1970s. See Louis Althusser, "Marx in his Limits," in *Philosophy of the Encounter: Later Writings, 1978–1987*, ed. François

Matheron and Oliver Corpet, trans. G. M. Goshgarian (London: Verso, 2006), 7–162; Louis Althusser, *Que faire?* (Paris: PUF, 2018).

35. Poulantzas, *Political Power*, 226.

36. Nicos Poulantzas, *State, Power, Socialism* (London: NLB, 1978); particularly the concluding chapter, "Towards a Democratic Socialism."

37. While the notion of a "long march through the institutions" has frequently been ascribed to Gramsci, it is not to be found implicitly or explicitly in any of his writings. It was instead formulated in the late 1960s by the German Student leader Rudi Deutschke.

38. Poulantzas, *State, Power, Socialism*, 256.

39. Poulantzas, *State, Power, Socialism*, 252.

40. Poulantzas, *State, Power, Socialism*, 254, 252, 255.

41. Poulantzas, *State, Power, Socialism*, 257.

42. Poulantzas, *State, Power, Socialism*, 257–258.

43. Poulantzas, *State, Power, Socialism*, 258.

44. "Une révolution copernicienne dans la politique," in *La gauche, le pouvoir, le socialism: hommage a Nicos Poulantzas*, ed. C. Buci-Glucksmann (Paris: PUF, 1983), 37–41. The interview was originally published in in Italian in the influential PCI journal *Rinascita* on October 12, 1979, a few days after Poulantzas's untimely death.

45. It is not always remembered that the new "Crisis of Marxism," of which Althusser spoke at the Conference organized by *Il Manifesto* in Venice in 1977, signified for him not Marxism's failure (as it had for revisionists in Germany Social Democracy earlier in the century) but its opening up to new currents of growth. See "The Crisis of Marxism," trans. Grahame Lock, *Marxism Today* (July 1978), 215–220, 227.

46. Poulantzas, *State, Power, Socialism*, 159. A key stage in Poulantzas's transition from his earlier ambiguously structuralist to this relational conception of the state was constituted by Nicos Poulantzas, trans. David Fernbach, *Classes in Contemporary Capitalism* (London: NLB, 1975 [1973]). On this transition, see Panagiotis Sotiris, 'Althusser and Poulantzas: Hegemony and the State', *Materialismo Storico. Rivista di filosofia, storia e scienze umane* 1/2017, 115–163.

47. Poulantzas, *Political Power*, 44–45.

48. Poulantzas, 45. For Lacan's association of metaphor and condensation, see "The Instance of the Letter in the Unconscious, or Reason Since Freud," in *Écrits: a Selection*, trans. Alan Sheridan (London: Tavistock, 1977), 146–176.

49. Poulantzas, *State, Power, Socialism*, 39.

50. It is remarkable, given Poulantzas's emphasis on the diffused nature of power in the capitalist state as the precondition for its centralization, that he does not engage with Hegel's arguments concerning the nature of civil society as an "external state," or the institutions in which the state's rationality is durably realized in the regulation of daily life. See G. W. F. Hegel, *Philosophy of Right*, trans. T. M. Knox (Oxford: Oxford University Press, 1942), §183.

51. Poulantzas, *State, Power, Socialism*, 258.

52. Poulantzas, 258.

53. The most consequent of these critiques was arguably Colin Barker's argument that parliamentary democracy and workers' councils were "incompatible institutions," thus disabling Poulantzas's key innovation of a "mixed constitution" of socialist transformation and governance. See Colin Barker, "A 'New' Reformism? A Critique of the Political Theory of Nicos Poulantzas," *International Socialism* 2, no. 4 (Spring 1979).

54. Poulantzas, *State, Power, Socialism*, 258, 261.

55. Poulantzas, *State, Power, Socialism*, 68.

56. Gramsci, *Prison Notebooks*, Q6, §10, p. 691, November–December 1930; Q8, §142, p. 1028, April 1932.

57. Christine Buci-Glucksmann, *Gramsci et l'État: pour une theorie materialiste de la philosophie* (Paris: Fayard, 1975); and *Gramsci and the State*, trans. David Fernbach (London: Lawrence and Wishart, 1980).

58. Buci-Glucksmann, *Gramsci and the State*, 69–110.

59. In the Italian context, the 1997 conference hosted by the Fondazione Gramsci, including contributions by figures such as Buci-Glucksmann, de Giovanni, and Salvador, was decisive for affirming this reading. See Franco Ferri, ed., *Politica e storia in Gramsci*, 2 vols. (Rome: Editori Riuniti, 1977). The notion played a similarly important role at the famed seminar in Morelia in 1980 that brought together many significant theoreticians from across Latin America and beyond, including Aricó, Laclau, Portantiero, and Mouffe. See Julio Labastida Martin del Campo, ed., *Hegemonía y alternativas políticas en américa Latina* (Mexico City/UNAM: Siglo veintiuno editores, 1985).

60. Max Weber, "The Profession and Vocation of Politics," in *Political Writings* (Cambridge: Cambridge University Press, 1994), 309–369; Carl Schmitt, *Staat, Bewegung, Volk: die Dreigliederung der politischen Einheit* (Hamburg: Hanseatische Verlagsanstalt, 1933); Jürgen Habermas, *Theory of Communicative Action*, 2 vols. (Cambridge: Polity, 1986); Mario Tronti, *Sull'autonomia del politico* (Milan: Feltrinelli, 1977), and *La politica al tramonto* (Torino: Einaudi, 1998); Michel Foucault, *Security, Territory,*

Population: Lectures at the Collège de France, 1977–1978 (London: Palgrave Macmillan, 2009), and *The Birth of Biopolitics: Lectures at the Collège de France, 1978-1979* (London: Palgrave Macmillan, 2008); Quentin Skinner, "The State," in *Political Innovation and Conceptual Change*, ed. Terrence Ball, James Farr, and Russell Hanson (Cambridge: Cambridge University Press, 1989); Gianfranco Poggi, *The Development of the Modern State: A Sociological Introduction* (Stanford: Stanford University Press, 1978); Norbert Elias, *The Civilizing Process, vol. 2, State Formation and Civilization* (Oxford: Blackwell, 1982); Pierre Bourdieu, *On the State: Lectures at the College de France 1989-1992*, ed. Patrick Champagne, Remi Lenoir, Franck Poupeau, and Marie-Christine Riviere (Cambridge: Polity, 2014); Ranajit Guha, *Dominance without Hegemony. History and Power in Colonial India* (Harvard University Press, 1998); Michael Mann, *Sources of Social Power*, 4 vols. (New York: Cambridge University Press, 1986, 1993, 2012, 2012); Francis Fukuyama, *The Origins of Political Order* (New York: Farrar, Straus and Giroux, 2012), and *Political Order and Political Decay* (New York: Farrar, Straus and Giroux, 2015); Giorgio Agamben, *Homo Sacer: Sovereign Power and Bare Life* (Stanford: Stanford University Press, 1998), and *Stasis: Civil War as Political Paradigm* (Edinburgh: Edinburgh University Press, 2015).

61. The periodizing logic that underwrites such essentially retrospective narratives is thoroughly deconstructed in Kathleen Davis, *Periodization and Sovereignty: How Ideas of Feudalism and Secularization Govern the Politics of Time* (Philadelphia: University of Pennsylvania Press, 2008).

62. A contemporary example of this interpretation can be found in Álvaro García Linera, *Del Estado aparente al Estado integral* (La Paz: Vicepresidencia del Estado Plurinacional, 2009). A particularly sharp critique of Linera's theorization of the state, in the Bolivian context and in general, is offered in Anne Freeland, "Motley Society, Plurinationalism, and the Integral State. Álvaro García Linera's Use of Gramsci and Zavaleta," *Historical Materialism* 27, no. 3 (2019): 99–126.

63. While Francioni's path-breaking philological study of the *Prison Notebooks* acknowledges its indebtedness to Buci-Glucksmann's work, he does not follow her emphasis on the notion of a *stato allargato*. See Gianni Francioni, *L'officina gramsciana. Ipotesi sulla struttura dei 'Quaderni del carcere'* (Naples: Bibliopolis, 1984). For a reading that instead acknowledges Buci-Glucksmann's "forcing" of Gramsci's terminology while still seeing it as a legitimate inference, based on the accompanying historical contextualization, see Guido Liguori, *Sentieri gramsciani* (Rome: Carocci, 2006), 13–29.

64. Q8, §142, p. 1028, April 1932.

65. Q6, §88, pp. 763–764, March–August 1931.
66. Q15, §10, p. 1765, March 1933.
67. Jacques Lacan, *The Seminar of Jacques Lacan, The Other Side of Psychoanalysis: Other Side of Psychoanalysis, Book XVII*, trans. Russell Grigg (New York: W.W. Norton & Co., 2008), 207.
68. Dante Aligheri, *De Vulgari Eloquentia*, trans. Steven Botterill (Cambridge: Cambridge University Press, 1996), Book I, XVI, 1, 39.
69. Q1 §48, p. 58, February-March 1930. On Gramsci's analysis of the contradictions of Jacobinism, see André Tosel, "Gramsci et la Révolution française," *Modernité de Gramsci?*, ed. André Tosel (Université de Besançon/Paris: Les Belles Lettres, 1992), 97–108.
70. Q8, §236, p. 1089, April 1932. According to this reading, the structure of what Fabio Frosini has characterized as a type of "post-Jacobin" hegemony should not be limited to the passive revolutions of the second half of nineteenth century or the rise of "totalitarian" political systems in the early twentieth century, as it was already a feature of the original, contradictory Jacobin synthesis of mobilization and control. See Fabio Frosini, "L'egemonia e i "subalterni": utopia, religione, democrazia," *International Gramsci Journal* 2, no. 1 (2016): 126–166.
71. The relation of "politicization" and "depoliticization" in this sense is not one of progress (or regress) between distinct stages (as both Weber and Schmitt asserted) but a reinforcing dialectic in which "politicization" (within the bourgeois limits of "politics") is itself "depoliticizing" (of autonomous subaltern activity): a "depoliticizing politicization," "originary [ursprünglich] neutralization," or "constitutive subalternization" perpetually repeated within the dialectic of the bourgeois integral state.
72. See chapter 2 for a discussion of the process of subalternization, and chapter 3 for the relation of hegemony and passive revolution.
73. On the liberal tradition's earlier exclusionary policies and its effective revisionism in the context of the Cold War, see Domenico Losurdo, *Liberalism: A Counter-History* (London: Verso, 2011).
74. Poulantzas, *State, Power, Socialism*, 258. Interestingly, Poulantzas used precisely the same extreme formulation to criticize Foucault and Deleuze because they posit, according to Poulantzas, a "public kernel" of the state in the strict or juridical sense. He does not seem to notice that the topographical presuppositions of his own alternative notion of an extended "strategic field of the state," a space that is "traversed" by class forces at varying "depths" and "distances" from its center, is itself open in principle to the same objection (pp. 36–37). For key strategic lessons of the democratic road to socialism—the need to "occupy" key locations within the

state (apparatus), the coordination of forces "outside" and "inside" such a "strictly political state" (in the Hegelian sense), in order to impose pressure on the process of condensation by means of an encircling system of alliances—ironically depend on a localization of the state, in however "expanded" a sense, and therefore also a determination of its internal and external borders.

75. Poulantzas, *State, Power, Socialism*, 36–37, 149–150.
76. Bob Jessop, "Pouvoir et stratégies chez Poulantzas et Foucault," *Actuel Marx* 36, no. 2 (2004): 89–107.
77. See chapter 3 for a discussion of Gramsci's non- souverainist understanding of hegemony.
78. The most explicit formalization of hegemony in this sense was provided by Guha in *Dominance without Hegemony. History and Power in Colonial India.*
79. Q1, §44, p. 41, February–March 1930.
80. Q8, §227, p. 1084, April 1932.
81. Valentino Gerratana was the first to stress this crucial difference. See in particular Valentino Gerratana, "Le forme di egemonia," in *Problemi di metodo* (Rome: Editori Riunti, 1997), 119–126. Again, I refer to chapter 3 for a fuller discussion of this theme.
82. I refer here to the critique of the link between sovereignty and hegemony (in Laclau and Mouffe's sense, rather than that of Gramsci) offered by theorists of "posthegemony." See Alberto Moreiras, *The Exhaustion of Difference: The Politics of Latin American Cultural Studies* (Durham: Duke University Press, 2); Jon Beasley-Murray, *Posthegemony: Political Theory and Latin America*, Minneapolis: University of Minnesota Press, 2010).
83. *Contra* repeated claims that class was conceived primarily in economic terms in the classical Marxist tradition, for Lenin a class could only fully be regarded as such when it had elaborated an awareness of the political conditions that (over)determined its economic exploitation; anything less than this was mere "tred-iunionizm." See Lars Lih, *Lenin Rediscovered: "What is to be Done" in Context* (Leiden: Brill, 2006). It is this political emphasis that Gramsci developed further in his notion of a dialectic between subalternization and hegemonic politics.
84. On the concept of a "hegemonic apparatus," see Q1, §48, p. 59, February–March 1930; Q6, §136, §137, pp. 800–801, August 1931. For a succinct analysis of its significance, see Stefan Bollinger and Juha Koivisto, "Hegemonialapparat," in *Historisch-kritisches Wörterbuch des Marxismus* 5 (Hamburg/Berlin: Argument, 2001), 1258–1270.

85. For Lenin's argument that the Soviets in 1917 represented a "power of a completely different type," see Lenin, "On Dual Power," in *Collected Works* 24 (Moscow: Progress Publishers, 1964 [April 1917]), 38. In the same text, he elaborates the notion of the Paris Commune as a "special type of state" ("special" here being understood in the sense of "particular") on the basis of his ongoing commentary on Marx's analysis of the experience of 1871, belatedly published as *The State and Revolution*. For Gramsci's notion of a post-statist "regulated society," see Q6, §65, p. 734, December 1930–March 1931. The influence of debates in Italian economic science on the development of this concept is analyzed in Giuliano Guzzone, *Gramsci e la critica dell'economia politica: dal dibattito sul liberismo al paradigma della 'traducibilità'* (Rome: Viella, 2018).

86. See August H. Nimtz, *Lenin's Electoral Strategy from Marx and Engels Through the Revolution of 1905* (New York: Palgrave Macmillan, 2014); and, by the same author, *Lenin's Electoral Strategy from 1907 to the October Revolution of 1917* (New York: Palgrave Macmillan, 2014).

87. Poulantzas, *State, Power, Socialism*, p. 252.

88. For an excellent exploration of the wide spectrum of meanings associated with the notion of a proletarian *vlast'* in the Russian revolutionary experience, see Lars Lih, "*Vlast'* From the Past: Stories Told by Bolsheviks," *Left History* 6, no. 2 (Fall 1999): 29–52.

89. Lenin, "On Dual Power," in *Collected Works*, vol. 24 (Moscow: Progress Publishers, 1964), 38.

90. Lenin, "The Tasks of the Proletariat in our Revolution," in *Collected Works*, vol. 24 (Moscow: Progress Publishers, 1964), 61. In June, Lenin repeats the claim of dual power's instability and transitory nature in "Has Dual Power Disappeared?," in *Collected Works*, vol. 24 (Moscow: Progress Publishers, 1964), 445–448.

91. Slavoj Žižek, *The Indivisible Remainder: On Shelling and Related Matters* (London: Verso, 1996), 6.

92. Lenin, *The State and Revolution*, trans. Robert Service (London: Penguin, 1991).

93. For two recent very different attempts to think through the significance of dual power for contemporary politics, see George Ciccariello-Maher, *We Created Chávez: A People's History of the Venezuelan Revolution* (Durham: Duke University Press, 2013), 234–256; Fredric Jameson, *An American Utopia: Dual Power and the Universal Army* (London: Verso, 2016).

94. This is the approach proposed by Antonio Negri in *Insurgencies: Constituent Power and the Modern State*, trans. Maurizia

Boscagli (Minneapolis: University of Minnesota Press, 1999), 286ff (which draws directly on his earlier *La fabbrica della strategia: 33 lezioni su Lenin* (Padua: librirossi, 1977), reprinted by Manifestolibri in 2004 under the original subtitle; see pp. 130ff). Negri's subsequent proposal of a qualitative distinction between *potentia* and *potestas* in his influential and contested reading of Spinoza represents the metaphysical continuation of this originally political argument. See Antonio Negri, *The Savage Anomaly: Power of Spinoza's Metaphysics and Politics*, trans. Michael Hardt (Minneapolis: University of Minnesota Press, 1991 [1981]).

95. Innovation here is understood not in the sense that Pocock famously proposed in his reading of *The Prince*, in which innovation is seen as an ordering response to the flux of *fortuna* (conceived as "pure, uncontrolled, and unlegitimated contingency"). Rather, Negri argues that the construction of the political itself is the product of "permanent innovation." Compare J. G. A. Pocock, *The Machiavellian Moment: Florentine Political Thought and the Atlantic Republican Tradition* (Princeton: Princeton University Press, 1975), 156f; and Negri, *Insurgencies*, 29.

96. This thesis of a situation of "permanent dual power" has been creatively explored in recent work by Panagiotis Sotiris. See "Rethinking Dual Power," paper presented at the 2017 London Historical Materialism Conference, available at https://www.academia.edu/35145688/Rethinking_Dual_Power.

97. If this difference is conceived in dialectical terms, constituent power appears as fundamentally internal to the modern sovereign state, in the sense of representing the historical and structural foundation that the consolidation of the state must sublate (in the dual Hegelian sense of reciprocal and simultaneous cancellation and preservation). If understood as a transcendental relation, on the other hand, constituent power, rather than preceding constitutional order, is depicted as the posited condition of possibility of the existing constitutional order, retrospectively determined in formalistic terms as "absented cause." For explorations of the paradoxical nature of constituent power, see Martin Loughlin and Neil Walker, ed., *The Paradox of Constitutionalism: Constituent Power and Constitutional Form* (Oxford: Oxford University Press, 2007).

98. Max Weber, *Gesamtausgabe, Band 23* (Tübingen: Mohr und Siebeck, 2013), 210.

99. René Zavaleta Mercado, "*El poder dual en América Latina*," in *Obra completa I: Ensayos 1957-1974*, ed. Mauricio Souza Crespo (La Paz: Plural editores, 2011 [1973]), 367-526. For an important contemporary discussion of the significance of this text, see Susana Draper,

"Hegemonía, poder dual, poshegemonía: las derives del concepto," in *Poshegemonía: El final de un paradigma de la filosofía política en América Latina*, ed. Rodrigo Castro Orellana (Madrid: Biblioteca Nueva, 2015), 93–112.

100. Mercado, *El poder dual*, 378.

101. *Pace* Antonio Negri, *Fabbrica di porcellana* (Milan: Feltrinelli, 2008), 11–15.

Chapter 2

1. Rosa Luxemburg, "Order Prevails in Berlin," *Rote Fahne*, January 14, 1919. "Learning process" is used here in the sense creatively valorized in Klaus Holzkamp's *kritische Psychologie* and its pedagogical elaboration. See Klaus Holzkamp, *Lernen: Subjektwissenschaftliche Grundlegung* (Frankfurt am Main: Campus, 1995).

2. Plato, *The Republic*, 7.514a–7.521a.

3. *Laws*, 3.701a.

4. Karl Marx, "Theses on Feuerbach," in *Marx Engels Collected Works*, vol. 5 (London: Lawrence and Wishart, 1975–2005), 5; Niccolò Machiavelli, *The Prince*, trans. George Bull (London: Penguin, 1961), chapter 15.

5. To put it in Leo Strauss's terms, Plato's cave was always already the "second, much deeper" or "'unnatural' cave" that Strauss himself feared the modern world had become. For a useful discussion of Strauss's allegory of an allegory, see Heinrich Meier, *Leo Strauss and the Theologico-Political Problem*, trans. Marcus Brainard (Cambridge: Cambridge University Press, 2006).

6. Not An Alternative, "Occupy the Party: The Sanders Campaign as a Site of Struggle," *ROAR Magazine*, February 16, 2016, https://roarmag.org/essays/occupy-democratic-party-sanders-campaign/

7. Reinhart Koselleck, *Critique and Crisis: Enlightenment and the Pathogenesis of Modern Society* (New York: Berg, 1988 [1959]).

8. Norberto Bobbio, "Esiste una dottrina marxista dello Stato?," *Mondoperaio* 28, nos. 8–9 (August–September 1975): 24–31. The subsequent debate rapidly overflowed the pages of *Mondoperaio* and shaped debates on the Italian and European left for much of the late 1970s. Its influence was evident, for instance, at both the Fondazione Gramsci's conference in Florence in 1997 and *Il Manifesto*'s conference on "Power and Opposition in Post-revolutionary Societies" in Venice in the same year.

9. Lucio Colletti, *Intervista politico-filosofico* (Bari: Laterza, 1975). For a critical contextualization of this interview (conducted by Perry Anderson and originally published in 1974 in *New Left Review*), see Cristina Corradi, *Storia dei marxismi in Italia* (Rome: Manifestolibri, 2011).

10. See, in particular, Franco De Felice, "Una chiave di lettura in 'Americanismo e fordismo'," *Rinascita - Il Contemporaneo* 29, no. 42 (October 27, 1972): 33–35; and the fundamental "Rivoluzione passiva, fascismo, americanismo in Gramsci," in *Politica e storia in Gramsci*, vol. 1, ed. Franco Ferri (Rome: Editori Riuniti, 1977), 161–220. I discuss some other dimensions of the context of de Felice's intervention in chapter 3.

11. For an account of the Italian "Marxisti Schmittiani," see Jan Werner Müller, *A Dangerous Mind: Carl Schmitt in Post-War European Thought* (New Haven: Yale University Press, 2003). What is arguably the most extensive study of Schmitt's thought emerged out of this broader culture; see Carlo Galli, *Genealogia della politica: Carl Schmitt e la crisi del pensiero politico moderno* (Bologna: Il Mulino, 1996). On the "impolitical" development of Tronti's proposal of an autonomy of the political, see Massimo Cacciari, *Krisis: Saggio sulla crisi del pensiero negativo da Nietzsche a Wittgenstein* (Milan: Feltrinelli, 1976); Roberto Esposito, *Categorie dell'impolitico* (Bologna: il Mulino, 1988).

12. Cornelius Castoriadis, *Political and Social Writings*, 3 vols. (Minneapolis: University of Minnesota Press, 1988–1992); Claude Lefort, *The Political Forms of Modern Society: Bureaucracy, Democracy, Totalitarianism* (Cambridge: MIT Press, 1986); Jean-Luc Nancy and Philippe Lacoue-Labarthe, *Retreating the Political* (London: Routledge, 1997); Jacques Derrida, *The Politics of Friendship* (London: Verso, 1994).

13. Daniel Bensaïd, *Marx for Our Times: Adventures and Misadventures of a Critique*, trans. Gregory Elliott (London: Verso, 2002 [1995]), 112. Clifford Geertz, "Thick Description: Toward an Interpretive Theory of Culture," in *The Interpretation of Cultures: Selected Essays* (New York: Basic Books, 1973), 3–30.

14. Louis Althusser, "Marx in his Limits," in *Philosophy of the Encounter: Later Writings 1978–1987* (London: Verso, 2006), 7–162. The text breaks off, symptomatically, with an excessively rhetorical question: "But what does one do in the Party, if not politics?" (p. 150).

15. Étienne Balibar, "Three Concepts of Politics," in *Politics and the Other Scene* (London: Verso, 2002), 1–39.

16. Alain Badiou, "Politics as Thought: The Work of Sylvain Lazarus," in *Metapolitics*, trans. Jason Barker (London: Verso, 2005), 26–57; Sylvain

Lazarus, *Anthropology of the Name*, trans. Gila Walker (London: Seagull Books, 2015 [1996]).

17. Alain Badiou, "Philosophy and Politics," in *Conditions*, trans. Steven Corcoran (New York: Continuum, 2008), 147–176. On the "middle Althusser's" conception of philosophy, see "Theory, Theoretical Practice and Theoretical Formation," in *Philosophy and the Spontaneous Philosophy of the Scientists*, trans. James Kavanaugh, ed. Gregory Elliott (London: Verso, 1990), 1–42.

18. Jacques Rancière, *Disagreement: Politics and Philosophy*, trans. Julie Rose (Minneapolis: University of Minnesota Press, 1999).

19. The extent of this incompatibility is only fleetingly registered in Axel Honneth and Jacques Rancière, *Recognition or Disagreement: A Critical Encounter on the Politics of Freedom, Equality, and Identity*, ed. Katia Genel and Jean-Philippe Deranty (New York: Columbia University Press, 2016). It is the rejection of any connection between "authentically political" politics and order as such (always a "police" order) that also marks the gulf separating Rancière's thought from the Kantian rigorism of Rainer Forst; see *The Right to Justification* (New York: Columbia University Press, 2014).

20. Carl Schmitt, *The Concept of the Political*, trans. George Schwab (Chicago: University of Chicago Press, 2007 [1932]).

21. The rapid transition between the autonomy of the Political to the heteronomous specificity of the Political can be tracked in Schmitt's (*Concept of the* Political) silent displacement of the friend–enemy distinction (p. 26) via the notion of antagonism ("the most intense and extreme antagonism"; p. 29) to his final communitarian emphasis ("the intensity of an association or dissociation"; p. 38).

22. Rancière, *Disagreement*, 139.

23. Raymond Geuss, *Philosophy and Real Politics* (Princeton: Princeton University Press, 2008); Lois McNay, *The Misguided Search for the Political* (Cambridge: Polity, 2014).

24. For important reflections on "style" as a philosophical and political category, see Daniel Hartley, *The Politics of Style: Towards a Marxist Poetics* (Leiden: Brill, 2016).

25. Chantal Mouffe, ed., *The Challenge of Carl Schmitt* (London: Verso, 1999). The themes explored in this volume have marked all of Mouffe's subsequent evolution, arguably nowhere more so than in the communitarian dimensions of her recent *For a Left Populism* (London: Verso, 2018).

26. Mouffe's move from the antagonism valorized in *Hegemony and Socialist Strategy* to this effectively formalist conception of agonism mirrors her collaborator Ernesto Laclau's positing of an ontological primacy

of "dislocation," which plays a similarly structural or even transhistorical role in his own later work. See Ernesto Laclau, *New Reflections on the Revolution of our Time* (London: Verso, 1990). For a critical reading of this development in Laclau's thought, see Fabio Frosini, *Da Gramsci a Marx: ideologia, verità e politica* (Rome: DeriveApprodi, 2009), 154 et seq..

27. Plato, *The Sophist*, 216a-236d.

28. See chapter 4 for a discussion of the aestheticized nature of Badiou's historicism.

29. Alain Badiou, *The Communist Hypothesis* (London: Verso, 2010), 234.

30. See Alain Badiou, *The Concept of Model: An Introduction to the Materialist Epistemology of Mathematics*, trans. and ed. Zachary Fraser and Tzuchien Tho (Melbourne: re.press, 2007 [1969]), particularly Badiou's discussion of the "dialectic of formalization" in the interview with Tzuchien Tho (90–93).

31. One of the most significant of such attempts is represented by Leonardo Paggi, "La teoria generale del marxismo in Gramsci," *Annali Feltrinelli* 15 (1973): 1318–1370.

32. Norberto Bobbio, "Gramsci e la concezione della società civile"; Jacques Texier, "Intervento," in *Gramsci e la cultura contemporanea. Atti del convegno internazionale di studi gramsciani tenuto a Cagliari il 23–27 aprile 1967*, vol. 1, ed. Pietro Rossi (Rome: Editori Riuniti-Istituto Gramsci, 1969).

33. Perry Anderson, "The Antinomies of Antonio Gramsci," *New Left Review* I, no. 100 (1976): 5–78.

34. Partha Chatterjee, *The Politics of the Governed. Reflections on Popular Politics in Most of the World* (New York: Columbia University Press, 2004), 51. See also Chatterjee's *Lineages of Political Society. Studies in Postcolonial Democracy* (New York: Columbia University Press, 2011); and *I am the People: Reflections on Popular Sovereignty Today* (New York: Columbia University Press, 2020).

35. For problematizations of Chatterjee's claims in the context of contemporary Indian politics, see Alf Gunvald Nilsen and Srila Roy, eds., *New Subaltern Politics. Reconceptualizing Hegemony and Resistance in Contemporary India* (New York: Oxford University Press, 2015).

36. I have explored the limitations of a notion of colonial difference in relation to Gramsci's theory of subalternization at greater length in Peter D. Thomas, "Il Cittadino *sive* subalterno," *Rivista italiana di filosofia politica* 1 (2021): 147–164.

37. A classic example of what I am referring to as an active sense of constitutionalization can be found in Negri's analysis of the distinctive

role of labor in the Constitution of the Italian Republic and his radicalization of Mortati's notion of a constitutive dialectic between formal and material constitutions. See Antonio Negri, "Il lavoro nella costituzione," in *La forma stato. Per a critica dell'economia politica della costituzione* (Milan: Feltrinelli, 1977); and Costantino Mortati, *La costituzione in senso materiale* (Milan: Giuffrè, 1940).

38. In particular, I refer to the attempt to reappropriate the notion of constitution from Habermas's influential formulation in the work of Hans-Jürgen Krahl; see Hans-Jürgen Krahl *Konstitution und Klassenkampf: Zur historischen Dialektik von bürgerlicher Emanzipation und proletarischer Revolution* (Frankfurt/M: Neue Kritik, 1971).

39. It is this relational and "post-foundationalist" emphasis that I see as the most enduringly vital dimension of Derrida's legacy today, themes that were especially prominent in his earliest works. See, in particular, *Of Grammatology*, trans. Gayatri Chakravorty Spivak (Baltimore: Johns Hopkins University Press, 1976 [1967]); and "From Restricted to General Economy: A Hegelianism without Reserve," *Writing and Difference*, trans. Alan Bass (London: Routledge, 1978 [1967]).

40. While a small selection of Gramsci's translations was included in Gerratana's critical edition of 1975, it was only with the publication of the relevant volumes of the *Edizione nazionale* in 2007 that the full range of Gramsci's activity as a translator—from Marx to Goethe to historical linguistics to the Grimm Brothers—became apparent to a wider audience. See Antonio Gramsci, *Quaderni del carcere*, Vol. 1 *Quaderni di traduzione*, ed. Gianni Francioni and Giuseppe Cospito (Rome: Istituto dell'Enciclopedia Italiana, 2007). A path-breaking study was that of Lucia Borghese, "Tia Alene in bicicletta. Gramsci traduttore dal tedesco e teorico della traduzione," *Belfagor* XXXVI (1981): 635–665.

41. See, in particular, Derek Boothman, *Traducibilità e processi traduttivi, un caso: A. Gramsci linguista* (Perugia: Guerra edizioni, 2004); Peter Ives and Rocco Lacorte, ed., *Gramsci, Language, and Translation* (Lanham, MD: Lexington Books, 2010); Fabio Frosini, *La religione dell'uomo moderno: Politica e verità nei Quaderni del carcere* (Rome: Carocci, 2010).

42. Q11, §46, p. 1468, August–December 1932. As Peter Ives notes, Gramsci both mistakenly dated Lenin's remark to 1921 and introduced the notion of translation where Lenin had instead spoken only of "presenting our [Russian] experience to foreigners." See Peter Ives, *Gramsci's Politics of Language: Engaging the Bakhtin Circle and The Frankfurt School* (Toronto: University of Toronto Press, 2004), 101.

43. See, for instance, Q1, §73, p. 81, February–March 1930.

44. *Q7*, §35, p. 886, February–November 1931.
45. On the dispute between Croce and Gentile over the [im]possibility and necessity of translation, see Domenico Jervolino, "Croce, Gentile e Gramsci sulla traduzione," *International Gramsci Journal* 1, no. 2 (2010): 21–28.
46. See, for instance, *Q3*, §48, p. 331, June–July 1930, in which Jacobinism is interpreted in terms of a reduction "to the principles of classical German philosophy."
47. Gramsci invokes the Marxian metaphors on a number of occasions; see, e.g., *Q8*, §208, pp. 1066–1067, February–March 1932.
48. Thus, for instance, Gramsci's earlier discussion of Jacobinism and German idealism is rephrased in non-foundational terms as the "parallel and reciprocally translatable" juridical-political languages. See *Q19*, §24, p. 2028, July–August 1934–February 1935.
49. On the distinction between mimetic and expressive theories of literary production (among others), see Meyer H. Abrams, *The Mirror and the Lamp. Romantic Theory and the Critical Tradition* (Oxford: Oxford University Press, 1953).
50. See Antonio Gramsci, "'La lingua unica e l'esperanto' (16 February 1918)," in *La città futura 1917–1918*, ed. Sergio Caprioglio (Turin: Einaudi, 1982). It is a polemic that Gramsci continues in the *Prison Notebooks*.
51. Widely invoked in contemporary translation studies, the distinction between source and target texts remains central even to Venuti's attempt to problematize it with the notions of "domesticating" and "foreignizing" translation strategies, which leaves the underlying problematic of "fidelity" in place even in its rejection. See Lawrence Venuti, *The Translator's Invisibility: A History of Translation* (London: Routledge, 1995).
52. See, in particular, *Q8*, §224, pp. 1081–1082, April 1932. The critique of the ultimately political function of speculation is developed in an intense fashion in Notebook 10 (in relation to Croce) and in Notebook 11 (in relation to Bukharin).
53. Benedetto Croce, *Materialismo storico ed economia marxistica*, 4th ed. (Bari: Laterza, 1921 [1900]).
54. Benedetto Croce, *Logica come scienza del concetto puro* (Bari: Laterza, 1967 [1908]), 212.
55. See Reinhart Koselleck, "Begriffsgeschichte and Social History," in *Futures Past: On the Semantics of Historical Times* (Cambridge: MIT Press, 1985), 84.
56. On the status of objectivity in (post) Kantian thought and its critical development by Marx, see Dominique Pradelle, "Gegenstand/Objekt," in *Vocabulaire Européen des Philosophies: Dictionnaire des Intraduisibles*,

ed. Barbara Casin (Paris: Editions du Seuil, 2004), 480–488; João Maria de Freitas-Branco, "Gegenstand," *Historisch-kritisches Wörterbuch des Marxismus*, vol. 5 (Hamburg/Berlin: Argument, 2001), 36–43.

57. I explore the limits of the notion of the "political subject" at greater length in chapter 4.

58. Q8, §238, p. 1090, May 1932.

59. See Ranajit Guha, "Preface," in *Subaltern Studies I: Writings on South Asian History and Society* (New York: Oxford University Press, 1982); Gayatri Chakravorty Spivak, "Can the Subaltern Speak?," in *Marxism and the Interpretation of Culture*, ed. Cary Nelson and Lawrence Grossberg (Urbana: University of Illinois Press, 1998), 271–314.

60. Max Weber, *Gesamtausgabe. Band 23* (Tübingen: Mohr und Siebeck, 2013), 210.

61. See Ranajit Guha, "On Some Aspects of the Historiography of Colonial India," in *Subaltern Studies I* (New Delhi: Oxford University Press, 1982), 4, 8.

62. Ranajit Guha, *Dominance without Hegemony. History and Power in Colonial India* (Oxford: Oxford University Press, 1998). The key programmatic essay in this collection dates from 1989; see Ranajit Guha, "Dominance without Hegemony and its Historiography," *Subaltern Studies VI* (Oxford: Oxford University Press, 1989), 210–309.

63. An account of the various iterations of this influential text (or rather, texts) is provided in Rosalind Morris, ed., *Can the Subaltern Speak: Reflections on the History of an Idea* (New York: Columbia University Press, 2010).

64. Gayatri Chakravorty Spivak, "Scattered speculations on the subaltern and the popular," *Postcolonial Studies* 8, no. 4 (2005): 475. See also "Discussion: An Afterword on the New Subaltern," in *Subaltern Studies XI: Community, Gender and Violence*, ed. Partha Chatterjee and Pradeep Jeganathan (Delhi: Permanent Black, 2000), 305–334; "Interview with Gayatri Chakravorty Spivak," in *The Postcolonial Gramsci*, ed. Neelam Srivastava and Baidik Bhattacharya (London: Routledge, 2012), 221–231.

65. See Marcus Green, "Gramsci Cannot Speak: Presentations and Interpretations of Gramsci's Concept of the Subaltern," *Rethinking Marxism* 14, no. 3 (2002): 1–24; "Rethinking the Subaltern and the Question of Censorship in Gramsci's *Prison Notebooks*," *Postcolonial Studies* 14, no. 4 (2011): 387–404; Peter D. Thomas, "Refiguring the Subaltern," *Political Theory* 46, no. 6 (2018): 861–864.

66. An excellent account of the process of subalternization can be found in Massimo Modonesi, *The Antagonistic Principle: Marxism and Political Action* (Leiden: Brill, 2018), 85–106.

67. See, e.g., Q3 §90, pp. 372–373, August 1930, in which Gramsci argues that "the historical unification of the ruling classes is in the state and their history is essentially the history of states and of groups of states. This unity has to be concrete, and thus the result of relations between the state and civil society."

68. The late Althusser in particular was concerned in emphasizing how the state-machine transforms an excess of force into "rights, laws, and norms"; see "Marx in his Limits," in *Philosophy of the Encounter: Later Writings, 1978–1987*, ed. François Matheron and Oliver Corpet, trans. G. M. Goshgarian (London: Verso, 2006), 109.

69. Judith Butler's work has powerfully explored the performative dimensions of politics over a long period; see Judith Butler, *Gender Trouble: Feminism and the Subversion of Identity* (London: Routledge, 1990); *Notes Toward a Performative Theory of Assembly* (Cambridge: Harvard University Press, 2015).

70. In the "late" Laclau, the seemingly "post-foundational" thesis of the political institution of the social is ultimately given an anthropological foundation—specifically, a libidinal-anthropological foundation, more Freudian than Lacanian—in a theory of the "drives" that subtend the "hegemonic construction of society." See Ernesto Laclau, "Glimpsing the Future," in *Laclau: A Critical Reader*, ed. Simon Critchley and Oliver Marchart (London: Routledge, 2004), 326.

71. Karl Marx, "Preface," in *Contribution to the Critique of Political Economy*, *Marx Engels Collected Works*, vol. 29 (London: Lawrence and Wishart, 1975–2005), 262.

72. For a critique of Negri and Hardt's formulation of the multitude that moves in this direction, see Vittorio Morfino, *Plural Temporality: Transindividuality and the Aleatory between Spinoza and Althusser* (Leiden: Brill, 2014), 16.

Chapter 3

1. *Manifesto of the Communist Party*, in *Marx/Engels Collected Works*, vol. 6 (London: Lawrence and Wishart, 1975–2005), 502.

2. Emmanuel Joseph Sieyès, "What is the Third Estate?," in *Political Writings*, trans. and ed. Michael Sonenscher (Indianapolis: Hackett, 2003).

3. On the origin of the name "Leveller" in the levelling of enclosure hedges in early seventeenth-century England, see Perez Zagorin, *Rebels and Rulers*

1500–1660, Volume II: Provincial Rebellion, Revolutionary Civil Wars, 1560–1660 (Cambridge: Cambridge University Press, 1982).

4. Karl Marx, *Capital Volume I*, trans. Ben Fowkes (Harmondsworth: Penguin, 1976), 280.

5. For a critical balance sheet of recent Latin American politics, see Franck Gaudichaud, Jeffery Webber, and Massimo Modonesi, *Los gobiernos progresistas latinoamericanos del siglo XXI: Ensayos de interpretación histórica* (Universidad Nacional Autónoma de México, Facultad de Ciencias Políticas y Sociales, 2019). The strategic blockages that plagued the movements in Greece are analyzed in Panagiotis Sotiris, ed., *Crisis, Movement, Strategy: The Greek Experience* (Leiden: Brill, 2018).

6. Through a lexical analysis of the occurrences of hegemony in the British National Corpus, Derek Boothman has demonstrated the strong influence of *Selections from the Prison Notebooks* from 1971 on the increasing use and changing meaning of the word "hegemony" in the English language in the wake of its publication. See Derek Boothman, "Translating the Lexical Item: Arguing over Dominance, Domination and Hegemony," *L'analisi linguistica e letteraria*, XVI, no. 2 (2008) (Special Issue of Proceedings of the IADA Workshop "Word Meaning in Argumentative Dialogue," ed. G. Gobber et al.).

7. The theorization of hegemony in terms of production of consent was central in particular to the reception of Gramsci in anglophone cultural studies. See Raymond Williams, *Marxism and Literature* (Oxford: Oxford University Press, 1977); Stuart Hall, "Gramsci and Us," in *The Hard Road to Renewal* (London: Verso, 1988), 161–174.

8. Ranajit Guha, *Dominance without Hegemony. History and Power in Colonial India* (Cambridge: Harvard University Press, 1997). In the same period, Nazih Ayubi theorized a similar relative weakness of hegemony in the Arab world; see *Over-stating the Arab State: Politics and Society in the Middle East* (London: I. B. Tauris, 1995).

9. On "populist" readings of hegemony on the "Italian road to socialism," see Roberto Dainotto, "Introduction," in *Gramsci in the World* (Durham: Duke University Press, 2020), 1–16. For pointed critical remarks on the later exportation of this perspective in international debates, particularly the "family resemblances" of Togliatti's and Laclau and Mouffe's reading of Gramsci, see Cesare Casarino and Antonio Negri, *In Praise of the Common: A Conversation on Philosophy and Politics* (Minneapolis: University of Minnesota Press, 2008), 162–164.

10. Simon Critchley provides a succinct formulation of this position: "This act of the aggregation of the political subject is the moment of hegemony." See

Simon Critchley, *Infinitely Demanding. Ethics of Commitment, Politics of Resistance* (London: Verso, 2007), 104. The notion that hegemony is fundamentally a theory of the formation of a political subject is one of the few perspectives shared by the interlocutors in Judith Butler, Ernesto Laclau, and Slavoj Žižek, *Contingency, Hegemony, Universality: Contemporary Dialogues On The Left* (London: Verso, 2000).

11. This interpretation was most influentially formulated by Norberto Bobbio in his intervention at the international Gramsci conference in 1967 in Cagliari. See "Gramsci e la concezione della società civile," in *Gramsci e la cultura contemporanea. Atti del convegno internazionale di studi gramsciani tenuto a Cagliari il 23–27 aprile 1967*, vol. 1, ed. Pietro Rossi (Rome: Editori Riuniti-Istituto Gramsci, 1969). Despite numerous critiques of the theoretical presuppositions of and limited textual foundation for this reading, Bobbio's approach remains widely influential in the general discussion of hegemony. Richard Day's argument for the superannuation of hegemony in the politics of the alternative globalization movement at the turn of the millennium, for instance, is effectively an unwitting re-proposal of Bobbio's presuppositions. See Richard J. F. Day, *Gramsci Is Dead. Anarchist Currents in the Newest Social Movements* (London: Pluto Press, 2005).

12. For a reconstruction of usages of hegemony among the Greek historians, see John Wickersham, *Hegemony and the Greek Historians* (Lanham, MD: Rowman and Littlefield, 1994). Perry Anderson, *The H-Word. The Peripeteia of Hegemony* (London: Verso, 2017) charts some of hegemony's transformations in the Cold War period. The most comprehensive reconstruction of hegemony's complicated conceptual history is Giuseppe Cospito, *Egemonia: Da Omero ai Gender Studies* (Bologna: Il Mulino, 2021).

13. The first generation of "neo-Gramscianism" in international relations theory is represented by Robert Cox, *Production, Power, and World Order: Social Forces in the Making of History* (New York: Columbia University Press, 1987); Stephen Gill, ed., *Gramsci, Historical Materialism and International Relations* (Cambridge: Cambridge University Press, 1993). More recent problematizations of the national/international nexus in Gramsci include Adam David Morton, *Unravelling Gramsci: Hegemony and Passive Revolution in the Global Political Economy* (London: Pluto Press, 2007); Lorenzo Fusaro, *Crises and Hegemonic Transitions: From Gramsci's Quaderni to the Contemporary World Economy* (Leiden: Brill, 2018).

14. Giovanni Arrighi, *The Geometry of Imperialism: The Limits of Hobson's Paradigm*, trans. Patrick Camiller (London: New Left Books, 1978).

Giulio Azzolini, *Capitale, egemonia, Sistema* (Macerata: Quolibet, 2018), provides the most comprehensive critical assessment of the evolution of Arrighi's thought.

15. On the presuppositions of Rousseau's argument for the necessity of this transition, see Augusto Illuminati, *J. J. Rousseau e la fondazione dei valori borghesi* (Milan: Il saggiatore, 1977); and for an argument that the notion of the "general will" reintroduces a representative logic surreptitiously behind the back of Rousseau's declared rejection of representation, see Michael Hardt and Antonio Negri, *Assembly* (New York: Oxford University Press, 2017), 27 et seq.

16. As previously noted, this has been the conception of hegemony presupposed by recent theorists of "posthegmeony." See Alberto Moreiras, *The Exhaustion of Difference: The Politics of Latin American Cultural Studies* (Durham: Duke University Press, 2001); Jon Beasley-Murray, *Posthegemony: Political Theory and Latin America* (Minneapolis: University of Minnesota Press, 2010); Rodrigo Castro Orellana, ed., *Poshegemonía: El final de un paradigma de la filosofía política en América Latina* (Madrid: Biblioteca Nueva, 2015).

17. Such a reading of hegemony as a form of domination is particularly noticeable in Michael Burawoy's project of a "sociological Marxism." See Michael Burawoy, "For a Sociological Marxism: The Complementary Convergence of Antonio Gramsci and Karl Polanyi," *Politics & Society* 31, no. 2 (2003): 193–261; "The Roots of Domination: Beyond Bourdieu and Gramsci," *Sociology* 46, no. 2 (2012): 187–206.

18. In a paper delivered in Vienna in October 1917, Weber briefly considered the possibility of such a fourth type of domination, albeit in a theoretically undeveloped form that did not find its way into the manuscripts later published as *Economy and Society*—perhaps because it directly contradicts the self-foundational dimension of charismatic power, which increasingly occupied Weber in his last years. See Max Weber, "Ein Vortrag Max Webers über die Probleme der Staatssoziologie," *Neue Freie Presse*, no. 19102 (October 25, 1917). For critical discussions of this fascinating but widely neglected late development in Weber's thinking, see Stefan Breuer, "The Concept of Democracy in Weber's Political Sociology," in *Max Weber, Democracy and Modernization*, ed. Ralph Schroeder (Basingstoke: Palgrave Macmillan, 1998), 1–13; Iván Szelenyi, "Weber's theory of domination and post-communist capitalisms," *Theory and Society* 45, no. 1 (2016): 1–24.

19. Francesca Chiarotto, *Operazione Gramsci. Alla conquista degli intellettuali nell'Italia del dopoguerra* (Milan: Bruno Mondadori, 2011).

20. These priorities were particularly noticeable in the organization and order of publication of the thematic edition, which began with volumes on Croce's philosophy, the political and cultural role of intellectuals, the Risorgimento, and Machiavelli. On the changing emphases of the initial postwar Italian discussion of Gramsci, see Guido Liguori, *Gramsci conteso. Interpretazioni, dibattiti e polemiche 1922–2012* (Rome: Editori Riuniti University Press, 2012).

21. For a critical contextualization of Togliatti's ongoing reassessment of the significance of hegemony in Gramsci's thought, see Aldo Agosti, *Palmiro Togliatti: A Biography* (London: I. B. Tauris, 2008 [1996]). A more polemical reading, drawing on the workerist tradition, can be found in Paolo Capuzzo and Sandro Mezzadra, "Provincializing the Italian Reading of Gramsci," in *The Postcolonial Gramsci*, ed. Neelam Srivastava and Baidik Bhattacharya (London: Routledge, 2012), 34–54.

22. Regarding the debate on force and consent in Italy in the 1920s, particularly in relation to contemporary Machiavelli scholarship and commentary, see Leonardo Paggi, *Antonio Gramsci e il moderno principe* (Rome: Editori Riuniti, 1970), 372 et seq.; Michele Fiorillo, "Dalla machiavellistica 'elitista' al moderno Principe 'democratico'," *Gramsci nel suo tempo*, vol. 2, ed. Francesco Giasi (Rome: Carocci, 2008).

23. This was undoubtedly the case in Tom Nairn and Perry Anderson's path-breaking attempts in the 1960s to use the notion of hegemony to analyze the origins of British (or rather, English) "exceptionalism," where both force and particularly consent were conceived in totalizing terms. For the initial studies that launched this enterprise, see Tom Nairn, "The British Political Elite," *New Left Review* I, no. 23 (1964): 19–25; Perry Anderson, "Origins of the Present Crisis," *New Left Review* I, no. 24 (1964): 26–53. Over half a century later, Anderson projected the couplet of force and consent backward as the definitional terms of his history of hegemony from Thucydides onward in *The H-Word. The Peripeteia of Hegemony.* The emphasis on force and consent as constitutive of hegemony reached what is arguably its most sophisticated formalization in Guha's typology of varying combinations of "coercion" and "persuasion." Guha, *Dominance without Hegemony*, particularly p. 20 et seq.

24. Among the most significant philological explorations of the role of passive revolution in the *Prison Notebook* are Dora Kanoussi, *Una introducción a los Cuadernos de la cárcel de Antonio Gramsci* (Madrid: Plaza y Valdés editores, 2000); Pasquale Voza, "Rivoluzione passive," in *Le parole di Gramsci: per un lessico dei 'Quaderni del carcere'*, ed. Fabio Frosini and Guido Liguori (Rome: Carocci, 2004), 189–207; Alvaro Bianchi, *O*

laboratório de Gramsci Filosofia, História e Política (São Paolo: Alameda, 2009); Antonio di Meo, "La «rivoluzione passiva» da Cuoco a Gramsci. Appunti per un'interpretazione," *Filosofia italiana* (2014); Fabio Frosini, "Rivoluzione passiva e laboratorio politico: appunti sull'analisi del fascismo nei *Quaderni del carcere*," *Studi Storici* 2 (2017): 297–328.

25. Among a wide range of studies, see Jan Rehmann, *Max Weber: Modernisierung als passive Revolution* (Hamburg/Berlin: Argument, 1998); Partha Chatterjee, *Nationalist Thought and the Colonial World—a Derivative Discourse?* (London: Zed Books, 1986); Adam Morton, *Revolution and State in Modern Mexico: The Political Economy of Uneven Development* (Lanham MD: Rowman and Littlefield, 2011); Massimo Modonesi, "Revoluciones pasivas en América Latina. Una approximación gramsciana a la caracterización de los gobiernos progresistas de inicio de siglo," in *Horizontes gramscianos. Estudios en torno al pensammiento de Antonio Gramsci* (Facultad de Ciencias Políticas y Sociales, UNAM, 2013); Adam David Morton, "The Continuum of Passive Revolution," *Capital & Class* 34, no. 3 (2010): 315–342. Marcos Del Roio, "Translating Passive Revolution in Brazil," *Capital & Class*, 36, no. 2 (2010): 215–234; Carlos Nelson Coutinho, *Gramsci's Political Thought* (Leiden: Brill, 2012); Cihan Tuğal, *Passive Revolution: Absorbing the Islamic Challenge to Capitalism* (Stanford: Stanford University Press, 2009); Gillian Hart, *Rethinking the South African Crisis: Nationalism, Populism, Hegemony* (Athens: University of Georgia Press, 2014); Brecht De Smet, *Gramsci on Tahrir: Revolution and Counter-Revolution in Egypt* (London: Pluto, 2016); Partha Chatterjee, *I am the People: Reflections on Popular Sovereignty Today* (New York: Columbia University Press, 2020).

26. De Felice's "*Una chiave di lettura in 'Americanismo e fordismo'*" from 1972 does not directly deal with the notion of passive revolution but establishes coordinates that he would employ later in the decade for its exploration. The concept is instead central to Buci-Glucksmann's *Gramsci et l'État* from 1975. Both authors made seminal contributions to the 1977 Istituto Gramsci conference, the papers from which are collected in Franco Ferri, ed., *Politica e storia in Gramsci: Atti del convegno internazionale organizzato dall'Istituto Gramsci, Firenze 9-11 dicembre 1977*, 2 vols. (Rome: Editori Riuniti, 1977): see Franco de Felice, "Rivoluzione passiva, fascismo, americanismo in Gramsci," 161–220; Christine Buci-Glucksmann, "Sui problemi politici della transizione: classe operaia e rivoluzione passiva," 99–126. A critical contextualization of the debates about conference organization leading up to this event can be found in Franco De Felice, *Il presente come storia*, ed. Gregorio Sorgonà and Ermanno Taviani (Rome: Carocci, 2017).

27. This was particularly the case in Latin America, where the problematic of passive revolution was read in relation to themes of possible paths of transition from the dictatorships of those years. In particular, the legendary seminar of Morelia of 1980 gathered activists and scholars of Gramsci from across the continent and beyond; see Julio Labastida Martin del Campo, ed., *Hegemonía y alternativas políticas en américa Latina* (Mexico City/UNAM: Siglo veintiuno editores, 1985).

28. For the argument that passive revolution constitutes the "historiographical paradigm" of the theory of hegemony, see Giuseppe Vacca, *Modernità alternative: Il novecento di Antonio Gramsci* (Turin: Einaudi, 2017), 95.

29. Fabio Frosini, "Beyond the Crisis of Marxism: Thirty Years Contesting Gramsci's Legacy," in *Critical Companion to Contemporary Marxism*, ed. Jacques Bidet and Stathis Kouvelakis (Leiden: Brill 2008), 667.

30. This transition back to a Hobbesian model of order was explicitly theorized by Leondaro Paggi, *Le strategie del potere in Gramsci. Tra fascismo e socialismo in un solo paese 1923–26* (Rome: Editori Riuniti, 1984), x.

31. Fabio Frosini, "Beyond the Crisis of Marxism: Thirty Years Contesting Gramsci's Legacy," in *Critical Companion to Contemporary Marxism*, ed. Jacques Bidet and Stathis Kouvelakis (Leiden: Brill, 2008), 667.

32. See Juan Carlos Portantiero, *Los usos de Gramsci* (Mexico: Folios ediciones, 1981); Stuart Hall, "Gramsci and Us," in *The Hard Road to Renewal* (London: Verso, 1988), 161–174; Guha, *Dominance without Hegemony*.

33. Ernesto Laclau and Chantal Mouffe, *Hegemony and Socialist Strategy: Towards a Radical Democratic Politics*, trans. Winston Moore and Paul Cammack (London: Verso, 1985), 7 et seq.

34. *Hegemony and Socialist Strategy*, 134.

35. *Hegemony and Socialist Strategy*, 138. In different ways, both Mouffe and Laclau in their later individually authored works were tempted to expand hegemony in a transhistorical way—by way of Schmitt's formalism, for Mouffe, or by way of a psychoanalytic anthropology, for Laclau. The ambivalences in Laclau's evolving characterization of the historical delimitation of hegemony are carefully noted in Samuele Mazzolini, "Laclau lo stratega: Populismo ed egemonia tra spazio e tempo," in *Il momento populista. Ernesto Laclau in discussione*, ed. Fortunato Cacciatore (Milan: Mimesis, 2019), 33–74.

36. See Fabio Frosini, "Reformation, Renaissance and the State: the Hegemonic Fabric of Modern Sovereignty," *Journal of Romance Studies* 12, no. 3 (2012): 63–77.

37. The most influential critiques of Laclau and Mouffe on the basis of a presumed defense of class analysis were perhaps those of Meiksins Wood

and Geras. See Ellen Meiksins Wood, *The Retreat from Class: A New "True" Socialism* (London: Verso, 1986); Norman Geras, "Post-Marxism?," *New Left Review* I, no. 163 (1987): 40–82.

38. *Hegemony and Socialist Strategy*, 139.

39. Gramsci's notion of a "collective will" has frequently been understood in broadly Rousseauvian terms, despite the limited references to Rousseau throughout all of Gramsci's works; see, for instance, Carlos Nelson Coutinho, "General Will and Democracy in Rousseau, Hegel, and Gramsci," *Rethinking Marxism* 12, no. 2 (2000): 1–17. A Rousseauvian perspective is presupposed but not entirely explicated in Laclau and especially Mouffe's understanding of the term. Despite the shared etymological root, however, there is a significant distance between Rousseau's *volonté* and Gramsci's *volontà*: while the former's secularization of theological motifs emphasizes a shared volition or willing of the common good, the latter is conceived throughout Gramsci's writings in organizational and practical terms, resulting in an almost Spinozian notion of "will as operative awareness of historical necessity" (Q13, §1, p. 1559, May 1932). On the background to Rousseau's notion, see Patrick Riley, *The General Will before Rousseau: The Transformation of the Divine into the Civic* (Princeton: Princeton University Press, 1986); regarding the sources of Gramsci's concept in philology, psychology, and the natural sciences of the late nineteenth century, see Fabio Frosini's introduction to Antonio Gramsci, *Filosofia e politica. Antologia dei "Quaderni del carcere,"* ed. Fabio Frosini and Franco Consiglio (Florence: La Nuova Italia, 1999); and Antonio Di Meo, "'La tela tessuta nell'ombra arriva a compimento.' Processi molecolari, psicologia e storia nel pensiero di Gramsci," *Il cannocchiale. Rivista di studi filosofici* 3 (2012): 77–139.

40. *Hegemony and Socialist Strategy*, 67, 105 et seq.; Chantal Mouffe, *For a Left Populism* (London: Verso, 2018); Ernesto Laclau, "Why Constructing a People is the Main Task of Radical Politics," in *The Rhetorical Foundations of Society* (London: Verso, 2014) (originally published in *Critical Inquiry* 32, Summer 2006).

41. The formalist dimensions of this conception of universality were carefully analyzed in Judith Butler, "Restaging the Universal: Hegemony and the Limits of Formalism," in Judith Butler, Ernesto Laclau, and Slavoj Zizek, *Contingency, Hegemony, Universality: Contemporary Dialogues on the Left* (London: Verso, 2000), 22 et seq.

42. The extension of Laclau and Mouffe's discourse theory by scholars associated with the "Essex School" into a wide variety of fields has been the most notable of these initiatives.

43. Laclau and Mouffe, *Hegemony and Socialist Strategy*, 76.

44. Laclau and Mouffe, *Hegemony and Socialist Strategy* (67–68, 89), in fact cited selected passages of only three notes from the *Prison Notebooks* to support their interpretation of Gramsci: Q10II, §44, pp. 1330–1331 (incorrectly referenced as "p. 349"), from August–December 1932; Q8, §196, p. 1058, from February 1932; and Q16, §12, p. 1875, written anywhere between June–July 1932 and the second half of 1934 but based on Q8, §153, p. 1033, from April 1932. These passages do not directly refer to hegemony but are instead used by Laclau and Mouffe to support their arguments regarding the contingent articulation of political subjects, in opposition to any class reductionism. Rather than a textually founded engagement with Gramsci's writings themselves, the interpretations of Gramsci and of hegemony presented in *Hegemony and Socialist Strategy* were developed in a closer critical dialogue with the influential studies from the mid to late 1970s of Buci-Glucksmann, de Giovanni, and Salvadori (see pp. 89–90). Contributions from these three theorists had figured prominently in an important volume of translations into English of Gramscian scholarship edited by Mouffe; see *Gramsci and Marxist Theory* (London: Routledge & Kegan Paul, 1979).

45. Mouffe's "Hegemony and ideology in Gramsci" (published in *Gramsci and Marxist Theory*) was a particularly significant attempt to engage in a close reading of Gramsci's texts, particularly in relation to themes of ideology and subject constitution. Mouffe's study was referred to by Laclau on a number of occasions as an influence on his own arguments of a more general conceptual nature.

46. Ernesto Laclau, "Tesis acerca de la forma hegemónica de la política," in *Hegemonía y alternativas políticas en américa Latina*, ed. Julio Labastida Martin del Campo (Mexico City/UNAM: Siglo veintiuno editores, 1985), 20–21.

47. Laclau, "Tesis acerca forma hegemónica," 21.

48. "Tesis acerca forma hegemónica," 21, 23–24.

49. Given this emphasis, it is unsurprising that "the final act in the dissolution of [the] Jacobin imaginary" provocatively announced in *Hegemony and Socialist Strategy* was followed in Laclau and Mouffe's subsequent works by implicit and explicit turns to the most rigorous elaboration of a subjectivist theory of politics, in the decisionism of Carl Schmitt. The limits of such a position are brilliantly dissected in Yoshihiko Ichida, "Subject to Subject: Are We all Schmittians in Politics?," *Borderlands* 4, no. 2 (2005).

50. See, in particular, the tension between a Wittgensteinian emphasis on efficacy and an Austinian focus on intentionality that emerges in

Skinner's reply to his critics in *Meaning and Context*, ed. James Tully (Princeton: Princeton University Press, 1998), 231–288.

51. See, in particular, Gerratana's classic study "Le forme dell'egemonia," in *Problemi di metodo* (Rome: Editori Riuniti, 1997), 119–126. More recently, Derek Boothman has explored the diversity of Gramscian hegemony's origins in "The sources for Gramsci's Concept of Hegemony," *Rethinking Marxism* 20, no. 2 (2008): 201–215; while Fabio Frosini has highlighted the transition between different understandings of hegemony during the years in which the *Prison Notebooks* were composed in "Hégémonie: une approche génétique," *Actuel Marx* 57 (2015): 27–42. A fundamental study of the plurality of meanings expressed in the notion of hegemony in Russian Marxism is Craig Brandist's *The Dimensions of Hegemony: Language, Culture and Politics in Revolutionary Russia* (Leiden: Brill, 2015).

52. For Rawls's assertion of the purely regulative nature of his hypothesis of an original position of equality, see John Rawls, *A Theory of Justice. Original Edition* (Cambridge: Belknap Press, 1971), 12, 120; for his understanding of the role of a "thought experiment" as one of clarification, see John Rawls, *Justice as Fairness: A Restatement*, ed. Erin Kelly (Cambridge: Belknap Press, 2001), 17.

53. Franz Fanon, *The Wretched of the Earth* (New York: Grove Press, 1963), 40.

54. This note telling concludes with reflections of the "actuality" of the Jacobin experience in the practice of hegemony; see Q1, §44, p. 54.

55. The use of hegemony to unravel the contradictions of modern democracy is perhaps the starkest example of this type of analytic focus. Rather than proposing a generic equation of "hegemony" with "democracy," as some positions in the debates of the 1970s rushed to conclude, Gramsci's (brief) reflections on this topic from 1931, when read in context, suggest instead a more limited focus. His interest was the way in which the organic transitions between the governing and the governed that the practice of hegemonic politics in revolutionary Russia had aimed to promote could help to provide a more concrete conception of the limits of the type of representative democratic politics in the West that had fallen prey to the rise of Fascism, conceived as a "populist" short-circuiting of representative mechanisms that left the paradigm of representation in place. See Q8, §191, p. 1056, December 1931.

56. Guha, *Dominance without Hegemony*, 72 et seq.

57. See, in particular, Gramsci's problematization of the Jacobin tradition that begins in Q1, §48, p. 58, February–March 1930.

58. See André Tosel, "Gramsci et la Révolution française" and the discussion of Gramsci's distinctive understanding of the strengths and limitations of the Jacobin tradition in chapter 1.

59. Important dimensions of this dynamic have been detected by some of Gramsci's later readers, in very different contexts. Ranajit Guha's characterization of the failures of hegemony in the colonial state in India, for instance, built on Gramsci's metaphor of a possible "Piedmont-type function" in modern state formation by suggesting the provocative notion of a "dominance without hegemony." Partha Chatterjee has further extended this perspective of passive revolution as a process that in a certain sense "subtends" the "normal" structure of the modern (western and imperialist) state; for Chatterjee, passive revolution can be understood as the "general form" of the transition from colonial to postcolonial national states in the twentieth century. See Chatterjee, *Nationalist Thought*, particularly p. 50; and for the development of this argument in relation to contemporary populist politics, *I am the People*, particularly pp. 73–81.

60. The founding note is Q1, §44, from February–March 1930; but it is a theme and narrative to which Gramsci returns in intensified and attenuated forms a number of times in the following years. Gramsci inserted the formulation of passive revolution in the margins of Q1, §44 at a later date, clearly under the influence of his later considerations.

61. The first note in which Gramsci employed the formula of passive revolution was Q4, §57, p. 504. On the evolution of passive revolution throughout the *Prison Notebooks*, see Pasquale Voza, "Rivoluzione passive," in *Le parole di Gramsci: per un lessico dei "Quaderni del carcere,"* ed. Fabio Frosini and Guido Liguori (Rome: Carocci, 2004), 189–207. I return to the vigorous antithesis of the modern Prince in chapter 4.

62. For Labriola, Marxism constituted not a doctrine but a critical and partisan "visual angle" on the development of capitalist society, insofar as it viewed this development from the perspective of the "proletarian revolution" (or in Gramsci's terms, from the standpoint of the subaltern classes). Similar optical and perspectival metaphors are distinctively used throughout Labriola's work; see, for instance, Antonio Labriola, *Del materialismo storico. Dilucidazione preliminare*, in *La concezione materialistica della storia*, ed. Eugenio Garin (Bari: Laterza, 1965), 123.

63. Ernesto Laclau and Chantal Mouffe, *Hegemony and Socialist Strategy: Towards a Radical Democratic Politics*, 2nd ed. (London: Verso, 2001), ix. Laclau and Mouffe's earlier emphasis on the substantive over the modifier in post-Marxism (4) in fact makes their position closer to what

could today, when the Marxist traditions are conceived in a more expansive and less doctrinal sense, be characterized as a type of "neo-Marxism."

64. Q1, §44, pp. 53–54, February–March 1930.

65. Marx and Engels, *Collected Works*, vol. 10 (London: Lawrence and Wishart, 1975–2005), 281–287.

66. Q1, §44, p. 54, February–March 1930. The consistency of this metaphor can be noted in its retention and attenuation in Gramsci's revised transcription over 5 years later, in Q19, §24, p. 2034. The conjugation of the revolution in permanence and hegemony can seem counterintuitive if not bewildering today, particularly given the way in which a variant of the former term has become so strongly associated with Leon Trotsky, from whose views Gramsci himself famously took his distance in the *Prison Notebooks*. It was, however, a common perspective in the Bolshevik discussions in the early 1920s, and one to which Gramsci was amply exposed during his work in the offices of the Third International. I have explored these linkages in more detail in Peter D. Thomas, "Gramsci's Revolutions: Passive and Permanent," *Modern Intellectual History* 17, no. 1 (2020): 117–146.

67. See, for instance, the linkage of hegemony and the revolution in permanence in Q8, §52, p. 973, February 1932; Q10I, §12, pp. 1234–1235, April–May 1932; and Q13, §7, §17, §18, §27, §37, pp. 1565–1650, May 1932–November 1933.

68. Q8, §21, p. 953, January–February 1932.

69. See, in particular, the nostalgic letters that Gramsci sent to his wife following his departure from Moscow for Vienna and later return to Italy in 1923–1924 in Antonio Gramsci, *A Great and Terrible World. The Pre-Prison Letters 1908–1926*, ed. and trans. Derek Boothman (London: Lawrence and Wishart, 2014).

70. On the specificity of the figure of the modern Prince in the development of the *Prison Notebooks*, see chapter 4.

71. This theme is extensively explored in Alberto Burgio, *Gramsci storico. Una lettura dei "Quaderni del carcere"* (Bari: Laterza, 2002).

72. Walter Benjamin, "On the Concept of History," trans. Harry Zohn, in *Selected Writings, Vol. 4: 1938–1940*, ed. Howard Eiland and Michael W. Jennings (Cambridge: Belknap Press, 2003). For an important critical commentary on this famous text, see Michael Löwy, *Fire Alarm: Reading Walter Benjamin's "On the Concept of History"* (London: Verso, 2005).

73. Dipesh Chakrabarty, *Provincializing Europe: Postcolonial Thought and Historical Difference* (Princeton: Princeton University Press, 2000); Amy Allen, *The End of Progress: Decolonizing the Normative Foundations of Critical Theory* (New York: Columbia University Press, 2016).

74. The constitutive limits of liberalism and their critique in the critical communist tradition is highlighted in Domenico Losurdo, *Antonio Gramsci: dal liberalismo al "comunismo critico"* (Rome: Gamberetti, 1997).

75. Q10I, §13, p. 1238, late May 1932.

76. This affiliation was highlighted by Quintin Hoare and Geoffrey Nowell Smith in their notes to Antonio Gramsci, *Selections from the Prison Notebooks* (London: Lawrence and Wishart, 1971), 55.

77. The importance of Gramsci's university study of historical linguistics for his later political vocabulary was first explored by Franco Lo Piparo, *Lingua, intellettuali, egemonia in Gramsci* (Bari: Laterza, 1979). More recently, see the important studies of Peter Ives, *Gramsci's Politics of Language* (Toronto: University of Toronto Press, 2004); Giancarlo Schirru, "Antonio Gramsci, student di linguistica," *Studi storici* LII (2011): 925–973; Alessandro Carlucci, *Gramsci and Languages: Unification, Diversity, Hegemony* (Leiden: Brill, 2013).

78. For this reason, Laclau and Mouffe's repeated assertion that the notion of an alliance of pre-constituted (economic) classes constitutes the central feature of Lenin's notion of hegemony says more about the subjectivist presuppositions of their own theory than it does about the function of hegemony in the Russian revolutionary movement.

79. Q15, §4, p. 1752, February 1933. Attempts to reduce Gramsci to a variant of the elitist paradigm need to neglect the way in which his conception of self-emancipatory politics as a pedagogical relation works to deconstruct these hierarchies, including in their democratic-representative forms. See Maurice Finnochiaro, *Beyond Right and Left: Democratic Elitism in Mosca and Gramsci* (New Haven: Yale University Press, 1997).

80. Fabio Frosini, "Luigi Russo e Georges Sorel: sulla genesi del 'moderno Principe' nei *Quaderni del carcere* di Antonio Gramsci," *Studi storici* LIV, no. 3 (2013): 545–589. I have explored the relation between the modern Prince and Gramsci's "constituentism" in Peter D. Thomas, "Towards the Modern Prince," in *Gramsci in the World*, ed. Roberto Dainotto and Fredric Jameson (Durham: Duke University Press, 2020), 17–37. I explore this theme further in chapter 4.

81. For my initial exploration of this theme, see Peter D. Thomas, "Η ιδέα του κομμουνισμού και το ζήτημα της οργάνωσης," (The Idea of Communism and the Question of Organization) *ΟΥΤΟΠΙΑ* 100 (2012): 117–134; and "Hegemony, Passive Revolution and the Modern Prince," *Thesis Eleven* 117 (2013): 20–39. The notion is also powerfully developed in relation to Gramsci by Panagiotis Sotiris, "Hegemony and Mass Critical Intellectuality," *International Socialism Journal* 137 (2013); and "The

Modern Prince as Laboratory of Political Intellectuality," *International Gramsci Journal* 3, no. 2 (2019): 2–38.

82. On the limits of the representative paradigm for emancipatory politics, particularly in its Rousseauvian formulation, see Michael Hardt and Antonio Negri, *Assembly* (New York: Oxford University Press, 2017), 27 et seq.

83. For an interesting discussion of the Uffizi laboratories in relation to the alchemical tradition, see Fanny Kieffer, "The Laboratories of Art and Alchemy at the Uffizi Gallery in Renaissance Florence: Some Material Aspects," in *Laboratories of Art: Alchemy and Art Technology from Antiquity to the 18th Century*, ed. Sven Dupré (Dordrecht/London: Springer, 2014), 105–127.

84. Q6, §138, p. 802, August 1931.

Chapter 4

1. Naomi Klein, *No Logo: Taking Aim at the Brand Bullies* (New York: Picador, 2000); Michael Hardt and Antonio Negri, *Empire* (Cambridge: Harvard University Press, 2000); John Holloway, *Change the World without Taking Power* (London: Pluto, 2002); Daniel Bensaïd, "On a Recent Book by John Holloway," *Historical Materialism* 13, no. 4 (2005): 169–192.

2. Slavoj Žižek, *First as Tragedy, Then as Farce* (London: Verso, 2009), 87; Alain Badiou, *The Communist Hypothesis* (London: Verso, 2010), 258–260.

3. For critical reflections on Badiou's relationship to the debates of the "movement of movements," see Alberto Toscano, "From the State to the World?: Badiou and Anti-Capitalism," *Communication and Cognition* 37, no. 3–4 (2004): 199–223.

4. Louis Althusser, "On the Young Marx," in *For Marx*, trans. Ben Brewster (Harmondsworth: Penguin, 1969 [1961]), 75.

5. In addition to the various conferences on the Idea of Communism in London (2009), Berlin (2010), New York (2011), Seoul (2013), and Rome (2017), among others, Badiou's intervention coincided with a proliferation of international initiatives that aimed to reassess the legacy and potential of twentieth-century communism. Among some of the most significant were an issue of the journal *ContreTemps* under the editorship of Daniel Bensaïd in 2009, and a subsequent conference in Paris in January 2010 (*"Puissance du communisme"*); the conference *"Quale comunismo oggi?,"* held at the University of Urbino in 2010; and special issues of the Athens-based journal *Utopia* in 2012 and *South Atlantic Quarterly* in 2014.

6. A significant and regrettable limitation of both Badiou's and Žižek's interventions has been the lack of a rigorous analysis of the non-Communist nature of the historically existing regimes that appropriated its name for an entire historical period; in the absence of such an account, the re-assertion of the idea of communism today will continue to be haunted by its misappropriation in the past.

7. For analyses of the emergence in Badiou's thought in the 1980s of the notion of "politics without a party," see Alberto Toscano, "Marxism Expatriated: Alain Badiou's Turn," in *Critical Companion to Contemporary Marxism*, ed. Jacques Bidet and Stathis Kouvelakis (Leiden: Brill, 2008); Bruno Bosteels, *The Actuality of Communism* (London: Verso, 2011), 105–106, 118–128.

8. For a powerful discussion of recent liberal- and left-egalitarianisms, see Tony Smith, *Beyond Liberal Egalitarianism: Marx and Normative Social Theory in the Twenty-First Century* (Leiden: Brill, 2017).

9. A focus on inequality is as central to Thomas Piketty's *Capital in the Twenty-First Century* (Cambridge: Belknap Press, 2014) as is his advocacy of statist solutions to it.

10. This point was forcefully highlighted by SYRIZA MP Costas Lapavitsas's claim, one made not without regrets, that the concepts of Keynesianism "remains the most powerful tools we've got" for dealing with immediate policy issues; see https://www.jacobinmag.com/2015/03/lapavitsas-var oufakis-grexit-syriza/

11. The most consequential formulation of this perspective is provided by Andreas Malm's championing of the contemporary relevance of the type of state socialism that characterized the historical experience of "war communism" in the early 1920s: *Corona, Climate, Chronic Emergency: War Communism in the Twenty-First Century* (London: Verso, 2020).

12. See, in particular, Axel Honneth, *Die Idee des Sozialismus: Versuch einer Aktualisierung* (Frankfurt/M: Suhrkamp, 2015); Nancy Fraser, *The Old Is Dying and the New Cannot Be Born: From Progressive Neoliberalism to Trump and Beyond* (New York: Verso, 2019).

13. A similar formulation can be found in Badiou's much earlier *Peut-on penser la politique* of 1985. For a discussion of the significance of this text for Badiou's organizational rethinking, see Gavin Walker, "The Body of Politics: On the Concept of the Party," *Theory and Event* 16, no. 4 (2013).

14. Daniel Bensaïd, "Puissance du communisme," *Contretemps* 4 (2009).

15. Remobilizing a concept from the early Rancière, via Badiou, Bruno Bosteels regards "speculative leftism" as 'a name for the philosophical appropriation of radical emancipatory politics." Bruno Bosteels, *The*

Actuality of Communism (London: Verso, 2011), 33. For an earlier version of this argument, see Bruno Bosteels, "The Speculative Left," *The South Atlantic Quarterly* 104, no. 4 (2005).

16. See chapter 3.

17. Alain Badiou, *The Rebirth of History: Times of Riots and Uprisings* (London: Verso, 2012). On the background of the so-called Arab Spring, see the fundamental works of Adam Hanieh, *Lineages of Revolt: Issues of Contemporary Capitalism in the Middle East* (Chicago: Haymarket, 2013); and *Money, Markets, and Monarchies: The Gulf Cooperation Council and the Political Economy of the Contemporary Middle East* (Cambridge: Cambridge University Press, 2018).

18. These themes are concretely highlighted in the remarkable interviews and analyses in Keeanga-Yamahtta Taylor, ed., *How We Get Free: Black Feminism and the Combahee River Collective* (Chicago: Haymarket, 2017).

19. For Badiou, "It will always be a question of communism, even if the word, soiled, is replaced by some other designation of the concept that it covers, the philosophical and thus eternal concept of religious subjectivity." See Alain Badiou, *Infinite Thought: Truth and the Return of Philosophy* (New York: Continuum, 2003), 131. For Žižek, what is missing today is a "privileged link of the Idea to a singular historical moment"; surviving the "failure of its realization as a specter," the communist idea thereafter subsists as an "endless persistence." See Slavoj Žižek, "How to Begin from the Beginning," *New Left Review* II, no. 57 (2009): 125–126.

20. Alain Badiou, *The Communist Hypothesis* (London: Verso, 2010), 234.

21. Badiou's notion of different phases of the Idea of Communism's historical existence implicitly presupposes a broader theory of history, but his (post-Althusserian) reliance on an undifferentiated critique of "historicism" tends to work against its coherent presentation. At times, he seems to comprehend history in a purely formal manner, as a "symbolic place" into which the Communist Idea projects the individual that has become a (political) Subject, or as a "narrative constructed after the fact." See Alain Badiou, *The Communist Hypothesis* (London: Verso, 2010), 252, 237–238. As Badiou remarkably writes, in a quasi-Benjaminian tone, in *Logic of Worlds* (recalling a formulation in *Theory of the Subject*), "History does not exist. There are disparate presents whose radiance is measured by the power they preserve to unfold a past that matches up to them." See Alain Badiou, *Logic of Worlds*, trans. Alberto Toscano (New York: Continuum, 2009), 509. In this formulation, Badiou runs the risk of falling into what Althusser himself had condemned as the type of "expressivist" historicism

that conceives of each present as an "essential section," which can be retrospectively articulated into a series of discrete conjunctures by what is effectively a theory of periodization, but cannot, on these terms, be concretely studied in terms of the causal relations that define their interrelationship and mutual constitution. See Louis Althusser and Étienne Balibar, *Reading "Capital,"* trans. Ben Brewster (London: NLB, 1970), 132. For critical reflections on the tension between historicity and historicism in contemporary radical thought, see the conclusion to Bosteels's *Actuality of Communism*.

22. Alain Badiou, *The Communist Hypothesis* (London: Verso, 2010), 234.
23. Daniel Bensaïd, "Puissance du communisme," *Contretemps* 4 (2009).
24. It was Badiou himself who originally suggest the Kantian comparison, which he just as quickly retracted, though without elaborating a detailed rationale or suggesting a more convincing alternative metaphor. See Alain Badiou, *The Communist Hypothesis* (London, Verso, 2010), 246.
25. Immanuel Kant, *Critique of Pure Reason*, trans. Norman Kemp Smith (Basingstoke: Macmillan, 1933), B 672.
26. Slavoj Žižek, *First as Tragedy, Then as Farce* (London: Verso, 2009), 87.
27. Reinhart Koselleck, "'Erfahrungsraum' und 'Erwartungshorizont' – zwei historische Kategorien," in *Vergangene Zukunft. Zur Semantik geschichtlichen Zeiten* (Frankfurt/M: Suhrkamp, 1979), 354–359; Giorgio Agamben, "What is Destituent Power?," *Environment and Planning D: Space and Society*, 32, no. 1 (2014): 65–74.
28. Cinzia Arruzza, Tithi Bhattacharya, and Nancy Fraser, *Feminism for the 99%: A Manifesto* (London: Verso, 2019); Verónica Gago, *Feminist International: How to Change Everything* (London: Verso, 2020).
29. Bensaïd, "Recent Book by Hollaway," 169–192.
30. Alain Badiou, *The Communist Hypothesis* (London: Verso, 2010), 66, 234. Badiou develops this distinctive vocabulary across *Logics of Worlds*, *Second Manifesto for Philosophy*, and his "hypertranslation" of Plato's *Republic*, though it was arguably prefigured in earlier works such as *The Theory of the Subject* with the similarly platonic notion of "courage."
31. Alberto Toscano, "The Politics of Abstraction. Communism and Philosophy," in *The Idea of Communism*, ed. Costas Douzinas and Slavoj Žižek (London: Verso, 2010), 202.
32. Peter Hallward, "The Will of the People: Notes Towards a Dialectical Voluntarism," *Radical Philosophy* 155 (May/June 2009); Bruno Bosteels, *The Actuality of Communism* (London: Verso, 2011); Jodi Dean, *Crowds and Party* (London: Verso, 2016).
33. Jodi Dean, *The Communist Horizon* (London: Verso, 2012), 207.

34. Hans-Jürgen Urban, "Die Mosaik-Linke. Vom Aufbruch der Gewerkschaften zur Erneuerung der Bewegung," *Blätter für deutsche und internationale Politik* 5 (2009); Mimmo Porcaro, "Occupy Lenin," *Socialist Register 2013: The Question of Strategy*, vol. 49, 2012.

35. Regarding the latter, see in particular Richard Seymour, *Corbyn: The Strange Rebirth of Radical Politics* (London: Verso, 2017).

36. Keeanga-Yamahtta Taylor, *From Black Liberation to Black Lives Matter* (Chicago: Haymarket, 2016).

37. The notion of the "party-form" itself has a precise conjunctural history, particularly in debates in Italian Marxism in the 1970s, some elements of which are usefully reconstructed in Étienne Balibar, "The Genre of the Party," *Viewpoint* 15 (March 2017). For Balibar's own contribution to those older debates, see Étienne Balibar, "Interrogativi sul 'partito fuori dello Stato," in *Discutere lo stato: posizioni e confronto su una tesi di Louis Althusser* (Bari: De Donato, 1978), 271–290; Étienne Balibar, "Etat, parti, idéologie" in André Tosel, Cesare Luporini, and Etienne Balibar, *Marx et sa critique du politique* (Paris: Maspero, 1979).

38. This judgment has been codified in the analytically unhelpful neologism of "autonomism," used polemically in order to describe a wide variety of contemporary political practices. Their common feature, supposedly, consists in a "rejection of the Leninist conception of organization," which in turn is asserted to represent a much more stable normative model that the historical record suggests. See Alex Callinicos, "Toni Negri in Perspective," *International Socialism Journal* 92 (2001). These ahistorical notions group together indiscriminately many experiences and orientations that would be better comprehended on the basis of their particular organizational proposals; contemporary "autonomist" politics vary among themselves just as much as do different understandings of the "Leninist" conception of organization itself.

39. Mario Tronti, *Noi operaisti* (Rome: Deriveapprodi, 2012).

40. Constitution of the Italian Republic, Fundamental Principles, Article 1.

41. Machiavelli, *The Prince*, Dedicatory Letter.

42. See Antonio Negri, "Il lavoro nella costituzione," in *La forma stato. Per la critica dell'economia politica della costituzione* (Milan: Feltrinelli, 1977).

43. Key historical documents from this development are collected in *L'Operaismo degli anni sessanta: Da "Quaderni rossi" a "classe operaia"* (Rome: DeriveApprodi, 2008). Wright's *Storming Heaven* focuses on the development of the notion of class composition as both analytical method and political orientation, while an excellent overview of Alquati's contribution can be found in Devi Sacchetto, Emiliana Armano, and Steve Wright,

"Coresearch and Counter-Research: Romano Alquati's Itinerary Within and Beyond Italian Radical Political Thought," *Viewpoint* (September 27, 2013).

44. This was clearly highlighted in the important "Panzieri-Tronti Theses" of 1962: "4.3 The class party as indispensable moment of revolutionary strategy." See Raniero Panzieri and Mario Tronti, "Panzieri-Tronti Theses," Aut, 149–150 (1975). See also Panzieri's "Spontaneità e organizzazione," *Quaderni rossi – Cronache operaie* (July 15, 1963), now in Raniero Panzieri, *Spontaneità e organizzazione. Gli anni dei "Quaderni rossi*," ed. Stefano Merli (Pisa: Biblioteca Franco Seratini, 1994).

45. On the division in the 1970s between an *operaismo* of the "left" and of the "right," See Cristina Corradi, *Storia dei marxismi in Italia* (Rome: manifestolibri, 2011).

46. Mario Tronti, *La politica al tramonto* (Rome: Einaudi, 1998); Mario Tronti et al., *Politica e destino* (Milan/Bologna: Luca Sossella Editore, 2006). I refer here to Tronti's support, for which he barely even attempted to offer an excuse, for the Democratic Party's "Jobs Act" in 2014 in the Senate of the Italian Parliament.

47. The fundamental text on these years remains that of Nanni Balestrini and Primo Moroni, *L'orda d'oro 1968-1977: La grande ondata rivoluzionaria e creativa, politica ed esistenziale*, 3rd ed. (Milan: Feltrinelli, 2003 [1988]).

48. Hardt and Negri, *Empire*, 394, 407–411, where the *posse* of the multitude is thought in terms of "biopolitical self-organization"; Michael Hardt and Antonio Negri, *Multitude: War and Democracy in the Age of Empire* (New York: Penguin, 2004), 219–227, 250, 339, where they claim that the "common production of the multitude itself produces the political organization of society," according to the model of "a language that can express itself."

49. Antonio Negri, "What to Do Today with What Is to Be Done?, or Rather: The Body of the General Intellect," in *Lenin Reloaded: Towards a Politics of Truth*, ed. Sebastian Budgen, Stathis Kouvelakis, and Slavoj Žižek (Durham: Duke University Press, 2007), 302.

50. For a problematization of the "traditional" reading of Lenin's adoption of Kautsky's formulation regarding the "exteriority" of socialist consciousness to the working classes, see Lars Lih, *Lenin Rediscovered: "What Is to Be Done" in Context* (Leiden: Brill, 2006).

51. In another text from the same period, Negri discussed the possible "body" of the multitude and its struggle for "self-governance of itself." See Antonio Negri, "Kairos. Alma Venus. Multitudo," in *Time for Revolution* (New York: Continuum, 2007 [2003]), 144.

52. Michael Hardt and Antonio Negri, *Commonwealth* (Cambridge: Belknap Press, 2009), vii, 361ff.

53. Hardt and Negri, *Commonwealth*, 350.

54. *Commonwealth*, 350.

55. *Commonwealth*, 8 et seq.; 159–164.

56. Rather than the type of political ontology that has been so prominent throughout Negri's earlier works, or an attempt to ground political action as an organic consequence of the already given, this notion of the common represents something much closer to a "political imaginary," in the fullest sense of the term; that is, as an attempt to imagine political action as a transformation of the existing relations of force, as a "monstrous" intervention. A similarly institutionalist conception of the common is at work in Pierre Dardot and Christian Laval's, *Common: On Revolution in the 21st Century* (New York: Bloomsbury, 2019).

57. Hardt and Negri, *Assembly* (New York: Oxford University Press, 2017), 37–46.

58. Organization in this vision thus becomes the articulation of "exodus" at the social level, "antagonistic reformism" at the governmental-institutional level, and hegemony at a more comprehensive political-strategic level, though precisely which agency would undertake this articulation remains unspecified. See *Assembly*, 274–280.

59. For the critique of previous party-forms, see in particular Hardt and Negri, *Commonwealth*, 161–162, 276–277. For a survey of Negri's changing conception of the party and political organization, see Timothy Murphy, *Antonio Negri* (Cambridge: Polity, 2012), 65–103. In terms of Negri's overall political evolution, this compositional turn in *Commonwealth* should be understood as an effective re-turn to the project of thinking the contours of a "neo-organization" outside the paradigm of (sovereign) representation, after a long detour through the debates on the obsolescence of the party-form that occupied the energy of so many on the European far left in the 1970s and 1980s. This return also marks a precise difference between the contemporary positions of Negri and Badiou. It does not consist in the philosophical opposition that Badiou has argued exists between his own "materialist dialectic" and Negri's supposed "democratic materialism." See Alain Badiou, *Logic of Worlds* (New York: Continuum, 2009), 2. Rather, their difference is fundamentally a political one. Badiou strives to keep faith with a far leftist moment of the late 1970s and early 1980s that argued, in the wake of the collapse of the Chinese Cultural Revolution and the consequent disillusionment of many "Western Maoists," for the need to move beyond the party-form as such. Badiou's subjectivity without a

subject at the philosophical level in this sense mirrors his notion of organization without a party at the political level; see in particular "Rancière
and Apolitics," in *Metapolitics*, trans. Jason Barker (London: Verso, 2005
[1998]), 122. Negri, on the other hand, returning to the more expansive energies of the late 1950s and 1960s, appears to be attempting to
re-articulate the question of the party-form in Machiavellian terms, as a
question of partisanship. For a brief but suggestive attempt to think the
notion of organization in these terms, as an organization of difference, see
Antonio Negri, *Fabbrica di porcellana* (Milan: Feltrinelli, 2008), 129–144.

60. Hardt and Negri, *Commonwealth*, 351 et seq.
61. Hardt and Negri, *Assembly*, 17, 65–66, 238.
62. *Assembly*, 19–24.
63. The self-foundational presuppositions of Weber's notion of charismatic
power are explored in Sara R. Farris, *Max Weber's Theory of Personality.
Individuation. Politics and Orientalism in the Sociology of Religion*
(Leiden: Brill, 2013). This dimension of the organizational reflections
of *Assembly* draws on an enduring aporia in Negri's thought. In his
book on Lenin from 1977, he had formulated it with remarkable clarity
(and equally remarkable confidence): "Organization is spontaneity that
reflects upon itself"; *33 lezioni su Lenin* (Rome: Manifestolibri, 2004),
42. Expressed in such starkly tautological terms, it issues in an austere
model of political ontology: spontaneity is spontaneity is spontaneity, in
an indeterminate repetition, suddenly transmogrifying into organization through an excess of reflection on itself. Precisely how such a transformation could occur, if not yet again in a caricatured Hegelian mode of
the teleological emergence of self-consciousness, remains unclear. For a
pointed analysis of similarities and differences in Negri's formulation of
the question of organization, particularly in relation to Lenin, from the
1970s to the present, see Matteo Mandarini, "Organising Communism,"
in Felix Guattari and Antonio Negri, *New Lines of Alliance. New Spaces
of Liberty* (New York: Minor Compositions/Autonomedia/Mayfly
Books), 2010.
64. In terms that seem remarkably similar to those sometimes adopted by
Badiou and Žižek, Negri even argues that "the revolution is an acceleration of historical time, the realization of a subjective conditions, of an
event, of an opening, which contribute to making possible a production
of an irreducible and radical subjectivity"; Antonio Negri, *Fabbrica di
porcellana* (Milan: Feltrinelli, 2008), 142. Though he insists that this subjectivity needs to be distinguished from individual acts of will, and its constituent (as opposed to "instituted") dimensions valorized, his proposal to

think this problem in terms of the constitutive elements of a "collective" or "common" decision remains frustratingly underdeveloped.

65. Georg Lukács, *History and Class Consciousness* (London: Merlin Press, 1971), 299.

66. *Class Consciousness*, 300.

67. *Class Consciousness*, 317.

68. *Class Consciousness*, 326.

69. Lukács, *Class Consciousness*, 330.

70. Lucio Magri provides a precise characterization of this process of reforging and its resulting party-form. It "does not represent a mere 'instrument of action' in the hands of a pre-existent historical subject with its own precise character and goals, but instead represents the mediation through which this subject constitutes itself, defining its own aims and historic goal"; Lucio Magri, "Problems of the Marxist Theory of the Revolutionary Party," *New Left Review* I, no. 60 (1970): 100–101. Magri's conception of the party as a process of subjectivation bears decisive resemblances to Daniel Bensaïd's reflections on the party-form as a problem of interpretation just as a much as a problem of unification, coordination, and decision. Freely drawing on psychoanalytical themes, Bensaïd argues that it is the specificity of the overdetermined field of political relations and its irreducibility to the social that continually reproposes the question of the party-form—not as a solution but as a problem that each upsurge of social and political struggle involving diverging and sometimes conflicting component elements inevitably confronts. According to Bensaïd, this constitutive tension generates the need for continuous interpretative and analytical labor, in the attempt to discover the party-form adequate to the specificity of the social movements to which it gives expression, at the same time as it transforms them by translating their demands into the distinctive register of politics. See Daniel Bensaïd, *A Marx for Our Times: Adventures and Misadventures of a Critique* (London: Verso, 2002), 112ff.

71. Lukács's theory of organization in this sense is a coherent and organic extension of his notion of an "ascribed" class consciousness, the consciousness that the working class should have of its true position in the social relations of production.

72. Terry Eagleton, "Lenin in the Postmodern Age," in *Lenin Reloaded: Towards a Politics of Truth*, ed. Sebastian Budgen, Stathis Kouvelakis, and Slavoj Žižek (Durham: Duke University Press, 2007).

73. The inherently political nature of the modern concept of the subject is explored extensively in Étienne Balibar, Barbara Cassin, and Alain de

Libera, "Sujet," in *Vocabulaire européen des philosophies: Dictionnaire des intraduisibles*, ed. Barbara Cassin (Paris: Seuil, 2004).

74. Karl Marx, *Capital*, Volume I (London: Penguin, 1990), 255. Interestingly, the concept of "subject," let alone "political subject," does not appear as a discrete entry in Georges Labica and Gérard Bensussan's 1982, *Dictionnaire critique du marxisme* (Paris: PUF). The ascription of the concept of the "political subject" to Marx should, in my view, be regarded as a paradigmatic instance of what Olivier Boulnois has referred to as the "retrospective illusion of the interpreters and translators who slip the new concept into old texts." See Oliver Boulnois, "Objet," in *Vocabulaire européen des philosophies. Dictionnaire des intraduisibles*, ed. Barbara Cassin (Paris: Seuil, 2004).

75. On the status of the slogan in Lenin, see Jean-Jacques Lecercle, *The Violence of Language* (London: Routledge, 1990); "Lenin the Just, or Marxism Unrecycled," in *Lenin Reloaded*, ed. Sebastian Budgen, Stathis Kouvelakis, and Slavoj Žižek (Durham: Duke University Press, 2007).

76. I have previously explored the curious absence of the philosophical vocabulary of the subject in Gramsci's *Prison Notebooks* inPeter D. Thomas, *The Gramscian Moment: Philosophy, Hegemony and Marxism* (Leiden: Brill, 2009), 386ff.

77. Slavoj Žižek, "How to Begin from the Beginning," *New Left Review* II, no. 57 (2009): 51.

78. For a discussion of the neo-Kantian dimensions of the young Lukács's thought, see Tom Rockmore, "Fichte, Lask, and Lukács's Hegelian Marxism," *Journal of the History of Philosophy* 30, no. 4 (1992); Gillian Rose, *Hegel Contra Sociology* (London: Verso, 2009), 29–39. For a critique that characterizes Lukács's theory of the party as "a kind of communist Cartesianism," see Joseph Fracchia, "The Philosophical Leninism and Eastern 'Western Marxism' of Georg Lukács," *Historical Materialism* 21, no. 1 (2013).

79. Jacques-Alain Miller, "Action of the Structure," in *Selections from the "Cahiers pour l'Analyse," Volume 1 of Concept and Form*, ed. Peter Hallward and Knox Peden (London: Verso, 2012 [1968]), 69–84.

80. There is also a direct genealogical connection, in the sense that many of the key features of radical thought over the last decades, particularly in its decisionist and voluntarist dimensions, were influentially formulated in Žižek's rediscovery and championing of Lukács's defense of *History and Class Consciousness* against its condemnation in the 1920s. See, in particular, Žižek's "Afterword" to Georg Lukács, *A Defence of History and Class Consciousness: Tailism and the Dialectic* (London: Verso, 2002).

81. Jodi Dean, *Crowds and Party* (London: Verso, 2016), 73. Bruno Bosteels' reading of the notion of the subaltern provides a variant of this approach by conceiving of the subaltern as a type of subject that escapes the action of the structure; "Theses on Antagonism, Hybridity, and the Subaltern in Latin America," *Dispositio/n* 25, no. 52 (2005): 147–158.

82. Ernesto Laclau, "Subject of Politics, Politics of the Subject," in *Emancipation(s)* (London: Verso, 1996), 47–59; "Why Constructing a People is the Main Task of Radical Politics," in *The Rhetorical Foundations of Society* (London: Verso, 2014), 139–180. Among the many critiques of Laclau's equation of hegemony, populism, and politics, see, in particular, Benjamin Arditi, "Populism Is Hegemony Is Politics? On Ernesto Laclau's *On Populist Reason,*" *Constellations* 17, no. 3 (2010): 488–497.

83. Chantal Mouffe, *On the Political* (London: Routledge, 2005); *Agonistics: Thinking the World Politically* (London: Verso, 2013), 1–18; *For a Left Populism* (London: Verso, 2018), 59–78.

84. Étienne Balibar, "Structuralism: A destitution of the subject?," *Differences: A Journal of Feminist Cultural Studies* 14, no. 1 (2003): 1–21, at p. 10.

85. For this reason, the early Althusser should also be distinguished from what Balibar (see note 84 above) has described as a "typical movement of structuralism," insofar as he offered the possibility for thinking a "deconstruction" of the (category of the) subject that would not be simultaneously a "reconstruction of the subject" (10).

86. See, in particular, the following formulation from Althusser's contribution to *Reading Capital*: "The true 'subjects' (in the sense of constitutive subjects of the process) are therefore not these occupants or functionaries, are not, despite all appearances, the 'obviousness' of the 'given' of naïve anthropology, 'concrete individuals,' 'real men'—but *the definition and distribution of these places and functions. The true 'subjects' are these definers and distributors: the relations of production* (and political and ideological social relations). But since these are 'relations,' they cannot be thought within the category *subject*"; Althusser and Balibar, *Reading Capital* (London: Verso, 1970), 180.

87. See, in particular, "The Transformation of Philosophy," in *Philosophy and the Spontaneous Philosophy of the Scientists*, trans. Thomas E. Lewis, ed. Gregory Elliott (London: Verso, 1990 [1976]), 241–265.

88. Jan Werner Müller, *What Is Populism?* (Philadelphia: University of Pennsylvania Press, 2016); Chantal Mouffe, *For a Left Populism* (London: Verso, 2018).

89. Laclau and Mouffe's reformulation of hegemony as a process of contingent and relative universalization in order to describe the constitution of modern sovereignty grasped this dynamic well. Their error was to ascribe this populist dimension to politics as such, rather than to politics conducted within the bounds of the subalternization of the integral state.

90. Q8, §21, pp. 951–953; written in January–February 1932.

91. Q13, §1, p. 1561, May 1932.

92. For a reading of the modern Prince in terms of universalization and synchronization, see Vittorio Morfino, *Spinoza e il non contemporaneo* (Verona: Ombre corte, 2009), 99. For a reading of *The Prince* in terms of innovation, see Pocock, *The Machiavellian Moment*, 158. Elective affinities between Gramsci and Mosca are central to Maurice A. Finocchiario's *Beyond Right and Left: Democratic Elitism in Mosca and Gramsci* (New Haven: Yale University Press, 1999); while the modern Prince is conceived in decisionistic terms in Andreas Kalyvas, "Hegemonic Sovereignty: Carl Schmitt. Antonio Gramsci and the Constituent Prince," *Journal of Political Ideologies* 5, no. 3 (2000), 343–376. Negri's belated encounter with Gramsci has been dominated by an effective fusion of these approaches: "What a formidable image [of the modern Prince] this is— the image of a new subjectivity that is born from the nothingness of any determination or preconstituted destiny and that preconstitutes collectively each determination and destiny!"; see *Insurgencies*, 320.

93. For Platone and Togliatti's influential interpretation, see the editorial preface to Antonio Gramsci, *Note su Machiavelli, sulla politica e sullo stato moderno* (Turin: Einaudi, 1949), xix.

94. See chapter 3.

95. Machiavelli, *The Prince*, Dedicatory Letter.

96. I have explored the significance of these developments in greater detail in Peter D. Thomas, "The Modern Prince: Gramsci's Reading of Machiavelli," *History of Political Thought* 38, no. 3 (2017): 523–544.

97. Q 8, §21, p. 951, January–February 1932. On the "new" conception of politics in Gramsci's last notebooks, see Francesca Antonini, "Pessimism of the Intellect, Optimism of the Will: Gramsci's Political Thought in the Last Miscellaneous Notebooks," *Rethinking Marxism* 31, no. 1 (2019): 42–57.

98. Machiavelli, *The Prince*, 81.

99. Q7, §6, p. 857, November 1930.

100. Q11, §25, p. 1430, July–August 1932.

101. Q6, §138, p. 802, August 1931.

102. Q5, §127, p. 662, late 1931.
103. This is effectively the reading proposed by the late Althusser, in a continuation of some of the central interpretative themes of the *Risorgimento* tradition against which Gramsci's reading was developed. See Louis Althusser, *Machiavelli and Us* (London: Verso, 1999 [1995]). Such a reading is also present in Claude Lefort's *Le travail de l'œuvre Machiavel* (Paris: Gallimard, 1986 [1972]), 242; and Maurizio Virolli's *Redeeming The Prince. The Meaning of Machiavelli's Masterpiece* (Princeton: Princeton University Press, 2014), 141.
104. Q13, §1, p. 1561, May 1932. In this argument, the classically Jacobin project of the "formation of a national popular collective will" is immediately supplemented by an expansive ("metajacobin") process of "intellectual and moral reform ... tied to a programme of economic reform," to the point that the modern Prince takes the place of a "categorical imperative" revolutionizing and de-subalternizing all social relations, including that national popular collective will itself. See also Q 8, §21, p. 953, January–February 1932.
105. "A collective awareness—that is, a living organism—is not formed until after the multiplicity has been united through the friction of individuals: nor can it be said that 'silence' is not multiplicity. An orchestra that rehearses, each instrument on its own, gives the impression of the most horrible cacophony; yet these rehearsals are the condition for the orchestra to live as a single 'instrument'" (Q15, §13, p. 1771, April 1933). For recent reflections on the relevance of this famous metaphor for contemporary movements, see Michael Denning, "Everyone a Legislator," *New Left Review* II, no. 129 (2021): 29–44.
106. Q15, §13, p. 1771, April 1933.

Conclusion

1. "Of you the tale is told." Marx famously adopted Horace's words as advice for the German readers of *Capital*, despite the fact that it drew heavily on the experience of capitalist industrialization in England for illustrative material. See Karl Marx, *Capital Volume I*, trans. Ben Fowkes (Harmondsworth: Penguin, 1976), 90.

Index

For the benefit of digital users, indexed terms that span two pages (e.g., 52–53) may, on occasion, appear on only one of those pages.